Steven TÖTÖSY de ZEPETNEK

The Social Dimensions
of Fiction

KONZEPTION EMPIRISCHE LITERATURWISSENSCHAFT / THE SYSTEMIC AND EMPIRICAL APPROACH TO LITERATURE

Herausgegeben von der Arbeitsgruppe NIKOL / Edited by the NIKOL Group – Achim Barsch, Helmut Hauptmeier, Gebhard Rusch, Siegfried J. Schmidt, Reinhold Viehoff

Steven TÖTÖSY de ZEPETNEK

The Social Dimensions of Fiction

On the Rhetoric and Function
of Prefacing Novels
in the Nineteenth-Century Canadas

Edited by Achim Barsch

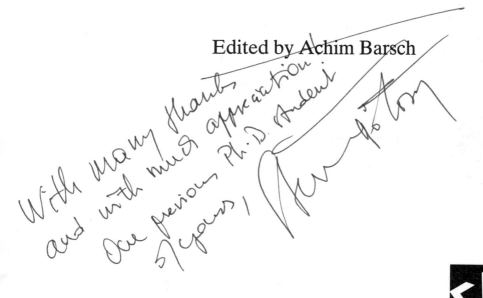

Professor Steven Tötösy de Zepetnek
Research Institute for Comparative Literature
University of Alberta
Edmonton, Alberta, Canada T6G 2R6

Die Deutsche Bibliothek – CIP-Einheitsaufnahme

Konzeption empirische Literaturwissenschaft = The systemic
and empirical approach to literature / hrsg. von der
Arbeitsgruppe NIKOL. Achim Barsch ... – Braunschweig;
Wiesbaden: Vieweg.
    Teilw. hrsg. von Peter Finke
NE: Barsch, Achim [Hrsg.]; Finke, Peter [Hrsg.];
Arbeitsgruppe NIKOL; PT
Bd. 15. Tötösy de Zepetnek, Steven: The social dimensions
of fiction. – 1993

Tötösy de Zepetnek, Steven:
The social dimensions of fiction: on the rhetoric and function
of prefacing novels in the nineteenth century Canadas / Steven
Tötösy de Zepetnek. Ed. by Achim Barsch. – Braunschweig;
Wiesbaden: Vieweg, 1993
    (Konzeption empirische Literaturwissenschaft; Bd. 15)
    ISBN 3-528-07335-7

Printing and binding: W. Langelüddecke, Braunschweig
Printed on acid-free paper
Printed in Germany

ISSN 0939-6691
ISBN 3-528-07335-7

TABLE OF CONTENTS

Préfacer une étude de préfaces
ou
Le troisième ciel du métadiscours

En tête de *Fortunio*, Théophile Gautier écrit: "Depuis bien longtemps, l'on se récrie sur l'inutilité des préfaces — et pourtant l'on fait toujours des préfaces. Il est bien connu que les lecteurs (pluriel ambitieux) les passent avec soin, ce qui paraîtrait une raison valable de n'en point écrire". Ou plutôt d'en écrire encore, si tant est qu'écrire ne veut pas dire nécessairement être lu. Il arrive que si les contemporains ne prennent connaissance ni des préfaces ni des livres, la postérité s'en charge, comme c'est le cas de Professeur Steven Tötösy qui non seulment a rassemblé avec peine et dépouillé toutes les préfaces des romans de langue anglaise et française du XIXe siècle canadien, mais les a catégorisées et systématisées. Cela donne au moins un lecteur, et mieux, un lecteur vraiment averti. Il y en a d'autres. Pour ma part, je dirige avec un de mes collègues une recherche subventionnée sur les préfaces et documents d'accompagnement aux rééditions d'oeuvres québécoises des origines à nos jours; cette expérience me permet d'affirmer qu'outre nous-mêmes, au moins une dizaine d'étudiants et d'étudiantes les on lus, dont certains en ont fait le sujet de leurs travaux de maîtrise et de doctorat. Le présent ouvrage est lui aussi le fruit d'une thèse de doctorat soutenue à Department of Comparative Literature and Film Studies de University of Alberta (Edmonton). Comme quoi l'Institution se charge parfois d'une occupation qu'on prétend laissée pour compte!

Écrire une préface à un ouvrage qui étudie le système des préfaces est toutefois un paradoxe qu'il faut d'abord souligner avant de tenter de le réduire. Même si elle introduit un livre savant, ma présentation n'échappe pas au classement taxonomique que Professeur Tötösy a construit pour traiter les éléments de son corpus. Il a d'ailleurs préalablement contrôlé toutes les définitions du terme et de ses équivalents dans les trois corpus français, anglais et allemand, où l'idée plus récente de *discours préfaciel* permet une extension des précédés d'analyse. Si je voulais sortir de la typologie des préfaces élaborée dans le chapitre 2 de cette étude, il me faudrait éviter les catégories de son protocole de lecture, par exemple, ne pas entrer dans l'un ou l'autre de des types, d'abord de nature axiologique, *apologetic, ethical, critical* (qui s'appuient les jugements de valeur morale, sociale, nationale, la préface est le "réceptacle naturel de l'idéologie", affirme Henri Mitterand), puis de nature stratégique, *acknowledgement* (reconnaissance, remerciement), *dedicatory* (cherche appui et autorité), *preemptive* (prédispose le lectorat, anticipe son accueil), les deux séries servant à des fins promotionelles, explicatives, voire subversives. Mais peut-on vraiment se soustraire aux nécessités d'un genre qui impose ses normes, ses règles et ses démarches? Je pourrais certes imiter ces préfaces où l'auteur s'adresse directement à son lecteur ("To the Reader", "Encore un mot, cher lecteur..".), pour l'enjoindre de lire le livre: "Lecteur, qui que tu sois: prends, lis et prononce". Non sans toutefois devoir revenir à cette obsédante constatation: "Reader, did you ever observe the manner in which a boy ignores the preface in his schoolbooks? If not, you do not know how much scorn a boy's face is capable of displaying". Quoi qu'il en soit, la fiche analytique de Professeur Tötösy repérerait facilement mon "type" de préface, ainsi que ses données systémique: références à la théorie et au genre littéraires, renvois à des textes célèbres, clins d'oeil ou appels au lecteur, et bien d'autres particularités, en somme un peu d'apologie, une pointe de critique, beaucoup d'explication en vue d'une certaine promotion, sans oublier l'intention de convaincre le lecteur de la validité du travail, sinon de le convertir à une nouvelle conception des études littéraires.

Toute ces précautions prises, inutiles sans doute, les risques demeurent. Et un devoir supplémentaire s'impose afin que la pensée de Vauvenargues (encore une référence à un texte littéraire!) ne se vérifie pas: "Une mauvaise préface allonge considérablement un mauvais livre". Car il s'agit d'un ouvrage solidement étayé par une documentation répertoriée de manière systémique et traitée selon des concepts théorique et des outils méthodologiques les plus affinés aujourd'hui. *The Social Dimensions of Fiction* a les qualités des travaux issus des théories systémiques actuelles, dont le polysystème d'Itamar Even-Zohar et l'étude (théorie) empirique de la littérature de Siegfried J. Schmidt. Cette dernière développée depuis plus d'une décennie en Allemagne, a la préférence de Professeur Tötösy. Deux orientations du travail en font foi, qui relèvent du "constructivism" de Siegfried J. Schmidt dont l'objectif est de déplacer la recherche du sens immanent des oeuvres vers celle des systèmes qui constituent et produisent le phénomène social et culturel de la littérature.[1] En premier lieu, l'auteur considère les textes de son corpus comme un ensemble de pratiques littéraires qui se rapportent à un genre (la préface), d'ailleurs "problématique", et non pas l'inverse, à savoir un genre qui définirait une série de textes. La recherche systémique et empirique le conduit à fixer les structures, les mécanismes, les processus et les valeurs qui gouvernent les opérations cognitives et communicatives entourant le phénomène des préfaces à cette époque donnée du XIXe siècle canadien. Il s'agit d'une opération de construction d'une réalité passée inscrite dans une perspective actuelle, celle de l'auteur et des développements théoriques de son temps. D'où le choix d'envisager le domaine d'étude comme un système de communication esthétique active où les interactions entre les pratiques esthétiques fondées sur la polyvalence des textes littéraires ne constituent pas un phénomène isolé mais au contraire sont comprises et intégrées dans ce système même dont les régularités lui sont propres. Reprenant ensuite le schéma théorique et méthodologique de Siegfried J. Schmidt, l'auteur analyse les données typologiques et systémiques des textes dans tous les lieux et les conditions de leur interaction, de la production (Produktionsbereich) à la médiation (Vermittlungsbereich), en passant par les processus de réception (Rezeptions-bereich) et de la "re-production" (Verarbeitungsbereich) (Chapter 4: "Analysis of the Systemic Dimensions of the Preface Typologies and of the Systemic Data of the Prefaces"). Le modèle a bien servi le buts de cet ouvrage et il permet une interprétation des données qui, en regard de la théorie générale (impossiblité d'objectiver la réalité, de trouver un sens dans le texte même), se présente comme une activité voisine de l'essai et non la simple application d'un procédure "scientifique".

Cette recherche systémique et empirique aboutit non pas à recopier la réalité, mais, pour le répéter encore, à construire le phénomène et les interactions de ses constituants, afin de saisir l'objet d'étude et de déterminer sa signification dans l'ensemble des autres phénomènes sociaux et culturels. La conclusion du travail fournit des résultats qu'on

---

1   Siegfried J. Schmidt, "The Logic of Observation: An Introduction to Constructivism", *Canadian Review of Comparative Literature/Revue Canadienne de Littérature Comparée*, Vol. XIX, No. 3, September/Septembre 1992, 295-311.

soupçonnait, mais que la démarche rend plus probants. D'abord, l'hypothèse de départ se vérifie: la préface de roman dans ce corpus et durant cette période est un "genre". L'homogénité du public lecteur (peu nombreux à l'époque), l'absence d'appel à un lecteur spécifique, l'attitude autoritaire du préfacier, marquée par la prédominance du récit au "je", ses soucis de reproduire les valeurs morales et sociales, mais non intellectuelles, économiques ou littéraires, tout cela définit un modèle de "Préface" qui serait commun aux deux littératures. Pourtant, si la comparaison montre que les similarités génériques semblent dominer, on aurait crû qu'entre les deux systèmes littéraires les différences seraient plus importantes au plan de l'interaction des données elles-mêmes qui marquerait ainsi une certaine "frontière" entre eux. C'est que l'analyse des deux systèmes préfaciels se présente de façon paradigmatique plus que de façon syntagmatique, c'est-à-dire plus dans une perspective de contiguïtés que d'interférences intra- ou intersystématiques. De sorte que les propriétés des deux littératures en question, si elles sont assez semblables dans le sous-système de préfaces de romans, le deviendraient peut-être moins si on les reliait aux autres éléments du système ou du polysystème global. C'est sans doute ce que laisse entendre la dernière phrase de la conclusion: "Having said this, the prefaces also reveal specific English-Canadian or French-Canadian properties which, in turn, point to differences in the mechanisms of the Canadian literary system". À la condition toutefois d'entendre "Canadian literary system" comme celui des deux systèmes littéraires de langues et de cultures différentes, encore en situation de dépendance au XIXᵉ siècle par rapport aux littératures anglaise, française, américaine, situation qui crée d'autres formes d'interférences pouvant jouer un rôle dans le fonctionnement de leurs quatre composantes (production, médiation, réception, re-production).

L'auteur de ce travail ne sera pas chagriné d'apprendre qu'il n'a pas fini ses recherches et qu'un autre programme se présente à lui, qui étudierait dans une perspective semblable les préfaces des autres genres canonique et non canonique: poésie, essai, théâtre, littérature religieuse, récits de voyage, légendes, mémoires, histoire, etc. Cette recherche apporterait sans doute des variations au modèle des préfaces de romans qu'il a défini. Dans ces cas de figure, le visage du lecteur serait peut-être autre, les intentions et les buts du préfacier se fonderaient sur des processus de valorisation différents et ainsi de suite. Si Professeur Tötösy a pu montrer de façon convaincante qu'il y un *genre* de préface de roman durant le XIXᵉ siècle canadien, il est permis de faire l'hypothèse qu'il n'existe pas un tel genre pour les recueils de poésie, d'essai, d'oeuvres historiques, etc., et qu'il ne soit pas possible d'assimiler partout et toujours les données ou les propriétés des deux systèmes littéraires en présence. Comme on le voit, cette étude est *séminale* en ce sens qu'elle en suscite d'autres, qu'elle renouvelle les question-nements, qu'elle trace des voies différentes de recherche. C'est une qualité qu'on ne retrouve pas dans toutes les thèses universitaires.

Clément Moisan
Centre de recherche en littérature québécoise (CRELIQ)
Université Laval (Québec)

Prefacing a Study of Prefaces,
Or,
the Nth Degree of Metadiscourse

Théophile Gautier's epigraph at the head of *Fortunio* reads: "For a very long time everyone has decried the futility of prefaces — yet everyone keeps writing them. We all know that readers (an already optimistic plural) skip them, which should itself be valid reason not to write any more". Or rather to keep writing them, if indeed writing be not necessarily destined to be read. It does happen, moreover, when the intended readers neglect both preface and book that posterity intervenes, as in the case of Professor Steven Tötösy, who has with great care not only gathered and inventoried all the prefaces in English and in French in Canada during the nineteenth century, but has also categorized and made them accessible to systemic and systematic analysis. Which means that there has been at least one reader of these prefaces, and a particularly lucid one. Still, there have been a few other readers. Myself and a colleague, for example, have a continuing research project on prefaces and related texts in re-editions of Québécois literature from the beginnings to present times. This experience allows me to attest that, apart from ourselves, at least a dozen students have read the texts in question, and several have taken them as subject for academic theses. In fact, this present work is the fruit of a doctoral dissertation in the Department of Comparative Literature and Film Studies at the University of Alberta (Edmonton). Decidedly, the academic institution does sometimes take charge of activities others have neglected!

In any event, writing a preface to a study of prefaces involves a paradox that must be addressed at the outset. Although mine is an introduction to a scholarly book rather than to a work of fiction, it does not stand outside the taxonomy Steven Tötösy devised to treat his subject matter. This taxonomy, the result of an exhaustive study of the definitions of the term and its synonyms in English, French, and German, uses the recent conceived notion of *prefatorial discourse* to expand the possibilities of analysis far beyond traditional criticism. If I wished to escape the typology of prefaces drawn up in chapter two of this study, I would first of all have to avoid falling into one or another of his categories of reading protocol he calls axiological, those founded on moral, social, or national grounds, be they *apologetic, ethical,* or *critical* — as Henri Mitterand states, "the preface is the natural receptacle of ideology". To the axiological must be adduced strategic protocols that offer *acknowledgement* (recognition or thanks), that are *dedicatory* (that seek support or endorsement), or *preemptive* (that predispose the reader, or anticipate his or her reaction). All of these strategic types can serve promotional, explanatory, or even subversive functions. Is there any possible way to escape the requirements of a genre like the preface, one that imposes its norms, rules, and sequences? To be sure, I could imitate those prefaces whose authors interpellate the reader ("To the Reader", "One final word, Dear Reader"), enjoining that he or she read the book that follows: "Dear Reader, whoever you may be, turn the page and read aloud". Though I would not go as far, I trust, as an author who would say: "Reader, did you ever observe how a boy ignores the preface in his school-books? If not, you do not know how much scorn a boy's face is capable of displaying". In any event, Professor Tötösy's analytical procedure would easily identify the category to which this very preface belongs, and would place it within the larger prefatorial system: my inevitable reference to literary theory and genre, learned references to famous texts, winks and similar appeals to the reader, and numerous other peculiarities, a pinch of apologia, a touch of critique, much explanation in prospect of some promotion or another, not to mention the endeavor to convince the reader of the validity of the work, if not that of converting him or her to a new conception of literary studies.

Yet, however much I strive to fulfill these terms, some risk of failure remains. And there is an additional duty in this case: since Vauvenargues (yet another learned reference!) has claimed that "a bad preface makes a bad book considerably longer", any ineptitude on my part might reflect poorly on the book in our hands. Let it be said then that this work is solidly backed up by documentation and proof laid out systematically and in accordance with the most up-to-date theoretical concepts and methodological tools. *The Social Dimensions of Fiction* has the quality of studies that have emerged from contemporary systemic theories of literature, the Empirical Theory of Literature as championned by Siegfried J. Schmidt and the Polysystem Theory of Itamar Even-Zohar. Professor Tötösy himself inclines towards the former, as can be seen, for example, in two of his concerns that derive from the "constructivism" of Siegfried J. Schmidt, whose goal is to shift attention away from study of the immanent meaning of works toward the systems that constitute and produce the social and cultural phenomenon of literature.[2] In the first place, the author considers the texts in his corpus as a set of literary practices related to a given genre, the preface, one that is moreover problematic — not the inverse, that is as a series of texts defined by a genre. Systemic and empirical research thus lead him to determine the structures, the devices, the procedures, and the values that govern the cognitive and communicative operations surrounding the phenomenon of prefaces in a given time and place, the nineteenth-century Canadas. This means constructing a past reality within a contemporary conceptual framework, that of the author and the theoretical currents of his/her time: hence the author's decision to treat his field of study as a system of active aesthetic communication wherein the relationships among the aesthetic practices manifest in the polyvalent literary texts are not understood as isolated phenomena but rather seized and integrated into the very system those regularities exemplify. Applying Schmidt's systemic and empirical theory and methodology, Tötösy analyzes the typological and systemic data at every site and circumstance of their interaction: production (Produktionsbereich), processing (Vermittlungsbereich), reception (Rezeptionsbereich), and post-production-processing (Verarbeitungsbereich) (cf. e.g., chapter four, "Analysis of the Systemic Dimensions of the Preface Typologies and of the Systemic Data of the Prefaces"). This model serves the author well and leaves room for an interpretation which, from a theoretical point of view (the impossibility of objectifying reality, of finding immanent meaning in the texts themselves), is closer in feeling to the essay than to any single minded application of a "scientific" method.

---

2   Siegfried J. Schmidt, "The Logic of Observation: An Introduction to Constructivism", *Canadian Review of Comparative Literature/Revue Canadienne de Littérature Comparée* 19.3 (September/Septembre 1992): 295-311.

This kind of systemic and empirical research does not pretend to produce a copy of reality, rather, it should be repeated, intends to construct the phenomenon itself and the interaction of its constituent elements, in order to grasp the object of study and to determine its significance within the context of other social and cultural phenomena. The conclusions reached are not altogether unsuspected, but procedural rigor makes them all the more persuasive. First of all, the initial hypothesis is verified: the novel preface in this corpus and at this period is indeed a genre. The homogeneity of the reading public (quite small at the time), the lack of appeal to a specific reader, the authoritarian attitude of the authors, suggested by the predominance of first person narrative, all of these features evincing moral and social — but not intellectual, economic, or literary values — set the parameters of a genre of the "Preface" that the two literatures had in common. Nonetheless, although comparison shows that generic similarities did prevail, one would have expected that differences between the two literary systems on the level of interaction of the data itself would be more pronounced, such that a certain "frontier" would appear. The reason is that this analysis of the two prefatorial systems is paradigmatic rather than syntagmatic in nature, that is more concerned with contiguities than with intra- or intersystemic interference. Although the properties of the two literatures in question are rather similar, at least within the novel preface sub-system, this would perhaps be much less the case if these traits were related to different features of the respective systems or the whole "polysystem". Such is suggested in the final sentence of the conclusion: "Having said this, the prefaces also reveal specific English-Canadian or French-Canadian properties which, in turn, point to differences in the mechanisms of the Canadian literary system". "Canadian literary system" must here be understood as one comprising two literary systems of different languages and cultures still dependent in the nineteenth century on English, French, and American literature, a situation generating other forms of interference touching on the four functions as defined above in the four systemic categories of production, processing, reception, and post-production processing.

The author of this study would not be unduly disturbed to be told that his work is far from over and that another project is waiting, a similar study of the prefaces of other canonical and non-canonical genres: poetry, essay, theatre, religious literature, travel literature, legends, memoires, history, etc. Such a project would further nuance the model of novel prefaces here constructed. In these hypothetical cases, the readers would perhaps be different, the aims and intentions of the preface writer would involve different procedures and values, and so on. Steven Tötösy has shown irrefutably that there was a novel preface *genre* during the nineteenth century in Canada, but this does not mean that there necessarily exist such a genre for collections of poetry, essays, historical studies, etc., or that the facts and the properties of the two literatures in question always coincide. This work is accordingly *seminal* in the sense that it calls for future study, renovates and reorients our thinking, and shows new directions for research. This is a quality not to be found in all university dissertations.

Clément Moisan
Centre de recherche en littérature québécoise (CRELIQ)
Université Laval (Québec)
(George Lang [University of Alberta], trans.)

INTRODUCTION

This work is a comparative study of nineteenth-century English-Canadian and French-Canadian novel prefaces, a previously unexplored literary topic. As a study in Comparative Literature — with the application of a specific literary framework and methodology — the study conforms to theoretical and methodological postulates formulated in and prescribed by this framework when applied. This *a priori* postulate necessitates that the research on and the presentation of the Canadian novel preface be carried out in a specific manner, as follows.

First, the study will establish the hypothesis that the preface to nineteenth-century English-Canadian and French-Canadian novels is a genre in its own right. This hypothesis will rest on the following: 1) a taxonomical survey of related terms meaning "preface"; 2) a survey of secondary literature of works dealing with the preface; 3) a discussion of the theoretical framework and methodology of the *Empirical Theory of Literature* and its appropriateness for the study of the preface; and 4) a discussion of the process of the compilation of the corpus of nineteenth-century Canadian novel prefaces (Chapter one). In a second step, the theoretical postulate outlined in the hypothesis will be put into practice by the development and production of a preface typology (Chapter two). In a third step, further tenets of the *Empirical Theory of Literature* will be tested on the corpus of the prefaces (Chapter three). In a fourth step, the prefaces will be analysed following the tenets formulated in and prescribed by the systemic framework applied (Chapter four).

The systemic framework and methodology that will be applied in this study is Siegfried J. Schmidt's work, known as the *Empirical Theory of Literature*, as presented in his book *Grundriß der empirischen Literaturwissenschaft* Vol. I *Der gesellschaftliche Handlungsbereich Literatur (Foundations for the Empirical Study of Literature: The Components of a Basic Theory*, R. de Beaugrande, trans. 1982) and Vol. II *Zur Rekonstruktion literaturwissenschaftlicher Fragestellungen in einer Empirischen Theorie der Literatur* (1980-82 and 1991).

As mentioned, the hypothesis that the preface is a genre will be built on four lines of reasoning. The first line involves a taxonomical survey. English, French, and German terms which have or have had the meaning "preface" indicate the literary historically autonomous status of the preface, i.e., that it is a genre in form and content. In addition, the taxonomical survey will implicitly sketch a *possible* history of the preface. The second argument derives from the examination of a selected but representative corpus of scholarly preface studies in German-, English-, and French-language scholarship. This survey will include such studies on the preface as Hermann Riefstahl's *Dichter und Publikum in der ersten Hälfte des 18. Jahrhunderts, dargestellt an der Geschichte der Vorrede* (1934), Hans Ehrenzeller's *Studien zur Romanvorrede von Grimmelshausen bis Jean Paul* (1955), Ulrich Busch's "Vorwort und Nachwort" (1961), Henri Mitterand's "Le Discours préfaciel" (1975), Claude Duchet's "L'Illusion historique: l'enseignement des préfaces (1815-1832)" (1975), Ulf Heyden's *Zielgruppen des Romans: Analysen französischer Romanvorworte des 19. Jahrhunderts* (1986), François Rigolot's "Prolégomènes à une étude du statut de l'appareil liminaire des textes littéraires" (1987), and the small number of English-Canadian and Québécois-Canadian studies existing on the preface in the Canadian literatures, as well as selected studies dealing with prefaces of specific authors. The third part of the hypothesis is the presentation of the *Empirical Theory of Literature* framework and methodology. On the one hand, this framework forms the base and point of departure of the whole of the present work. On the other hand, it is employed for the hypothesis of this study, namely for the notion that the application of this theoretical framework will produce new insights into the the Canadian literatures of the nineteenth century via the study of the novel preface. It is a contention here that the choice of the *Empirical Theory of Literature* as a theoretical model is appropriate because it allows for the study of the Canadian literatures in the context of social *and* literary relevance rather than in a one-dimensional aesthetically oriented one, which would lead, in the case of the preface, to one-sided and, consequently, limited results. Briefly, the *Empirical Theory of Literature* framework is based on the postulate that literature should be studied systemically, thus involving the research and study of literature *and* literary life. This systemic orientation of the *Empirical Theory of Literature* framework allows for the positioning of the prefaces in a more sophisticated context than a strictly aesthetically or text-only oriented context. Further, it is an important postulate of the *Empirical Theory of Literature* that literary analysis should be based on (constructivist) empirical research, while attention must be paid to avoiding the danger of a neo-positivist analysis. The empirical study of literature should follow the tenets of scientific inquiry: the "forming of a hypothesis, the putting it into practice, testing, and evaluation" (van Gorp *et al.* 116-17). This succession of scientific inquiry has been analogously carried out in the present study's four chapters. Among further postulates of the *Empirical Theory of Literature* framework is that its results should be presented in non-metaphorical language. The fourth point of the hypothesis that the Canadian novel preface is a genre documents the process by which the prefaces were compiled and touches on such problems as periodization, classification, canonization, etc.

The second step in the research on the Canadian preface, i.e. the level of "putting it into practice", concerns the development and production of a preface typology. In a good number of theoretical and critical studies about the preface there is a call for a corpus-based typology of this genre, as for example in Jacques Derrida's *La Dissémination* (1972) and Gérard Genette's *Seuils* (1987). To date, no study has appeared which offers a typology of a specific corpus of novel prefaces, or of other types of preface. Thus, the present work will respond not only to the *Empirical Theory of Literature* theoretical and methodological postulate requiring the classification, i.e. a typology of the preface, but it will also respond to scholarly interest demonstrated by scholars not involved with the *Empirical Theory of Literature*. The typology is based on a relatively large corpus of prefaces, particularly in the case of the English-Canadian prefaces. It is noteworthy that whereas the corpus of French-Canadian novel prefaces has previously been compiled and has undergone a (limited) amount of scholarly scrutiny, the large English-Canadian novel preface corpus has neither been compiled, nor studied until the present work.

The construction of the preface typology will be based to a lesser extent on selected theoretical works on novel prefaces, and largely on the specific characteristics of nineteenth-century English-Canadian and French-Canadian novel prefaces. These characteristics will be established by preliminary readings of selected prefaces. The structure of the preface typology will be intrinsically analytical in that it will rest on decisions of preface type that depend on pre-designed categories. These categories will include main categories and sub-categories of preface characteristics.

In a third step, specific tenets of the *Empiricial Theory of Literature*, as well as areas of interest discovered in the typology of the prefaces, will be applied in a further testing of the prefaces. This third step is to be understood, largely, as the testing of the specifically systemic characteristics and contents of the prefaces.

In the fourth and last step of the work, following the presentation of the preface typologies and their systemic characteristics, the data thus developed and produced will be analysed according to areas of the literary system as postulated in the *Empirical Theory of Literature* framework. This systemic framework consists of four areas: 1) Production (Author and Text); 2) Reception (Readership); 3) Processing (Publication); and 4) Post-Production Processing (Criticism and Scholarship). The prefaces will be analysed in each of these four areas.

The analysis proper (Chapter four) of the prefaces will be limited. The limitation is an unavoidable consequence of the large gaps existing in the secondary literature about the nineteenth-century Canadian literatures. As a successful application of the *Empirical Theory of Literature* is contingent upon the existence of a significant corpus of secondary literature, the lack of this corpus unavoidably curtails the success of the framework's application. For example, a discussion of readership must be based on, among other things, information about literacy levels. Unfortunately, English-Canadian scholarship about the nineteenth century has not as yet produced nearly enough on this subject and the situation is much the same in many other aspects of the nineteenth-century Canadian literatures. On the other hand, while this limitation will have to be recognized, the present study will augment the slowly expanding scholarship about the period. It will do so for several reasons: it will present an unrecognized and largely unknown literary genre not only in its Canadian context, but also in relation to the Western literary tradition; the typology of prefaces will be a first attempt to present this genre, based on a specific corpus; and the use of the *Empirical Theory of Literature* theoretical framework will demonstrate the applicability of a *systemic* socio-literary theory in comparative Canadian scholarship. It should be noted that although in Québécois-Canadian scholarship systemic studies are not unknown and much and excellent work has been done with research based on an institutional view of literature, the *Empirical Theory of Literature* framework has not yet been exploited.

Some — but by no means all — of the the results of this study confirm what has already been established in scholarship and thus the frequent criticism of the empirical study of literature — that it produces confirmation of what has been found intuitively — would appear to be justified to a limited extent. In response to such criticism the following can briefly be put. For one, the importance of this study lies in the application of a new theoretical framework to a hitherto undiscovered text type — at least as far as English-Canadian prefaces are concerned. Further, there is good reason to state what is *perhaps* obvious but has not been spelled out — and here is where the "scientific" tenets of the framework applied play an important role — in this case by the study of newly established texts in Canadian literary scholarship. The compilation of the prefaces; their typologization and consequently the establishing of their status as a genre in form, content, and function; the description of their relationship with a number of literary factors are further areas of this work which demonstrate both the appropriateness of the application of the *Empirical Theory of Literature* framework and methodology and the usefulness of the results of the application.

Clearly, there is still much work to be done in the nineteenth-century Canadian literatures, including the novel prefaces. For instance, in this study the relationship between the preface and the novel has been left unresolved. This was deemed necessary because of the self-imposed limits of the study and the argument that the preface is a text on its own. Similarly, many aspects of the *Empirical Theory of Literature* analysis could be expanded, once more published work emerges from the study of the nineteenth-century Canadian literatures or more time and effort can be spared for the scrutiny of primary sources.

In sum, this study increases our knowledge of an important period of the Canadian literatures and it will, it is hoped, interest scholars in studying these literatures with the use of a systemic framework and methodology of literature.

CHAPTER ONE

THE THEORETICAL FOUNDATIONS OF THE STUDY OF PREFACES AND
THE CORPUS OF THE NINETEENTH-CENTURY CANADIAN NOVEL
PREFACES

1. A Hypothesis: The Preface as a Genre

Preamble

A discussion of the preface as a genre is necessary for several reasons: a comparative study, this work is based on theoretical and methodological assumptions and these must be stated. In addition, the relatively unexplored state of the subject, the preface, necessitates a more detailed introduction to the object of the study. The theoretical position that the preface is a genre will be introduced by a taxonomical survey and with examples from the secondary literature. Further, a section arguing for the appropriateness of the application of the framework and methodology of the *Empirical Theory of Literature* for the study of the preface — and for the study of literature *per se* — will be presented. Lastly, the matter of the corpus of the prefaces will also be discussed. As the claim will be made that the *Empirical Theory of Literature* is a most appropriate framework and methodology for the study of the Canadian novel preface and as this framework prescribes that the steps of research taken be the "forming [of] a hypothesis, putting it into practice, testing, and evaluation" (van Gorp *et al.* 117), the structure of and sequence in this work will conform to this theoretical postulate. This is the more necessary, because such an approach to literature is, at large, most uncommon in literary scholarship.

1.1 Taxonomy

In the two languages and literatures, French and English, and consequently, in both English-Canadian and French-Canadian literatures,[1] there are terms that mean some type of "preface" or "préface". In other European languages and literatures the taxonomy of the term is similar. Here, English, French, and German prefatory taxonomies will be presented.[2]

In the history of prefatorial taxonomy, some terms were more frequently used at a particular time, while some were used more specifically than others. In the nineteenth century, but also at present, in both English and French it is the term "preface" or "préface", which best expresses and is most used for this type of text. In German the

---

1 A distinction is made between French-Canadian and Québécois-Canadian literature. While French-Canadian literature is used in reference to the nineteenth century, Québécois-Canadian literature is in reference to the twentieth century.

2 German-language scholarship in particular has contributed much to the study of the preface. Also, the volume of German-language prefatory taxonomy is significant. For these reasons, although this study is on the English-Canadian and French-Canadian novel preface, German-language prefatorial terminology and secondary literature will be included in this introductory chapter.

most often used term is "Vorwort", whose meaning is analogous to "preface" and "préface".

In one of the more recent theoretical studies of the preface G. Genette indicates the variety of French terms used for "préface":

Je nommerai ici préface, par généralisation du terme le plus fréquemment employé en français, toute espèce de texte liminaire (préliminaire ou postliminaire), auctorial ou allographe, consistant en un discours produit à propos du texte qui suit ou qui précède. ... J'ai dit "le plus fréquemment employé": la liste de ses parasynonymes français est fort longue, au gré des modes et innovations diverses, comme peut le suggérer cet échantillon désordonné et nullement exhaustif: introduction, avant-propos, prologue, note, avis, présentation, examen, préambule, avertissement, prélude, discours préliminaire, exorde, avant-dire, proème.... (150)[3]

This multitude of terms with almost synonymous meaning is, as mentioned, similar in English and in German. The taxonomical state of the preface, as will become clear, is an indication of a certain indecision as to what to call a type of text placed typographically separate at the beginning of a more clearly definable type of text, the main body of a novel or an anthology, for instance. At the same time, the multitude of terms must be understood in their relation to their usage in the different periods of literary history and, to a point, in their significance as different types of preface. It is for this reason that a taxonomical outline will be useful for an indication that the preface has a history, a typology, and as a preliminary argument for the notion that the preface is a genre.

Generally speaking, dictionaries are at best incomplete on the preface and its related terms. One does not need to go as far as H. Ehrenzeller, who, in reference to German-language dictionaries, wrote that "Die Wörterbücher sind schlecht auf die Vorrede zu sprechen. Sie bringen ihr Mißtrauen, wenn nicht gar Verachtung entgegen und sprechen ihr im Grunde die Daseinsberechtigung ab" (14), but he makes a point that is also valid for English and French dictionaries.

To begin with German prefatorial taxonomy, "Einleitung" seems to be seldom used in conjunction with a literary text. It is more often placed at the beginning of an instructional text. For example, an "Einleitung" may serve to introduce Kant's works (*Der Sprach-Brockhaus* 1935, 140). However, the earlier usage of the term "Einleitung" seems to have been somewhat different: "Einleitung ... schon seit vielen jahren schrieb man in Deutschland nach Klopstocks einleitung sehr läßliche hexameter" (Grimm VII 2164) while in the last decades its meaning and usage have changed again. The above example referring to the works of Kant appeared in the 1935 edition of the *Der Sprach-Brockhaus*, while in the 1984 edition it is defined thus: "Einleitung, die. ... gebe eine Einführung, verfasse ein Vorwort" (209).

The "Prolog" is defined specifically with reference to drama and as a text that clarifies the play for the readers:

---

3   Genette included, in addition to the preface, several other "paratextuals", such as the title, the epilogue, etc.

Prolog ... der prolog (zu Olint und Sophronia) zeiget das schauspiel in seiner höchsten würde, in dem er es als das supplement der gesetze betrachten läßt. ... denn es ist ganz klar, daß alle die stücke (des Euripides), deren prologe ihnen (den tadlern) so viel ärgerniß machen, auch ohne diese prologe vollkommen ganz und vollkommen verständlich sind. (Grimm VII 2164)

The *Reallexikon* places the "Prolog" in relation to plays as well and the article presents a history of the "Prolog" not only in the literature of Antiquity, but also in those of England and other European countries (262-83). In contemporary usage the "Prolog" comes closer to the meaning of preface: "Prolog ... a) einleitende Vorrede, Vorspiel (im Drama): der P. zu Goethes Faust; ... b) Vorrede, Vorwort, Einleitung eines literarischen Werkes" (*Duden* 5 2051).

The "Vorbericht" is perhaps the oldest term from among the terms meaning preface: "Vorbericht ... in älterer sprache meist eingeschränkt auf die einleitung eines buches, einer abhandlung oder sonst einer schriftlichen aufzeichnung; ... verzeichnet nur diese bedeutung und meint, daß der v. kürzer sei als die vorrede, 'obgleich auch beyde häufig mit einander verwechselt werden'" (Grimm XII 2 895). "Vorsprache" is a term that is used in relation to literature in a limited sense. From nine types of usage it means preface in one case only, and then in a now antiquated sense: "Vorsprache... wie das ahd. forasprahha, vorrede, einleitung: vorsprache ..., 'die vorrede eines buches, der eingang einer rede' ... schon bei Adelung als veraltet, der diesen gebrauch wohl überhaupt nur aus forasprahha erschlossen hat" (Grimm XII 2 1620). The "Vorrede", along with the "Vorwort" of contemporary usage, is the German term closest to "preface". This view is substantiated by the etymological meaning of the word: "vorrede ist dem lat. praefatio nachgebildet" (Grimm XII 2 1404). Although "Vorrede" has a large number of meanings, several of these meanings are congruent with that of "preface": "8) gewöhnlich in neuerer sprache von einer gesonderten, einführenden, berichtigenden ausführung vor einer schriftlichen darlegung, einem druckwerk (vgl. vorwort). ... 10) beziehung zum leser. a) im entwickelten nhd. gewöhnlich mit an: eine vorrede machen an den leser" (Grimm XII 2 1406-08).

Although the "Vorrede" is close in its meaning to the preface, in its contemporary meaning there still is a differentiation, which is perhaps explicable only because of different usage in East and West Germany. The West German *Brockhaus Wahrig* denotes "Vorrede" thus: "1. kurze, einleitende Rede vor der eigentlichen Rede" and only further down classifies "Vorrede" as an antiquated term for "Vorwort" (Wahrig 6 615). On the other hand, the East German *Handwörterbuch der deutschen Gegenwartssprache* defines "Vorrede" identically with "Vorwort" as "1.1 die einleitende, erläuternde Bemerkungen vor dem eigentlichen Text eines Buches" (Kempcke 2 1297). The meaning of "Vorrede" as defined in the *Brockhaus Wahrig* appears only as a secondary meaning in the *Handwörterbuch der deutschen Gegenwartssprache*: "1.2 einleitende Mitteilung vor der eigentlichen mündlichen Äußerung" (Kempcke 2 1297). If "Vorbericht" is defined as shorter in length than "Vorrede", "Vorwort" is again shorter than "Vorrede". This typological differentiation is apparent in the choice of the title of H.-J. Ansorge's *Art und Funktion der Vorrede im Roman von der Mitte des 18. Jahrhunderts bis zum Ende des 19. Jahrhunderts*. The differentiation makes sense not only because of the related meaning between "Rede" and "Wort", but also because the type of preface found in novels of the eighteenth and early nineteenth centuries was longer, generally speaking, than in the twentieth century.

Ultimately, the meaning of "Vorwort" seems to be analogous to that of "Vorrede" and most other terms here introduced. In the 1862 edition of the Grimm Brothers' *Deutsches Wörterbuch*, "Vorwort" is defined as "prolog, vorrede, einleitende vorbemerkung; ältere sprache bezeichnet dies durch vorsprache ..., vorrede ..., und vorbericht ..., soweit nicht das lat. praefatio, proemium, praeloquium oder prologus verwendet wird, erst im frühhd. kommt vorwort dafür auf" (XII 2 1964). The Grimm Brothers' nineteenth-century definition of "Vorwort" appears to have been borrowed for its modern, contemporary usage. Thus the *Brockhaus Wahrig* defines "Vorwort" as "Einleitung zu einem Buch, in der der Verfasser, Herausgeber od. Mitarbeiter des Werkes Sinn u. Zweck der Veröffentlichung darlegt" (Wahrig 6 624) and the East German *Handwörterbuch der deutschen Gegenwartssprache*, similarly: "Vorwort, das ... einleitende, erläuternde Bemerkungen vor dem eigentlichen Text eines Buches" (Kempcke 2 1299).

In French it appears that "avant-propos" was first used in a specific text at a specific time. Its meaning is defined as a "Discours en tête d'un livre" and "Le premier qui mit en oeuvre avant-propos pour prologue, fut Louis Lecharrond en ses *Dialogues*" (Littré 259). This means also that the term "prologue" served before this time for "avant-propos". At the same time, "avant-propos" seems to differ from the "préface" in its length: "Avant-propos ... Courte préface" (Hatzfeld *et al.* 1 171). A more specific definition is to be found in the more recent *Grand Larousse*: "avant-propos ... Courte préface, placée en tête d'un livre, où l'auteur expose succinctement ses intentions" (1 339). The designation of a shorter preface and the fact that the "avant-propos" contains the author's explanations in relation to the following text is the contemporary meaning found also in the *Grand Robert*: "Avant-propos ... Courte introduction (présentation, avis au lecteur, etc.)" (I 754).

"Introduction" is a term which is used to mean, among other things, "préface". However, its usage is more varied than that of "avant-propos". Its meaning in the sense of a "préface" is usually listed further down in dictionaries, after its primary meanings: "introduction ... Discours préliminaire en tête d'un ouvrage" (Hatzfeld *et al.* 1330). It should be noted that here the meaning of "introduction" does not explicitly refer to literature but to a book in general (Hatzfeld *et al.* 1330). Thus an "introduction" may be written as instruction to a non-fictional / non-belletristic text. The more contemporary usage of "introduction" implies a similar instructional usage, although the examples illustrating its usage are curiously from literary texts:

Développement placé en tête d'un ouvrage et qui tend généralement à présenter le sujet, à en justifier l'importance ou le choix: Ce livre a six pages d'introduction. Une introduction est plus étroitement liée au sujet qu'une préface. Il était absolument nécessaire de consacrer spécialement quelques lignes d'avertissement, de préface ou d'introduction à cette seconde édition (Hugo). (*Grand Larousse* IV 2793)

The "préface" denotes an introductory function: "Préface ... Discours préliminaire mis à la téte d'un livre" (Littré 1276), and "Préface ... Exposé préliminaire placé par un auteur en tête de son livre, pour indiquer l'objet, le caractère, etc." (Hatzfeld *et al.*

1796), and "Praefatio *vorrede* ... préface ... exposé préliminaire placé en tête d'un livre pour préparer le lecteur..." (Wartburg 9 293), and "Préface ... texte placé en tête d'un ouvrage pour le présenter et le recommander au public" (*Grand Larousse* V 4563), and "Préface ... texte placé en tête (d'un livre) et qui sert à le présenter au lecteur" (*Grand Robert* VII 704).

In essence, the "préface" is defined similarly to "introduction" but with a subtle difference, which becomes apparent only when one observes the examples used to illustrate the definitions. The difference is that more literary examples are used to define the usage and meaning of the "préface" than in the case of the "introduction".

The "prologue" is perhaps best defined as a "préface" for plays: "Prologue ... Ouvrage qui sert de prélude à une pièce dramatique" (Littré 1277), and "Prologue ... Dans une pièce de théâtre, sorte d'introduction qui annonce et prépare l'action" (Hatzfeld *et al.* 1820), and "Prologue *vorrede* ... discours préliminaire, avant-propos ... morceau qui sert de prélude à une pièce dramatique ou narrative" (von Wartburg 9 440). The *Grand Larousse*, interestingly, differentiates between the meaning of the "prologue" when used for the text of a play and for other genres: "prologue ... petite pièce de vers ou de prose qui précède et prépare une pièce de théâtre ..." and "prologue ... première partie d'une oeuvre littéraire (pièce, roman) ou artistique (film) où sont présentés des événements antérieurs à ceux qui se déroulent dans l'oeuvre proprement dite" (V 4670). The *Grand Robert* defines "prologue" again in relation to plays: "Prologue ... Discours qui introduit une pièce de théâtre" (VII 816). Québécois-Canadian dictionaries define "préface" and the other terms mentioned here similarly (cf. Bélisle).

In English the "preface" and the "introduction" are defined similarly to the French "introduction" and "préface". Also similar to the French, the "preface" in English fulfills a more functional role — as opposed to a discursive one: "preface ... A statement or brief essay, usually by the author, included in the front matter of a book, etc., and dealing primarily with the purpose and scope of the work" (*Funk and Wagnalls Standard College Dictionary Canadian Edition* 1063), and in the *Oxford English Dictionary* (*OED*) "Preface ... to introduce or commence (a writing or speech) with a preface or introduction" (1961, VIII 1266) and "Preface ... a preliminary statement by the author or editor of a book, setting forth its purpose and scope, expressing acknowledgement of assistance from others, etc." (*Random House Dictionary* 1134). Overall, the term "preface" in English seems to have had a wider variety of meaning and usage than the French "préface" and the German "Vorwort". The *OED* also lists diverse non-literary meanings, such as several liturgical meanings and usages or the general usage of "Preface ... To place before or in front of; to front or face (with something)" (1961, VIII 1266). The use of the term in literature occurred very early. Chaucer employed it in 1386 in his *Nun's Tale* (*OED* 1989, XII 343). The definition here is that a preface is the "introduction to a literary work, usually containing some explanation of its subject, purpose, and scope, and the method of treatment" (1989, XII 343). Interestingly, only the 1989 edition of the *OED* includes one single example of a preface written for a literary text (XII 343) and no literary examples are shown for "foreword" (1961, IV 447). "Prologue" in English, similar to its usage and meaning in French, is defined in relation to theatre: "Prologue ... The preface or introduction to a discourse or performance; a preliminary discourse, proem, preface, preamble; *esp.* a discourse or proem spoken as the introduction to a dramatic performance" (*OED* 1961, VIII 1450). On the other hand, in the *Random House* — an American dictionary — the meaning and usage of "prologue" is defined more in relation to prose than to dramatic works: "Prologue ... a preliminary discourse; a preface or introductory part of a discourse, poem, novel" and only further down, in its fourth position, is it related to theatre (1150). Disappointingly, as mentioned above in the case of the *OED*, English and American dictionaries do not give a historical perspective on the use of the preface as a text written to introduce the main body of a literary text, although the linguistic usage of the term "preface" and its related terms is documented at length. Similarly to Québécois-Canadian dictionaries, English-Canadian dictionaries do not define "preface" or the other terms differently from English or American dictionaries (e.g. *The Gage Canadian Dictionary*).

This brief but representative taxonomical survey of terms in German, English, and French, leads to the following general observation. In the nineteenth and twentieth centuries the term "Vorwort" / "preface" / "préface" is used in all three languages as the most frequent term to define a text placed before a literary text. Other terms, such as "Einleitung", "prologue", "introduction", etc., are used less often and denote slightly different types of the preface. The definitions of terms with the meaning of preface indicate that there are, in all three languages and literatures, several types of prefaces.

The uncertain state of the taxonomy raises questions, although it also underscores one essential proposition. The taxonomy proves the possibility of the postulate that prefaces may be viewed as at least texts "connected" with literature, even if one is party to a traditional, "canonical" definition of literature. Having taken this step, the question in the context of this present work may be formulated this way: if the *preface* is a term that is largely used to define texts that are placed, typographically separate, before a larger, the main, and literary, text of a book; if this "preface" is usually written by either the author of the main text or by someone who is from a similar "persuasion" as the author of the main text; and if there is, in addition, a variety of terms defining various types of the preface, can one postulate that the preface is a literary genre?

Although a metatheoretical discussion of whether classifications into genres in literature are justified or not would be interesting, this lies beyond the scope and objectives of the present work. However, it may be useful to refer to one recent work in which its author formulates a theory of genre that *a priori* allows for the designation of the preface as a genre. Adena Rosmarin writes in *The Power of Genre* that "once genre is defined as pragmatic rather than natural, as defined rather than found, and as used rather than described, then there are precisely as many genres as we need, genres whose conceptual shape is precisely determined by that need" (25). This notion has much validity, for instance, with respect to the nineteenth-century novel when a variety of terms was used in the preface, often calling a novel something else when it was, as we see it today, a novel (cf. Purdy). A pragmatic approach to the question of genre would indeed solve the terminological difficulties attendant upon the concept of genre. In the specific case of the preface, the taxonomical survey indicates this possibility: it is possible to distinguish the preface from other types of texts from a pragmatic and systemic point of view.

1.2 The Secondary Literature

The longevity of the preface is evident in both oral and written literature. This longevity vouches, among its other dimensions and characteristics usually associated with a genre, for its classification as a genre. For example, in the Gilgamesh epic the first tablet includes the author's "introduction" to the tale of Gilgamesh (*Gilgamesh* 57). Although obviously in this form one cannot speak of the preface as a genre but only of a concept of the preface as a genre, its existence strengthens the argument that the preface is a constant and significant part of all "telling". An early and clearly definable example of the preface as a genre is to be found in Martial's books of epigrams, that this author of Antiquity wrote:

"What is the good of a prologue," you say. "Is it not concession enough to you if I read the epigrams? And, besides, what do you mean to express in the said prologue that you could not express in verses? I see why tragedies and comedies are allowed one, because they cannot speak for themselves, but epigrams need no herald and are content with their own power of speech — and a hurtful one it is too; they can do their prologising on any page they will. I beseech you, if you think fit to listen, not to do an absurd thing, nor dress the dancer in a long robe. Furthermore consider whether a wooden sword satisfies you as a weapon against a fighter armed with a net. I, for my part, take my place with those spectators who protest against any such unfair conditions." I verily believe, Decianus, that you are right! Ah, if you only knew with what sort of prologue, and how long a one, you nearly had to deal! Be it then as you desire, and anyone who may chance to read this book shall owe it to you that he comes unwearied to page one. (Martial 43)

Ágnes Kenyeres interpreted Martial's preface as a "genre, a type of text in which the author by virtue of the last word speaks to the readers, contemporary and future, so that she/he himself be his/her own advocate and interpreter".[4] This specific aspect of the preface, namely the establishing of a personal relationship with the reader while advocating a particular point of view, is perhaps the most prevalent dimension of the preface in its history. Another early example is Petrarch's preface to his *De viris illustribus* in which he states that his address to the readership serves "the nature and goal of history" (Kohl 132).

The acceptance of the preface as a genre in manuals of literary terms or genres is limited. However, a few examples will illustrate the variety of perceptions of the preface. C. Hugh Holman's *A Handbook to Literature* contains the following two entries:

Preamble: An introduction. In formal sets of "resolutions" there is usually a *preamble* giving the occasion for the resolutions. This *preamble* is introduced by one or more statements beginning with "Whereas" and is followed by the resolutions proper, each article of which is introduced by the word "Therefore". (373)

---

4   "Az előszó — műfaj, olyan irásmű, amelyben a könyv szerzője az utolsó szó jogán áll a közönség, a kor és az utókor elé, hogy önmaga ügyvéde és interpretátora legyen" (my translation; Kenyeres 5).

This definition is obviously one for legal documents. Nevertheless, it is entered in a work of literary terms — most likely because the term "preamble" means "preface" as well, or, it functions here as part of a recognizable rhetoric and is formulaic in nature. The second entry in Holman's book is specifically on the preface:

Preface: A statement printed at the beginning of a book or article — and separate from it — which states the purpose of the work, makes necessary acknowledgements, and, in general, informs the reader of such facts as the author thinks pertinent. Some writers, notably Dryden, Shaw, and Henry James, have written *prefaces* that are really extended essays. Some whole books are called *prefaces*, as with C.S. Lewis's *A Preface to "Paradise Lost"*. (1992, 373)[5]

Gerald Prince's *Dictionary of Narratology* has one entry on the preface: "Prologue. An initial section in some narratives, preceding and not including the exposition or (part of) the complication" (78). Prince's definition, as many of his narratological terms, is related to Greek and Latin rhetorics. Similarly, Heinrich Lausberg's much earlier *Handbuch der literarischen Rhetorik* (1960) is based, in a more detailed and explicit manner, on the rhetorics of Antiquity. His book contains a precise definition and typology of the preface (I 150-63 and *passim*). Although Lausberg's work is based on Greek and Latin rhetorics, and thus his concept and examples are in reference to oratory, his statements about the preface as a concept and as a genre (*genus*) in Greek and Latin literature are applicable to the preface in general: "Das Exordium ..., prooemium ..., Principium ..., exorde ..., prologue ist der Anfang der Rede. Ziel des exordium ist es, die Sympathie des Richters (oder im weiteren Sinn: des Publikums) für den (parteimäßig vertretenen) Redegegenstand zu gewinnen" (I 150). Lausberg's typology of the "Exordium" is almost as detailed as Genette's. The main difference between Genette's typology of the preface and Lausberg's typology of the "Exordium" is that the several types of the "Exordium" all signify some relationship between "das Publikum" and the orator, but the different possibilities of the orator's voices in the context of narration are not developed.

Again in relation to speech rather than written prose, Wolfgang Kayser's *Das sprachliche Kunstwerk* contains a definition of the preface in the context of drama. The actor (speaker) performs the prologue on behalf of a designated protagonist:

Im älteren Drama gibt oft ein besonderer Sprecher in einer Art Prolog ans Publikum die Exposition; Tieck, der auch in diesem Fall alte Techniken zu beleben suchte, verband in seiner *Genoveva* Prolog und Drama, indem er als Prolog- (und Epilog-) Sprecher den Heiligen Bonifacius auftreten ließ. (199)

Alistair Fowler, in *Kinds of Literature*, discusses the concept of the preface in a section "Opening Formulas and Topics". Fowler briefly attempts to describe a history of the preface. His understanding of the preface, however, as indicated in the title of the

---

5 In previous editions, "statement" was further qualified by "short introductory statement", and "author" was deleted in the new edition, thus eliminating an ambiguity that allowed for the assumption that the preface was written largely by the author of the book itself (cf. Holman 1980, 349).

section "Opening Formulas and Topics", allows for the inclusion of, for example, the leading of the reader into the story within the narrative. In other words, he does not delineate the preface as a spatially (typographically) separated text (95-105). His discussion suggests that the preface as a genre is a later development and, at best, is a type of text that exists in relative dependence on the main text. His verdict, although he insists on the priority of the main text as the determining fact, implies that the preface is a genre in its form of "threshold", very much in the sense of Genette's "Seuils" (Fowler 105).

A concise dictionary definition of the "Vorwort" appears in Gero von Wilpert's *Sachwörterbuch der Literatur*:

Vorwort, einem Werk vorangestellte kurze und persönlicher gehaltene Vorbemerkung des Autors selbst (<Vorrede>), z.T. auch e. anderen Autors (<Geleitwort>) oder Herausgebers über Sinn, Aufgabe, Ziele, Methode, Anlage und Entstehung desselben, Rechfertigung des Verfassers und Erwiderung früherer Kritiken u.ä. für den Benutzer Wissenswertes. Teil der Autorenstrategie zur Leserlenkung, Korrektur des Erwartungshorizonts, Beteiligungsangebot und Einstimmung auf die ästhet. Erfahrung, gelegentl. auch Manifest e. neuen Richtung. Seit den antiken Historikern (Herodot, Thukydides, Plutarch, Livius) verbreitet. Berühmte Beispiele sind die langen V.e G.B. Shaws zu seinen Dramen. (1019)[6]

Theoretical scholarship and works on the history of the preface are scarce in general, and there is, apparently, no work on the history of the preface in any Western literature. That such a history is conceivable or, more than that, desirable, appears, interestingly, in a preface: "One could write a history of theories of translation, a history of the relationship between author and translator, indeed between author and reader, by writing a history of the preface as genre" (Godard 1).

In the three languages — and consequently in several national scholarships based in these languages — in the secondary literature there are, if not a large, at least a significant number of theoretical and historical works on the preface. In the following, a selection from these works will be presented. These works, of course, approach the preface from various points of view. It is possible to group these approaches into three: 1) The preface is discussed as a genre; 2) The preface is analysed from the point of view of discourse analysis; and 3) The preface is studied as written for a specific text or texts, e.g., the history of the preface to novels.

In German-language scholarship, one of the earlier works on the preface is Hermann Riefstahl's *Dichter und Publikum in der ersten Hälfte des 18. Jahrhunderts, dargestellt an der Geschichte der Vorrede* (1934). Riefstahl discusses the preface and its function in eighteenth-century German poetry:

In dem Zeitraum von etwa 1680 bis 1750 ist es stehender Gebrauch, der Veröffentlichung einer Dichtung oder Sammlung von Gedichten eine Widmung, ein Widmungsschreiben (genannt "Zuschrift") und eine Vorrede (auch "Vorbericht) voranzuschicken. Diese literarischen Gebilde

---

6   The entry also contains a short bibliography of German-language works on the preface.

sind in dieser Zeit sehr ausgeprägt; sie treten, voneinander und von der Dichtung getrennt, als äusserlich selbständige Teile auf.... (5)

What is of note here is that Riefstahl defines the preface by listing its variously used terms of "Widmung, Widmungsschreiben, Zuschrift, Vorrede, Vorbericht" as a "literarisches Gebilde". In other words, "literary structure" means genre.

Another early scholar of the preface, Hans Ehrenzeller, in his book *Studien zur Romanvorrede von Grimmelshausen bis Jean Paul* (1955), ventures to pinpoint the time and place when the preface became a convention and consequently a genre in German literature:

In der zweiten Hälfte des 18. Jahrhunderts wird — wohl hauptsächlich durch den Einfluß englischer Vorbilder[7] — die scherzhafte Verwendung der Romanvorrede zur eigentlichen Mode. Die Reflexionen über die Form häufen sich, und manche Schriftsteller scheuen sich nicht, die Vorrede zum Hauptgegenstand ihrer Vorrede zu erheben. Eine eigentliche Vorreden-Inzucht fängt an zu blühen, ein Kult der Vorrede um der Vorrede willen. (17)

Ulrich Busch, in his often cited article "Vorwort und Nachwort", accepts the definition of the preface as a genre but refers to the confusion surrounding its status, form, and function:

Es wäre nicht nötig, solch einen Vorgriff zu benutzen, wenn sich die Schriftsteller darüber einig wären, daß das Vorwort eine eigenartige literarische Erscheinung sei, dass es einen bestimmten Grund und bestimmte Formen habe und dass die eine Form so und jede andere Form anders zu nennen sei. (349)

Busch also acknowledges what became obvious in the taxonomical survey, namely that in different literary periods different terms were preferred for the preface. Nevertheless, the notion that the preface is a genre, is here too accepted.

Ansorge's book previously mentioned book, *Art und Funktion der Vorrede im Roman...*, is important because it is one that, in distinction to almost all other works on the preface including the present one, develops a prefatorial typology and discusses the preface in a discourse relation to and as an integral part of the novel itself. The prefatorial typology is developed along the lines of novel types. The first preface type is the "romanhafte Vorrede" to the "Ich-Roman" or to the auctorial novel. The second type is the preface ("Einleitung") to the "Er-Roman", characterized by its digressive function of providing information without an aesthetic narrative. The third and last prefatorial type is thought to be one of aesthetic functionality. This last type may, however, fulfill a function of the first type, thus situating these prefatorial types in various configurations and overlaps (220-21).

---

7   Since English scholarship on the preface is almost non-existent and most studies on the preface are about the modern period, one can only guess whom Ehrenzeller could have meant. He must have been referring to such texts as Sterne's *The Life and Opinions of Tristram Shandy*.

A theoretical work on genres, again in reference to a specific literary period, Fritz Nies's and Jürgen Rehbein's *Genres mineurs: Texte zur Theorie und Geschichte nichtkanonischer Literatur (vom 16. Jahrhundert bis zur Gegenwart)* recognizes one type of the preface, the "notice", as a genre:

Notice ... La *notice* peut se présenter sous deux formes, soit comme introduction à un livre, soit comme ouvrage séparé. Dans le premier cas, elle contient d'ordinaire la vie de l'auteur du livre, des éclaircissements sur son époque et sur les personnages avec lesquels il a été en relation, des jugements sur le fond et la forme de son ouvrage. (93-94)

The most important element of the notion that the preface is a genre is best formulated by the question "What does it do and how?" This question combines the notion that the preface is a genre, on the one hand, with a typology of the preface, the "how", on the other.

The works of two earlier scholars of the preface, H. Riefstahl and H. Ehrenzeller, contain answers to the above theoretical question, although they inquire into prefaces written to specific types of texts in specific literary periods. Jacques Derrida and, more so, Gérard Genette, formulate more theoretical answers to the above question. To begin with Riefstahl, he defines the main objectives and the main components of a preface as:

Die Hauptgegenstände der Vorrede sind: 1. der Autor selbst, 2. das veröffentlichte Werk: Inhalt und Absicht, Quellen und Vorgänger, Veranlassung und Entstehung, Stil ("Schreibart"), 3. die literarische Gattung: historische Entwicklung, theoretische Bestimmung, 4. das Publikum, 5. die Kritik, 6. Zeit und Volk. (5-6)

Although Riefstahl's work concerns the eighteenth century and prefaces to poems only, his observations are applicable to prefaces in general. His definition implicitly postulates a typology of the preface. At the same time, he concedes that the above categories are not part and parcel of all prefaces but that the prefacer's main objective is to obtain a favourable judgement (5). In other words, the main function of the preface in addressing the reader originates in the author's second-guessing and his authorial insecurity where he does not trust either his own value as author or the readership (64-65). Another important contribution made by Riefstahl is that he discusses what types of texts require a preface. He suggests that a preface is justified for those genres that require private reading ("private Lektüre"), such as poetry, the epic, and the novel (66).

Ehrenzeller, who also proposes a typology of the preface, derives prefatorial function from the innate insecurity of the author and contends that prefaces written to justify or excuse the work often contain an apology for the preface itself (14). But Ehrenzeller connects this innate authorial fear to a deeper discomfort, which exists in relation to one of the purposes of the preface. The basic authorial discomfort he sees in the author's perception that it is wrong to praise or to criticise one's own work, because that effectively becomes a way to influence critical judgement by the readership (15). It is from this insecurity and discomfort, which authors cannot escape and then attempt to override by writing the preface, where the main function of the preface, promotion, emanates.

The mechanism of the preface consists for Ehrenzeller in three factors: the author, the reader, and the main text. The author is involved because the contextual characteristics of a preface are explanations and biographical data about the author given by himself/herself. The statements could also extend to judgements on his/her work. Reader-contextual characteristics serve to regulate the relationship between the author and the readers. Here, the choice of the author's voice is of importance: does the author address the readership directly or indirectly? Advice to the readership as to when and how they should read the book are further characteristics. Text-contextual characteristics may consist of the main idea or theme of the book, its short summary, the genesis of the work. The latter may include the mention of secondary sources, previous similar works, the explanation of the title, etc. The text-contextual characteristics may also consist of justifications of an aesthetic, moral, or other nature. For example, in prefaces of the sixteenth and seventeenth centuries the justification of laughter based on health reasons was frequent. Also, the relationship between fact and fiction is included in this category. Ehrenzeller includes in this category defences against opponents, enemies, critics, colleagues, the pirating of prints, typographical mistakes by the printer, commercial dedications, and advertisements (35-38).

An important theoretical work dealing with the preface in German scholarship is Claus Träger's chapter "Vorwort-Geschichte als Spiegel bürgerlicher Ideologie- und Methodengeschichte" in his book *Studien zur Realismustheorie und Methodologie der Literaturwissenschaft* (183-248). Träger perceives the preface as a genre in which the science of literature ("Literaturwissenschaft") reaches its unity of literary history, theory, and criticism (185). This opinion is based, however, on the mechanisms of a specific type of preface, namely prefaces written for translated works and re-editions: generally, prefaces written by other than the author of the main text, critically appraising the work. Analyses of this type, in essence the second type in Ansorge's typology, provide an important perspective for the rarely assessed other-than-the-author-of-the-main-text preface type. It is important because the analysis extends to such areas as the role of the publisher, the publishing industry, manifestations of literary scholarship, etc.

In German scholarship in particular, in addition to the theoretical studies of the preface there is a sizable corpus of works dealing with prefaces of specific periods and genres. For example, Georg Jäger in his *Empfindsamkeit und Roman* (1969), Ernst Weber in his *Die poetologische Selbstreflexion im deutschen Roman des 18. Jahrhunderts* (1974), Sven-Aage Jørgensen in an article, "Warum und zu welchem Ende schreibt man eine Vorrede? Randbemerkungen zur Leserlenkung, besonders bei Wieland" (1976), and Peter Küpper in an article, "Author ad Lectorem: Vorreden im 18. Jahrhundert: Ein Forschungsvorschlag" (1978) deal with the preface written to novels of the eighteenth and early nineteenth centuries. An example of more recent prefatorial study when attention is paid to specific prefatorial characteristics is Harald Stang's *Einleitung — Fußnote — Kommentar* (1992). Stang discusses forms of paratextual discourse among which he places "Vorwortparodie" (227-35).

In more recent French scholarship, Jacques Derrida, in the chapter "Hors livre — préfaces" of his book *La Dissémination*, and Gérard Genette in a chapter on the preface in his book *Seuils*, designate the preface as a genre. Furthermore, both Derrida and

Genette reformulate the typological dimension of the preface. For Derrida, the necessity of a typology is based on the apriorial question:

Mais que font les préfaces? La logique n'en est-elle pas plus surprenante? Ne faudra-t-il pas en reconstituer un jour l'histoire et la typologie? Forment-elles un genre? S'y regroupent-elles selon la nécessité de tel prédicat commun ou bien sont-elles autrement et en elles-mêmes partagées? (14)

Derrida ultimately ascribes a directive and affirmative function to the preface:

La préface, mode synthétique de l'exposition, discours des thèmes, des thèses et des conclusions, précède ici, comme toujours, le texte analytique de l'invention qui l'aura lui-même effectivement devancée mais qui ne peut pas, sous peine de rester illisible, se présenter ou s'enseigner lui-même. (44)

and

Elle [la préface] ne deviendra discours de la méthode, exposé de la poétique, ensemble de règles formelles, qu'après le parcours irruptif d'une méthode pratiquée cette fois comme un chemein qui se fraye et se construit lui-même, sans itinéraire préalable. D'où l'artifice d'une préface qui "ne paraîtra peut-être pas assez naturelle" et qui en tout cas ne sera jamais simplement biffée. (45)

The preface and its discourse mechanisms and function are perhaps best summarized in the discussion of Hegel's prefaces:

Il [Hegel] problématise la préface selon ce que le mot veut dire: vouloir-dire, pré-dire, avant-dire (pre-fari) du prologue ou du prolégomène conçu (tel un vivant) et proclamé depuis l'acte final de son épilogue. Dans le discours, le logos reste auprès de soi. Ce qui devrait pourtant interdire de considérer l'écriture (ici le pro-gramme, la pré-scription, le pré-texte) comme le simple déchet empirique du concept, c'est que ce déchet (car il ne s'agit pas ici de le relever de cette condition mais de le questionner autrement) est coexistensif à toute la vie du discours. (57)

Genette, too, in his book *Seuils*, asks, "Mais que font les préfaces?" (182) and proceeds with a justification for a preface typology: "toutes les préfaces ne 'font' pas la même chose — autrement dit que les fonctions préfacielles diffèrent selon les types de préface" (182). Before presenting a typology of the preface, Genette sketches, more or less in strictly theoretical terms, a history of the preface in Western literature. In the section entitled "Les fonctions de la préface originale", he presents six main types of preface (87-218) and in "Autres préfaces, autres fonctions", he proposes several more types (219-70).[8]

To discuss Genette's typology here in its entirety would not be useful, more so, because his typology, as will become clear in the subsequent Chapters of the present work, does not seem appropriate for the analysis of English-Canadian and French-

---

8   For a recent study of the paratextual — apart from Genette's work — see John Pier's "Pragmatisme du paratexte et signification" (1988).

Canadian novel prefaces.[9] At the same time, it must be acknowledged that Genette's typology is detailed and sophisticated, and it could be used to analyse a different corpus than that of nineteenth-century Canadian novel prefaces.

Other important French contributions to the theoretical scholarship of the preface include studies by H. Mitterand, C. Duchet, and F. Rigolot. In an article titled "Le Discours préfaciel" (1975), H. Mitterand postulates the preface as a genre: "Ce genre, nous l'avons dénommé le discours préfaciel, parce qu'il nous ... a semblé qu'il avait des caractéristiques linguistiques spécifiques" (3). Mitterand then approaches the question of the function of the preface in the nineteenth-century French novel by proposing that it is ideological: "Il me semble en effet que la préface est un réceptacle naturel de l'idéologie" and the ideology of the preface is manifested in its "discours didactique" (7). This didacticism, according to Mitterand, possesses three major characteristics:

> Elle enseigne, sur le mode de l'universel — à l'aide du présent gnomique — ce qu'est la littérature, et ce qu'est en particulier le genre littéraire qui a le plus grand besoin d'être situé, étant donnée l'incertitude de son statut rhétorique: le roman. Comme le discours didactique, elle met en ordre l'exposé de ses arguments conformément aux règles des traités de belles-lettres. Elle suppose les problémes résolus et en indique les solutions. Son discours est résolument affirmatif. (7)

For Mitterand the main functions of the preface are: 1) the intention of didacticism, in particular in promoting and positioning the novel within literature; 2) the presentation of this promotion in a literary style and language; and 3) to present propositions for solutions to questions arising from the above two functions (10-11). He adds that the polemical preface usually attacks critics. Needless to say, the functional characteristics of the preface proposed by Mitterand are at the same time typological.

Overall, there are more studies on prefaces written for specific novels. The reason for this may lie in the coincidence of the prominence of the novel in the nineteenth century as far as publication and readership were concerned, when at the same time the novel was being resisted in scholarship, by "serious" critics, religion, the educational system, etc., and of the proliferation of prefaces written for this relatively new genre. This is not only evident when one is familiar with the novel literature of the nineteenth century, but is also clear from the secondary literature on the preface. Thus it should not come as a surprise that the notion of the preface as a genre can be found most explicitly in studies with reference to specific novels with prefaces. Henri Mitterand writes in his *Le Discours du roman* (1980): "La préface de roman, au XIXe siècle, est un document sur la théorie du genre romanesque" (21) and in his article "Le Discours préfaciel": l'étude des préfaces de roman au XIXe siècle, prises à la fois en tant que documents sur la théorie du genre romanesque, et en tant que spécimens d'un genre. Ce genre, nous l'avons dénommé le *discours préfaciel*" (1980, 3). A similar recognition of the purpose and function of the preface to the historical novel is discussed by Claude Duchet in his article "L'Illusion historique — L'Enseignement des préfaces (1815-1832)":

---

9   Genette's typology is mainly based on a differentiation of prefatorial-authorial voices. This having not been an important aspect of Canadian prefaces, his typology cannot be meaningfully implemented.

Tout se passe comme si par l'accumulation des références au Réel, à l'Histoire, le romancier ou le préfacier essayait de lutter contre un processus de déréalisation insidieuse. Le singulier, tentation et production du romanesque, éloigne du spécifique, domaine de l'histoire. Multiplier les références, les particularités, c'est produire l'étrangeté et sortir de l'Histoire. Et même, en exhibant ses preuves, en insistant sur son exactitude, le préfacier finit par mettre en question la capacité du roman à créer l'illusion de l'Histoire. (266)

Further, the journal *L'Esprit créateur* devoted a special issue in 1987 to the preface in French literature. Among the articles in the journal is François Rigolot's "Prolégomènes à une étude du statut de l'appareil liminaire des textes littéraires", a theoretical study. Here too, the specificity of the preface as a genre is recognized:

La nature et la fonction de l'appareil liminaire des textes littéraires (préfaces, introductions, ouvertures, prologues, avis, avant-propos, poèmes d'escorte ou pièces d'encadrement) font l'objet depuis quelques années d'analyses critiques dont l'enjeu ne saurait être sous-estimé. ... La préface étant, de ce point de vue, un genre codé.... (7-8)

And Rigolot, too, calls for a history of the preface, as well as studies on prefaces to specific literary texts: "Il faudrait d'ailleurs tenir compte non seulement des états synchroniques mais de la diachronie des préfaces dans les cas où le texte a subi de nombreux remaniements" (13).[10]

In English-language scholarship, studies on the preface are generally limited to the study of prefaces by particular authors. This is also the case with M.A. and Ph.D. dissertations. Here, a few examples of works on some of the major prefacers shall be mentioned. Walter Scott's prefaces are generally recognized as important texts and they are often used as illustrations of prefatorial functions. Weinstein's book, *The Prefaces to the Waverly Novels*, is such a study of prefatorial function and form. U. Brumm's article, "Hawthorne's *The Custom-House* and the Problem of Point of View in Historical Fiction", although a study on a single author and a specific genre, contains some theoretical discussion about the purpose and function of the preface:

The narrator of a fiction cannot quite express all that is necessary in order to establish a historical point of view toward his story. This is the reason why authors of the historical novel and, also, of the early novel which pretended to relate a true story, have often found it convincing and useful to create a frame which separates the functions of editor and narrator, or to add an "author" or "editor" who informs the reader about his sources, problems, or intentions, and is thus able to establish an additional, in most cases, a historical point of view, somewhat outside the narrative proper. (408)

G.G. Harpham's unpublished paper, "Joseph Conrad and the Art of the Preface", contains some theoretical discussion. This scholar defines the preface thus:

---

10 This article also includes a selected but very useful bibliography of preface studies in an appendix.

Prefaces are written after the book but are read before the book. In temporal terms, therefore, they occupy a liminal phase between the writing and the reading of the book, marking a frame and mediating between the two activities. This mediating function accounts for the disproportionate importance the preface can, on occasion, assume: although it is neither the writing nor the reading, it can serve to justify and rationalize the one and to circumscribe and direct the other. The preface is where the author asserts ownership of the book, directing the reader to use it only in certain ways. ... For both reader and writer, the preface is a space of reduced tension and correspondingly free communication. ... In terms of communication, the preface makes perfect sense; it accords with our most routine models of social exchange. (n.pag.)

K. Bales's article, "Hawthorne's Prefaces and Romantic Perspectivism", argues that the study of Hawthorne's prefaces has been limited to the discussion of romances and novels in the prefaces. Bales suggests that Hawthorne's prefaces are important in the context of his [Hawthorne's] perception of readers and of how the narrative of the prefaces relates to the narrative of the novels *per se*. T.D. Adams's article, "To Prepare a Preface to Meet the Faces That You Meet: Autobiographical Rhetoric in Hawthorne's Prefaces" is again a study on a single author. Adams asks the question whether Hawthorne was deliberately misleading about his autobiography and establishes that Hawthorne's prefaces are constructs between the fictional and the factual (non-fictional). In other words, Hawthorne wrote his prefaces in a combination of real and imaginary (fictitious) components. Th.C. Carlson, in an article on Melville that includes some aspects of this author's prefaces, argues in a similar manner: namely, that very little is to be taken literally in Melville's prefaces. He also points to differences in the prefaces to the American and English editions. W.R. Goetz's article, "Criticism and Autobiography in James's Prefaces" again argues that the prefaces are go-betweens of truth and fiction. He suggests that James's prefaces are characterized by a specific prefatory narrative. A literary historical study of James's prefaces is found in P.B. Labadie's *Critical Response to the Prefaces of Henry James: A History of the Development of Understanding and Appreciation of James's Theory of Fiction*. F. Kaplan, in his article "Fielding's Novel about Novels: The 'Prefaces' and the 'Plot' of *Tom Jones*", designates Fielding's narratological device of speaking to the reader in the first chapter of each of the eighteen books as a prefatorial device. A sign of the more recent interest in prefaces is J.R. Nabholtz's book *"My Reader My Fellow-Labourer": A Study of English Romantic Prose*, in which he discusses Coleridge's and Wordsworth's prefaces.

In English-language scholarship an analogue of the Genettian concept of the paratext is "frame narration", as postulated by Bernard Duyfhuizen in his *Narratives of Transmission* (1992). Duyfhuizen's study of the preface is, generally speaking, an adaptation of Genette's paratext but he focuses on the narrative interrelationship between the preface and the main text, i.e., the novel (cf. 157-78).

One of the most recent and largest corpus-based study of the preface is Ulf Heyden's *Zielgruppen des Romans: Analysen französischer Romanvorworte des 19. Jahrhunderts* (1986). Although Heyden's main concern is the addressing of different groups of readers in the prefaces, his book contains useful theoretical discussions for the study of English-Canadian and French-Canadian novel prefaces. He postulates a number of questions for his study. For example: are specific groups of readers addressed in the prefaces? Is there a relationship between the literary theoretical statements and statements about the author himself in the prefaces and the perception of author and literature in the readership? Do the prefaces contain socio-historical data, i.e., are the prefaces socio-historical sources and what do they contain with regard to the "business" of literature? Although Heyden rejects a typology of prefaces and does not discuss their semantic characteristics, his conclusions are important because they provide insights about the shape and form of the nineteenth-century French readership of novels. The various types of prefacers, e.g., their professions and their function in literary life ("Literaturbetrieb"), and their opinions as stated in the prefaces, are analysed in their relationship with the readership and the readership's literary interests and perceptions. The analysis is applied to various features of women prefacers as well as of the female readership. Heyden notes that the analysis of the prefaces cannot be understood as giving definitive results for the understanding of the readership. For example, he notes that the prefaces contain relatively few examples of the addressing of a readership in the lower classes. The last result of the analysis is that the prefaces exemplify the constantly changing composition of the readership. Prefaces are "facettenhaft" (16, 199-202).

In conclusion, a return to the original question, which is one of the most important of the theoretical and methodological bases of this study — can the preface be "classified" as a genre in its own right? — is appropriate. The above examples and brief discussions will suffice to allow theoretically and methodologically for such a classification. A general theoretical position-taking on the problem of genre and which supports the above arguments is provided, for example, by F. Nies, who writes in an article that since the 1970s genres are again appearing in literary scholarship and their value for systemic studies and the theory of the science of text is being rediscovered (1988, 326). Nies's perspective on the genre not only justifies the postulate that the preface is a genre in its own right, it also justifies its analysis from a systemic point of view. Finally, Genette's work most poignantly postulates the notion that the preface is a genre: "Des degrés divers, et avec des inflexions diverses selon les types, ... la préface est peut-être, de toutes les pratiques littéraires, la plus typiquement littéraire, parfois au meilleur, parfois au pire sens, et plus souvent aux deux à la fois" (270).

1.3 The Literary System and the Empirical Theory of Literature[11]

In the last two or three decades a number of innovative literary theories and methodologies have emerged which can be described, collectively, as a "systemic" approach to literature. This approach can be defined in alternative ways when the point

---

11 In English-language literary studies the terms "empirical" and "science" have negative connotative associations. For this reason, the term "science" from the more usual designation of *Empirical Science of Literature* is replaced with "theory". The term "empirical" — as an important element of the theoretical framework remains in the taxonomical designation of the framework and methodology (for a dictionary entry of the *Empirical Science of Literature* in English cf. Tötösy [1993a] and for a version of the following discussion dealing with systemic approaches for the study of literature, with an extensive bibliography, cf. Tötösy [1992a]).

of departure is taken from a variety of "predecessor" frameworks or simply points of view. For instance, the nineteenth-century notion of intellectual or cultural history, if taken in its approach to literary texts, or the notion of "literary life", may be two such large interpretative frameworks. In the general, the "macro" framework of cultural and/or historical approaches to literature are still prominent in some areas of literary scholarship. For example, in the current taxonomy of Anglo-American literary theory such approaches are often called "contextual", while "New Historicism" and "Cultural Materialism" are also such "macro" frameworks (cf. Hart 254-70); or, the more recent interest in interdisciplinarity and view of literature as a cultural activity as in, for example, A. Easthope's *Literary into Cultural Studies* (1991). While such theoretical approaches provide a point of departure and — at least — invite to a more open-ended view or a more definable view of literature than, for example, New Criticism or Deconstruction — to choose two ends of the spectrum of contemporary theory — they lack "scientific" *rigueur* in addition to a North American tendency to pay attention to scholarship elsewhere belatedly because works written in the major European languages are too often read in translation. This delay in the study of developments in theory and methodology often results in the unfortunate situation that theoretical frameworks are developed analogously and/or in parallel, so without the benefit or the advantageous incorporation of developments elsewhere.[12]

A more precisely circumscribed yet broader framework out of which the systemic approach may be viewed as having emanated is Structuralism. This discipline can be understood as an interdisciplinary approach and its intellectual roots are to be found in the works of F. de Saussure and in those of the Russian Formalists. It has since been developed in a variety of disciplines such as philosophy, ethnology, anthropology, psychoanalysis, and sociology with proponents such as C. Lévi-Strauss, J. Lacan, M. Foucault, L. Goldmann, R. Barthes, etc. (Wilpert 899). The relationship between Structuralism and the systemic approaches in general is often not clear. More specifically, Structuralism via the Russian Formalists and the Prague School has been a confessed departure for the *Polysystem theory* (I. Even-Zohar *passim*).[13] In the development of the *Empirical Theory of Literature* (S.J. Schmidt), the *l'institution littéraire* (J. Dubois), and other systemic approaches such as the *champ littéraire* (P. Bourdieu), this is much more indirect, and other disciplines such as the Sociology of Literature and theories of Communication, predominate as conceptual sources.

For the purpose of a clear delineation of "literature as system," definitions, as proposed by I. Even-Zohar and S.J. Schmidt, will be here presented. These definitions are clearly located within an *a priori* notion of *literature* but demonstrate advances in theoretical clarity and taxonomy, and, subsequently, in method than, for example, definitions presented by such as P. Caws in his *Structuralism: The Art of the Intelligible* (12-14 and *passim*).

Even-Zohar writes that

---

12 It has been suggested that North-American scholars often lack the knowledge of foreign languages and rely on translations, thus the delay in attention to new developments (cf. Blodgett 1986).

13 For a recent English-language dictionary entry see Dimić (1993).

If by "system" one is prepared to understand both the idea of a closed set-of-relations, in which the members receive their values through their respective oppositions, *and* the idea of an open structure consisting of several such concurrent nets-of-relations, then the term "system" is appropriate and quite adequate. (12)

This definition is, then, consolidated by Even-Zohar to "the network of relations that is hypothesized to obtain between a number of activities called 'literary', and consequently these activities themselves observed via that network", and "the complex of activities, or any section thereof, for which systemic relations can be hypothesized to support the option of considering them 'literary'" (28).

Schmidt has developed — although via alternate considerations such as a more closely scientific base borrowed from mathematics, biology, and general systems theory and with the epistemological base of Constructivism (cf. Schmidt 1985, 1992a, 1992b) — an even more carefully delineated description and precise taxonomy of the literary system within the postulates of literary communication and social interaction:

Als ein System Kommunikativer Handlungen muß das System Literarischer Kommunikationshand-lungen ... den Bedingungen genügen, die ... Kommunikations-systeme gennant ... sind: Es muß eine Außen-Innen-Differenzierung aufweisen [und] es muß eine Struktur sowie bestimmbare gesellschaftliche Funktionen haben. (1982, 131)

Schmidt further postulates that such a literary system rests on the conventions of aestheticity and polyvalence.

It is important to note in observing the *Empirical Theory of Literature*'s rapid growth on the international scene that its systemic approach to literature as postulated extends beyond the confines of literature to the larger area understood as media and communication studies. In other words, on the one hand the framework concerns primarily literature, on the other hand literature itself is understood as a *system of literary communication* within a larger *system of social interaction* i.e., *communication*:

In unserer Gesellschaft gibt es ein System von Kommunikationshandlungen, die dadurch ausgezeichnet sind, a) daß die Kommunikationshandlungen sich auf sprachliche Ästhetische thematische Kommunikate richten; b) daß Produktions- und Rezeptionshandlungen von Kommu-nikationsteilnehmern im System von Kommunikationshandlungen der Ästhetischen Literatur-Konvention und Polyvalenz-Konvention folgen, Vermittler- und Verarbeiterhandlungen daneben anderen Handlungsregularitäten folgen, die spezifisch für ein System von Kommunika-tionshandlungen betrachtet werden und mit der Ästhetischen Literatur-Konvention und der Polyvalenz-Konvention verträglich sein müssen; c) daß das System von Kommunikations-handlungen eine innere Struktur aufweist, über eine Innen-Außen-Differenzierung verfügt, die von keinem anderen Kommunikationssystem substituiert werden. (1982, 198)

Explicitly systemic theories and methodologies of literature, although developed from a range of disciplines such as mathematics, biology, and physics, and other theories from the humanities and social sciences, as well as other theories of literature, emanate mainly from the Sociology of Literature and theories of Communication. This should be noted because while it can be argued that although systemic theories of literature, such as the

Empirical Science of Literature — alternatively, *Empirical Theory of Literature* or the *Polysystem theory* and the *l'institution littéraire,* do not appear to have attracted much attention in Anglo-American scholarship, several recent works implicitly argue for such a systemic approach to literature. For example, in neo-Marxist works, such as J. Frow's *Marxism and Literary History* (1986) and T. Bennett's *Outside Literature* (1990), but also in such works as J.J. McGann's *The Textual Condition* (1991) and A. Easthope's *Literary into Cultural Studies* (1991)[14] this is clearly evident. Interestingly, an implicit systemic view, based for example on Barthes and Derrida's notions of "network", is also evident in the novel concept of reading and literary research resulting from computer technology as discussed by G.P. Landow in his *Hypertext: The Convergence of Contemporary Critical Theory and Technology* (1992).

To illustrate with one historical description of the development of the conception of the literary system, L. Vinge in her article "Ganzheit, System und Kontinuität — Eine Übersicht über einige Theorien zum Zusammenhang der Literatur" (1980) discusses several seminal works of the systemic approach to literature. She discusses systemic concepts by Schlegel, Guillén, Tynjanov and Jakobson, Wellek, Rosengren, and Jauß and she refers us to the fact that literary theoreticians habitually discuss at length whether the cohesion and continuity of literature is best analysed as historical continuity, abstract designations of norm, value systems, or as a function of society (1). Vinge's designation of the systemic approaches into two main groups has sound literary historical grounds and it also proves to be the case in the decade since the paper was published. The two main groups, then, are approaches which are Communication theory (including Semiotics) oriented and those of the Sociology of Literature orientation. The Communication and Semiotics theories oriented group includes the approaches of the Russian Formalists, of the Prague School, and of the more recent *Polysystem theory.* The Sociology of Literature groups include the French schools such as the *l'institution littéraire* and the *champ littéraire* groups, the *Empirical Theory of Literature,* and generally theories where the relationship between author and text, readership, and production is formulated.

The *Empirical Theory of Literature* originally attracted proponents particularly in the areas of reception studies, specifically by N. Groeben, and later in cognitive psychology when it is concerned with questions of reading. In these two areas research and studies based on the *Empirical Theory of Literature* framework are steadily growing (cf. Barsch 1992). It is also worth noting that a number of researchers in cognitive science and artificial intelligence have been attempting to articulate frameworks for the study of text, particularly those interested in narrative, most commonly called story grammars (e.g. Mandler). It has been claimed that such frameworks should be applicable to understanding all writing, including literary texts (e.g. Graesser 116), but the gap between their present abilities and the complexities of literary understanding remains a

---

14 For example, Easthope's book obviously widens the scope and understands literature similarly to Schmidt who proposes the notion of "media studies". Easthope's new paradigm for literary *recte* cultural analysis consists of the areas of sign system, ideology, gender, identification and subject position, the other, institution, readership, and pedagogy (129-39). These areas are analoguous to the tenets of the systemic frameworks and theories in question.

wide one (Ide and Véronis). Cognitive psychologists studying literary texts also often fall victim to disregarding the necessity of explicitly stating theoretical postulates and/or are mislead into focussing on empirical factors and thus run the risk of being neo-positivists — exactly the danger the framework and methodology of the *Empirical Theory of Literature* clearly states wanting to avoid.

As briefly mentioned, Anglo-American theoretical works which take a systemic approach tend to be much less explicit in theoretical and taxonomical precision. For example, the previously mentioned works of eminent scholars such as Bennett's *Outside Literature* and McGann's *The Textual Condition*, although of a sociological and system orientation, amazingly enough make no reference to any systemic (literary or other) theory except to that of Bourdieu (Bennett) and do not *explicitly* use a systemic taxonomy in their works. In general, systemic thinking for the study of literature is, although growing, more often often than not, is expressed in an exclusory manner. Another, more recent example of the Bennett and McGann type is Patti White's *Gatsby's Party: the System and the List in Contemporary Narrative* (1992). In this work, the author does not appear to be aware of any systemic theories and constructs her own postulates, often by way of re-inventing the wheel. Nevertheless, Bennett's, McGann's, and White's works — to name a few examples — are valuable contributions to the systemic study of literature. A similar case, although rare in German scholarship, occurs with the work of D. Schwanitz, *Systemtheorie und Literatur: ein neues Paradigma* (1990). Although Schwanitz clearly evolves his work from a base of a system of literature, he does not mention anyone of the system persuasion except Habermas (with works 1962-87) and Luhmann (with works 1970-88).

It may be of importance to call attention to the fact that the systemic approach to literature, in general, refers to a micro structure although it could also be understood in the context of literature as a macro structure. The latter, in the understanding of "national literatures", was the subject of D. Durišin's work *Vergleichende Literaturforschung* (1972) and I. Neupokoeva's "Dialectics of Historical Development of National and World Literature" (1973).

The systemic view of literature adopted by scholars of the Sociology of Literature orientation is less cohesive than that of the Communication/Semiotics oriented group. The more open-ended base of this group and its consequent variability is an obvious result of the wider field of the discipline of the Sociology of Literature. This can be illustrated by descriptions from works by two earlier Sociology of Literature scholars, whose concept of literature is clearly systemic. For example, J.L. Sammons states in the "Introduction" to his *Literary Sociology and Practical Criticism: An Inquiry* that

It may be helpful to say at the outset that the very term "literary sociology" is likely to have a different ring in American ears that in previous and contemporary Continental discussion. It will tend to denote to us a technical branch of the discipline of sociology dealing with the behavior of groups in what is sometimes called the "literary system": authors, producers (commissioning Maecenases and publishers), mediators and inhibitors (critics, scholars, educators, libraries, censors) and receivers or what, in more naive days, was called the reading public. (3)

Although Sammons means here to differentiate between a Continental-European and a North-American Sociology of Literature, a similar view is presented by the Continental-European scholar A. Silbermann in his *Einführung in die Literatursoziologie*:

Diese Konzeption des Literaturprozesses zeigt um einen, dass es bei der Literatursoziologie empirischer Ausrichtung vordringlich um Interaktionen und Interdependenzen von Individuen, Gruppen und Institutionen geht; zum anderen, daß die Analyse von Teilaspekten, so wie sie von anderen literatursoziologischen Ansätzen aus gepflegt wird, von seiten des empirischen Ansatzes erst in Angriff genommen werden kann, wenn der totale Literaturprozess, die Interaktion und Interdependenz von Autor, Werk und Publikum hinsichtlich seiner Bedeutung als Bezugsrahmen erkannt ist. (36)

Although, as the above examples illustrate it, the systemic approach to literature appeared early on, real innovation in the sense of T.S. Kuhn's paradigm occurred when the systemic view of literature was merged with the concept of Constructivist Empiricism and the postulate of social relevance in a clearly defined and explicated framework. The requirement that a systemic theory must be empirically testable (i.e. "observable") and that the results of the testing must have sociological relevance, appeared, although in a theoretically rudimentary form, already in K.E. Rosengren's *Sociological Aspects of the Literary System*, published in 1968.[15] A descriptive and detailed literary theoretical formulation of the above postulates, namely those of literary system, empirical testability and its sociological and socio-literary relevance first appeared in Siegfried J. Schmidt's *Grundriß der Empirischen Literaturwissenschaft*, with its two volumes, I: *Der gesellschaftliche Handlungsbereich Literatur* and II: *Zur Rekonstruktion literaturwissenschaftlicher Fragestellungen in einer Empirischen Theorie der Literatur* (1980-82 and 1991).[16] Schmidt's *Empirical Theory of Literature* theory soon found numerous followers first in Germany (West) at the Universität-Gesamthochschule Siegen and in other Continental European countries, in Japan, but also in Canada.[17] The vitality

---

15 R. Viehoff's (ed.) recent book, *Alternative Traditionen: Dokumente zur Entwicklung einer empirischen Literaturwissenschaft* (1991) documents the intellectual roots of the *ETL* theory with a large number of works. My selected bibliography (Tötösy, 1992a) contains additional titles in several categories.

16 The large corpus of both theoretical and applied works that followed and follows Schmidt's work is evident in the numbers of titles in my selective bibliography (Tötösy, 1992a), as already mentioned. For a recent discussion of the systemic approach to literature cf. Schmidt (1993).

17 In addition to the number of scholars who published works with the *ETL* theory, since the early 1980s several learned journals began to focus on this theory and methodology. For example, *Poetics Today* has published throughout the decade many articles written in the framework of the *ETL*. Also, the *ETL* approach has its own learned journal, the internationally recognized *Poetics*, as well as the biannual *SPIEL — Siegener Periodicum zur Internationalen Empirischen Literaturwissenschaft*, published by Peter Lang, and the Hungarian learned journal of literary theory *Helikon* devoted a special issue to the *ETL* in 1989. Scholars working with the *ETL* theory also have an international association (Internationale Gesellschaft der Empirischen Literaturwissenschaft, IGEL) that regularly holds international conferences, the first of which was held at the Universität-Gesamthochschule Siegen in 1984, the second in Amsterdam in 1989, the third at Memphis State University (USA) in 1992, and the fourth to be held in Budapest in 1994. Peer-reviewed articles selected from the presentations at these conferences were (*Poetics* and Ibsch, Schram, Steen [1991]) and will be published. In North American scholarship cognitive psychologists in particular showed interest

and importance of the *Empirical Theory of Literature* in literary theoretical scholarship is indicated, for example, by a separate entry in the recent seventh edition of G. von Wilpert's *Sachwörterbuch der Literatur* (1989) and in H. van Gorp *et al.*'s 5th edition of the *Lexicon van literaire termen* (1991). These two definitions of the *Empirical Theory of Literature* shall serve here as a concise introduction:

Empirical Science of Literature: Recent movement within the study of literature which is concerned with the study of literature as a social system of [inter]actions. The main question is what happens to literature: it is written, published, distributed, read, censored, imitated, etc. The empirical study of literature originated as a reaction to and an attempt at solving the basic problem of hermeneutics, i.e., how the validation of an interpretation can be demonstrated. From reception theory it had already become clear that interpretations are not only tied to the text, but also, and even to a great extent, to the reader (both in terms of the individual and of social conventions). This led to the theory of "cognitive constructivism", based on the thesis that the subject largely construes its empirical world itself. The logical consequence of all this, to be seen in the work [for example] of S.J. Schmidt, is the separation of interpretation and the strictly scientific study of literature (so-called "radical constructivism"). The literary system of actions is observed from the outside — not experienced — and roughly characterized as depending on two conventions (hypotheses) that are tested continually. These conventions are: the aesthetic convention (as opposed to the *convention of facts* in the daily *language of reference)* and the *polyvalency convention* (as opposed to the monovalency in the daily empirical world). Thus, the object of study of the empirical study of literature is not [only] the text in itself, but the *roles of action* within the literary system, namely production, distribution, reception, and the processing of texts. The methods used are primarily taken from psychology and the social sciences (reception theory). In general the steps to be taken in empirical research are: forming a hypothesis, putting it into practice, testing, and evaluation. More concretely, for the study of reader response a wide array of techniques are used, ranging from protocol techniques and thinking aloud to pre-structured techniques, such as the semantic seven point scale (C. Osgood) and the classification technique (card sorting), and forms of content analysis, association techniques, etc. Some objections that are often raised to the empirical study of literature are the triviality of many of its research results

---

in the *ETL* framework. As mentioned above, one handicap of North American Scholars often appears to be their lack of German and thus they are unfamiliar with the existing and large secondary literature in that language. At present, apart from the work of Tötösy (1989; 1990a-b; 1993b) no works have been published in North America in the specificity of the *ETL* applied to literary texts. The *ETL* theory and methodology has not appeared in English-language literary encyclopaedias and dictionaries apart from Tötösy (1993). The same is true in French-language reference works, but C. Moisan (Université Laval) has recently begun to translate some of S.J. Schmidt's work into French. In the area of readership research, on the other hand, the *ETL* framework and methodology has gained significant ground since Hintzenberg *et al.* (cf. e.g. Miall, Graesser, and the results of a readership survey in *Poetics* by Tötösy and Kreisel (1992). The *Polysystem theory*, in addition to scholars working at the Tel Aviv Porter Institute of Poetics and at Leuven University in Belgium and whose scholarship appears in (similarly to *Poetics* an internationally recognized journal) *Poetics Today* and attracted Canadian scholars affiliated with the University of Alberta Research Institute for Comparative Literature (Dimić 1989a-b; Pivato 1990, and Tötösy 1988) and scholars working at other Canadian universities some of whom employ the *Polysystem theory* in their work with the Institute's project "Towards a History of the Literary Institution in Canada". This project resulted to date in seven conferences whose proceedings were published and received very favourable reviews. The *l'institution littéraire* attracted mainly Québécois-Canadian scholars.

(confirmation of what was already known or suspected) and its reductionism (artificiality of the framework and set-up, and limitation to reader response instead of the study of the text). It is clear, however, that the empirical study of literature by its specific approach of the object and its methodology is an outstanding way to explore the socio-cultural aspects of the literary system. It makes an irreplaceable contribution to the development of a more scientific and socially relevant study of literature. (van Gorp, *et.al.* 116-17. A. Tadema, trans.)

Empirische Literaturwissenschaft, von S.J. Schmidt u.a. inaugurierte neue, systemat. Richtung der Literaturwissenschaft auf intersubjektiv überprüfbarer Grundlage. Sie betrachtet Lit. wiss. als empir. orientierte Sozialwissenschaft und als ihren Gegenstand den Gesamtbereich soz. Handlungen an und mit. lit. Werken, aufbauend auf einem System der ästhet. Kommunikation zwischen (Text-Produzent, Vermittler, Rezipient und Verarbeiter, das gesellschaftlich relevante Aspekte der Literaturgeschichtsschreibung, -soziologie, -psychologie, -kritik und -didaktik vereinen will. Kommunikation zwischen (Text-)Produzent, Vermittler, Rezipient und Verarbeiter, das gesellschaftlich relevante Aspekte der Literaturgeschichtsschreibung, -soziologie, -psychologie, -kritik und -didaktik vereinen will. (Wilpert 233)[18]

The *Empirical Theory of Literature* contains in its framework — a framework that clearly problematizes questions about literature in terms hitherto unexplored — several specific aspects which ought to be mentioned briefly, because they provide by virtue of their definitions important theoretical and methodological bases which distinguish this theory — by virtue of their detail, taxonomical exactitude, the explicitness of certain theoretical positions as opposed to implicit acceptance, and their position in the corpus of the entire theory — from other systemic theories, such as the previously mentioned *Polysystem theory*, the *l'institution littéraire* or the *champ littéraire* frameworks. For example, the *Empirical Theory of Literature* accepts the notion of literary period and literary genre and Schmidt notes that even a cursory reading of recent literary histories reveals that literary history cannot be written without periodization and classification and that the periodization of literature includes the acceptance of genre, among other literary, sociological, and artistic categories (II 17-18). Schmidt further explains his view that as the periodization of literature is an element of the writing of literary history, in the framework of the *Empirical Theory of Literature* no moment or act remains outside the categorizing perspective of historicity (II 31). A justification or argumentation for the concept of genre is also explained as the following two brief quotations demonstrate:

Die Entscheidung eines Literatur-Produzenten für bestimmte sprachliche Formen der Text-organisation (stilistische, rhetorische, kompositorische usw.) und bestimmte Ausschnitte aus dem sprachlichen Inventar einer Gesellschaft spiegelt seine Einstellung zu den jeweils herrschenden literatursprachlichen und textorganisatorischen Erwartungen. (II 103)

and

---

18 See also the more recent lexical entry of A. Barsch, "Empirische Literaturwissenschaft" (1992a, 206-09). In this entry, more than in other dictionary definitions, special attention is paid to the reception-theoretical focus of the *Empirical Theory of Literature*.

welche Lenkung des Rezeptionsprozesses ein Autor durch Anwendung bestimmter Vertextungs-
strategien bewußt intendieren kann und intendiert; welche er durch Übernahme gattungsspezifischer
Verfahren implizit übernimmt; wie Sozial- und Herrschaftsstrukturen zur Produktionszeit eingehen
in Gattungsstrukturen, Personenkonstellationen, stilistische Verfahren der Textorganisation usw.,
wie solche Momente von Literatur-Produzenten normativ bewertet werden und welche affektive
und kognitive Eistellung von Rezipienten der Literatur-Produzent damit bewriken will und
tatsächlich bewirken kann. (II 107)

The *Empirical Theory of Literature* defines literary relationships by four main fields
of social and literary interaction ("Handlungsbereich") — as already introduced in the
above translations from Wilpert's and van Gorp's literary dictionaries. The fields are
defined as a primary choice of those structures of literary and sociological areas of
interaction which proved themselves *a priori* relevant for the *Empirical Theory of
Literature* (I 60). These are production (Produktionsbereich), reception
(Rezeptionsbereich), processing (Vermittlungsbereich), and post-production processing
(Verarbeitungsbereich). A more precise formulation of these fields into systemic
categories then follows, after which the following agenda is postulated: "In einem zweiten
Schritt werden dann die Einzelprobleme auf den jeweiligen Analyseebenen der Theorie
Literarischer Kommunikationshandlungen untersucht" (I 60). This framework structure,
in other words, the systemic and empirical approach, results in a flexible, yet
"scientifically" exacting approach.

Importantly, this framework lends itself particularly well, for example, to feminist
literary research, although at the present time in both North America and in Europe
feminist scholars often reject systemic approaches to literature and prefer
deconstructionist, Lacanian, or other more "intuitive" and descriptive frameworks.
Contrary to the suggestion that the "systemic", "scientific" and/or "empirical" approach
is by definition closed, positivist, and reflective of patriarchal values embedded in literary
scholarship, the *Empirical Theory of Literature* theoretical configuration and methodology
can accommodate both the "objective" (i.e. male/patriarchal) and the "subjective" (i.e.
female/subjective/feminist) points of view (cf. "intersubjective testability").[19] As well,
other traditionally marginal literatures such as gay/lesbian writing and ethnic literature,
or minor genres such as the preface, can be studied resulting in important findings which,
in turn, provide new and valuable insights into the nature of literature as such.[20]

---

19 To date no study has been published where the *ETL* has been applied in feminist criticism, but Tötösy and
Tötösy are in the process of developing a study of gender specific representation in the modern novel where
literary discourse is analysed as showing masculine and feminine points of view.

20 Interestingly, one area of scholarship that appears to manifest exceptional resistance to systemic approaches
is scholarship involved with the literatures of visible minorities in the context of marginality and ethnicity.
The criticism that a systemic approach is in essence a "system building" approach, thus imposing unjustified
borders on literature and exposing the problem of theory transfer and Eurocentrism — systemic approaches
being of European origin — is misguided. Systemic approaches to literature do not "build" or impose a
system upon literature. It is the other way around: the "system(s)" is/are obviously there and because it is
there, the systemic approach is the best tool to disentangle literature's nature and problems. Interestingly,
in a recent discussion with scholars involved with research into the history of Canadian ethnic literature,
the criticism was raised that the systemic approach to Canadian ethnic literature is unacceptable because of

Some further instances from within the framework's systemic categories are useful to mention. For example, the *Empirical Theory of Literature* recognizes the problematic process and literary historical significance of canonization (II 18-19). This is important in view of recent developments with regard to Women's Literature and ethnic literatures, all having been traditionally, i.e., until recently, marginalized in literary studies and histories. Further, the postulates of the framework state that in the systemic view of literature the study and consequently the mutation of previously non-canonized types of literature will be the result (II 19). Another example of a systemic instance (otherwise generally neglected) is the role of the publisher and the publishing industry (I 115). A further area that the *Empirical Theory of Literature* intrinsically propagates is interdisciplinarity and team work. This is particularly important in the case of a larger or already more frequently researched topic with a large body of secondary literature.

The word "empirical" has specific associations.[21] It is clear that the *Empirical Theory of Literature* is in its concept, structure, and application, not neo-positivist. Schmidt explains his position with regards to possible accusations of neo-positivism in a section entitled "Exkurs: Hinweis für Neopositivismus Argwöhner" (I 7-11). In an important study on West German readership by Hintzenberg, Schmidt, and Zobel, based on the *Empirical Theory of Literature* theory, the authors again very carefully describe their position with regards to the concepts of empiricism and positivism (3-12. Also Schmidt 1992). Briefly put, empiricism in its *Empirical Theory of Literature* context is a postulate for the meaningful employment of observed and observable data in the analysis of *how* literature happens, i.e., *how* it is written, processed, read, received, etc. Of course, if empiricism is used in a manner of "number crunching" or without analytical context, it will indeed do disservice to literary studies. In the context of systemic approaches to literature, the postulate empiricity defines the *Empirical Theory of Literature* as distinct from and clearly more advanced than other systemic approaches. Aside theoretical and methodological demarcations internal to systemic approaches, here a brief discussion of parallel frameworks will demonstrate further the significance of the systemic approach

---

its Eurocentrism (the problem of theory transfer) and because it represents a "straight-jacket" approach to literature. While it is true that the systemic approaches are indeed Eurocentric, the deciding factor as to any theory's usefulnes should be the overriding question "does it bring about new knowledge?" If it does, it should not matter where the theory itself comes from. As to the question of the "straight-jacket" approach, this is a problem of any theory when applied, and to get around it only the total disregard of literary theory will be satisfactory — which, surely, cannot be a tenable notion because its ultimate consequence will be the implicit rejection of the meaning of the study of literature *in toto*. With reference to the problem of "Western" literary frameworks and the study of "colonial" literatures it is noteworthy that the *Polysystem theory* has been applied to the study of African and Caribbean literatures (cf. Awuyah, Jones).

21 The term itself — whether in its traditional context or in its Constructivist meaning — raises eyebrows in literary studies, especially in North America. Interestingly, one of North America's foremost literary critics, the Canadian Northrop Frye, said in an interview in 1986: "I think that criticism is still bound up with ideology, and consequently much more concerned to develop the language of argument and thesis than really embark on the empirical study of literature" (Salusinszky 32). Unfortunately, Frye has not demonstrated in his work, either in theory or in practice, what he cursorily referred to in the interview. However, one Canadian scholar considers Frye's work as consisting of a systemic view of literature, including some empirical tenets (cf. Hart 1993).

in general. A specific branch of systemic theory groups, most clearly originating in the Sociology of Literature, are the French and Québécois-Canadian groups which work with the concept of the literary institution. This approach is most often associated with J. Dubois's seminal book *L'Institution de la littérature: introduction à une sociologie* (1978)[22] and resulted in important Canadian-Québécois works such as G. Marcotte's "L'Institution: institution et courants d'air" (1981), C. Moisan's collection of essays in *Comparaison et raison* (1986) and *Qu'est-ce que l'histoire littéraire?* (1987),[23] and his *L'Histoire littéraire* (1990) with several sections devoted to the "institutional" and "champ" approaches (43-64),[24] M. Lemire and M. Lord's collection of essays in *L'Institution littéraire* (1986), L. Robert's *L'Institution du littéraire au Québec* (1989),[25] and St. Santerres-Sarkany's *Théorie de la littérature* (1990). Another, although to date less developed systemic approach in French scholarship is the *École bibliologique française*.[26] This approach too found Canadian-Québécois followers who published important works such as Y. Lamonde, V. Nadeau, and L. Robert, for example.[27] The German approach with a strong leaning towards hermeneutics should also be mentioned: the most prominent scholar of this group is J. Habermas with several important publications such as *Strukturwandel der Öffentlichkeit* (1962) which underwent nine reprintings up to 1987.

Clearly, in each of these frameworks there are "overlaps" with other systemic theories. An early example of such overlapping frameworks is P.E. Sørensen's *Elementare Literatursoziologie*, which takes both a systemic and an institutional view of literature (1976). But also the *Polysystem theory*, although it is, in the first instance, a Communication / Semiotic approach, contains many systemic components from the Sociology of Literature. Other examples may include a "general" systemic approach, in

---

22 Because of the lack of theoretical and methodological interest in the institutional — or systemic — view of literature in Anglo-American literary scholarship, it should be mentioned that Harry Levin, in his book *Gates of Horn: A Study of Five French Realists* (1963), wrote a section in his introduction with the subtitle "Literature as an Institution" (16-23. The piece was first published in *Accent* in 1946). Although thus Levin's notion of literature as institution may claim some genealogical precedence — pre-dating both Goldmann's notion of the novel as an institution and Dubois's book — his notion is not developed either in a theoretical framework or in a methodology beyond an undefined proposition of the notion.

23 This work may also be viewed as representing the *polysystem* theory.

24 The Québécois-Canadian groups of scholars also use many of the *champ littéraire* (Bourdieu) tenets. For a selected bibliography, divided into sections of general system theoretical works, works by the Russian Formalists and the Prague School, and other Communication theory approaches cf. Dimić and Garstin. This bibliography is more oriented towards the semiotic than the sociological body of secondary literature.

25 This work won the first prize of the Canadian Federation for the Humanities for best French-language scholarly work of 1989.

26 Cf. R. Estivals, éd., *Le livre en France* (1984), R. Estivals, *Le livre dans le monde* (1984), and St. Sarkany, *Québec Canada France: Le Canada littéraire à la croisée des cultures* (1985). There is of course also the disciple of Library Science in North America and the area of "Bücherkunde" in German-language scholarship. However, these are much further removed from the text *per se* than the *École bibliologique*.

27 Cf. Y. Lamonde, éd., *L'Imprimé au Québec: aspects historiques (18e-20ᵉ siècles)* (1983), V. Nadeau, *Au Commencement était le fascicule. Aux sources de l'édition québécoise contemporaine pour la masse* (1984), L. Robert, *Prolégomènes à une étude sur les transformations du marché du livre (1900-1940)* (1984).

the sense that the approach and methodology are not formulated explicitly. Such a work is the multivolume *Letteratura italiana* under the editorship of A. Asor Rosa (1982-.). Volume I of this work ("Il letterato e le istituzioni") contains a short theoretical outline which is based mainly on the works of the Russian Formalists (I xvii-xxii, 5-29). Although the theoretical and methodological postulates in Asor Rosa are less than satisfactory and demonstrate only cursory knowledge of or familiarity with even the Russian Formalists, the work nevertheless indicates a positive departure on the methodological side, in the context of the history of literary histories.

The more Semiotics and to a lesser extent Sociology of Literature oriented approach found its most cohesive expression in the *Polysystem theory*.[28] Theoreticians of this approach base the roots of the theory in the works of the Russian Formalists and in some early German theoretical texts (cf. Dimić 1991). It may be added here that perhaps one of the earliest systemic notions of literature — of a Semiotics orientation — may be found in Mme de Staël's essay "De la littérature considérée dans ses rapports avec les institutions sociales" (1800) where she discusses the influence and impact of law, virtue (morality), and religion on literature, and vice versa (196-334). In the 1861 edition, in her "Préface de la seconde édition" and the subsequent short history of literature, the terms and concepts of "system" (and "institution") are used, but again in a Semiotic, rather than in a sociological sense.[29]

Historically and genealogically, the formulation of the semiotic-systemic view of literature has been developed by the Russian Formalists and the Prague School.[30] In Anglo-American scholarship, this historical development is very well presented, for example, in J. Frow's book *Marxism and Literary History* (1986).[31]

Finally, one area in which the *Polysystem* theory clearly originated advances, to which neither the *Empirical Theory of Literature* nor the *l'institution littéraire* frameworks have given attention, is translation. As translation is obviously a prominent element of the literary system, both the *Empirical Theory of Literature* and the *l'institution littéraire* frameworks need to be explicated to include this literary and social activity.[32] Although it is necessary, to be fair, to make reference to this often elicited criticism of systemic approaches, the appeal must also be made to the need of a change of paradigm: the study of literature must be executed in the context of *system* in order to account for both the specificity of literature as an aesthetic matter that *socialises*, as a communicative

---

28 A selected bibliography is in the Dimić and Garstin bibliography. See also I. Even-Zohar, *Poetics Today* 11.1 *Polysystem Studies* (Spring 1990), and Tötösy (1992a) with recent titles.

29 U. Weisstein, in his *Einführung in die vergleichende Literaturwissenschaft* (23-24) interpretes Mme de Staël's work as "soziologische Interesse" in literatures. In my view this is hardly tenable.

30 It is of interest that there has been no link discussed to date between the Schlegelian and Staël concepts and that of the Russian Formalists — although the relationship between German, French, and Russian literatures in the sense of intellectual and literary history is well known.

31 Frow devotes two chapters to the view of literature as system.

32 However, the systemic significance and its accompanying inclusion into the study of literary phenomena can be easily demonstrated with both the *ETL* and the *l'institution littéraire* frameworks. Recently, I completed a "A Taxonomy for Literary Translation," based on works of the Nitra School (Slovakia) and merged their concepts and terminology with tenets of the *ETL* and of the *Polysystem* theory.

mechanism, with *socially* determined elements of human interactions. In addition, and this is the point where the *Empirical Theory of Literature* manifests innovation, i.e. "Paradigmawechsel", whenever possible this approach should be complemented by an empirical component. This way, the study of literature will arrive at a truly "scientific" niveau, one which defines itself in terms of *scholarship* first and *artistic/writerly creativity* second and not the other way around, while *intuition* is still given ample room.

In sum, while all three frameworks and methodologies provide the scholar with a *new theoretical paradigm* for the study of literature, there are differences among them which, beyond the obvious preferences of the scholar based on language, cultural background, academic training, etc., will attract variably different scholars.[33] The levels of structural, taxonomical, and descriptive elements and the different foci (i.e. Sociology of Literature, Semiotics, theories of Communication) divide these three frameworks. The *Empirical Theory of Literature* is the most explicit and scientific — as is clearly recognized, for example, in the above van Gorp, *et al.* dictionary definition — in both base and description in addition to the argument for the necessity of studying literature with a specific understanding of empiricism. In comparison, the *Polysystem* theoretical framework is the most open ended and thus allows the scholar to shift his/her focus of analysis, albeit to the detriment of "scientific" *rigueur*, while the *l'institution littéraire* framework is the least developed to date.[34]

1.4 The Corpus of Nineteenth-Century Canadian Novel Prefaces

A discussion of the corpus of the Canadian novel preface in detail is necessary for several reasons. For one, as the prefaces — particularly those written for English-Canadian novels — are an undiscovered entity, their number becomes one of the factors that determines the postulate of this work, namely that the Canadian preface is a genre in its

---

33 The "expansion" of the systemic approach to literature, as mentioned above in several instances, is steady. In addition to the cited areas such as Germany, Belgium, France, Israel, Canada, the U.S., etc., particularly in the Netherlands, Japan, and Hungary did scholars advance these frameworks theoretically and in their application. See, for example, D. Fokkema's and E. Ibsch's recent book *Literatuurwetenschap & Cultuuroverdracht* (1992).

34 With regard to discussions among scholars working with systemic approaches, proponents of the *Polysystem theory* and the *ETL* in particular, express divergent views. For example, the *Polysystem* group maintains that the *ETL* analyses "system" as a homogeneous and closed structure. Other criticisms include the contention that *ETL* uses classificatory criteria detrimentally and that it imposes "borderlines", and that the notion of "empiricity" is superfluous. Even-Zohar, for instance, contends that the *ETL* framework is "rigid, anachronistic, and unsatisfactory". At the same time, Even-Zohar acknowledges that the original Semiotics orientation, or, in his words "bias" of the *Polysystem theory* "has been conspicuously replaced by a 'socio-semiotic'" framework, and he describes the *Polysystem theory* as a "theory of *culture* [which is] an ensemble of socio-semiotic activities, where 'literature' is considered to be an integral activity" (Even-Zohar in a letter to the author, January 1992). This development, although it does not bridge the difference of opinions about concepts of literature as system and its empirical postulate, brings the *Polysystem theory* closer to the *ETL* with its notions and postulates of communication, social interaction, and social relevance still. It is ironic that the criticisms expressed with reference to the *ETL* by scholars working with the *Polysystem theory* are analoguous with the criticisms brought forward against all systemic frameworks by scholars, who *in toto* reject these approaches to literature.

own right. Further, the question of classification and periodization is an accepted notion in the framework of the *Empirical Theory of Literature*. Thus, the demonstration of the methodological process by which the prefaces were compiled is an integral and necessary part of the first step in the study, that of the "hypothesis". In addition, the discussion of the compilation of the prefaces propagates the possibilities of more research made now possible by the avenues chosen for this compilation, i.e. by electronic means. In more general terms, the discussion of the selection procedure of the prefaces from the primary corpus — the novels — is necessary because it relates to the reader the problematics of periodization and categorization in the case of the nineteenth-century Canadian literatures.

The typology of the prefaces, keeping in line with the tenets of *Empirical Theory of Literature*, demonstrates the genre specificities of the prefaces. In turn, this notion can be made acceptable only by the presentation of an approximately *full* corpus, as presented in Chapter two via the typology and in the Appendix containing the bibliographical data of the selected prefaces.

As mentioned previously, the preface in the Canadian literatures has not been researched in Canadian literary scholarship beyond a few studies on prefaces written for a limited number of canonical novels and, with few exceptions, these studies were written by Québécois-Canadian scholars about French-Canadian novel prefaces. There has been one Canadian Learned Societies section organized on the preface and one conference.[35] The section at the Canadian Learned Societies Conference was concerned with the preface as a topic in general and the conference was specifically on the preface and manifestoes in the Canadian literatures. The conference on Canadian prefaces and manifestoes resulted in several interesting studies, published as proceedings in 1990 (cf. Blodgett, Purdy, and Tötösy). For example, with regard to the Canadian preface corpus, Carole Gerson claims that "The vast majority of creative books published by nineteenth-century Canadian authors lack introductions" (Gerson 57).

There are other questions concerning the CIHM classification. For example, R.M. Ballantyne is classified as an English-Canadian author under the Dewey Number C813. As Ballantyne has never been classified in any Canadian literary history as an English-Canadian author, his classification as such is curious.[36] However, he did spend six years as a fur trader in Canada and Brian Moore, who lived for ten years in Canada, is often described as a Canadian author — at least in Canada.[37] While admittedly this classification is arbitrary, because Ballantyne was classified by the CIHM as an English-Canadian author and because he physically spent some time in Canada, in this study too

---

35   1. Canadian Learned Societies Conference at the University of British Columbia (Vancouver), June 1983; Section: Comparative Literature, Special Colloquium on the Preface and Manifestoes. 2. *Prefaces and Manifestoes*, 3rd Conference for "Towards a History of the Literary Institution in Canada, Research Institute for Comparative Literature, University of Alberta (Edmonton), November 1987.

36   One, although ambiguous, exception ought to be mentioned. W.H. New's *A History of Canadian Literature* lists Ballantyne's *Ungava* in a list of Canadian literary publications (311).

37   Cf. Selby (40-46) on Ballantyne and *The Canadian Encyclopedia* (3 1386) on Moore. The *Oxford Companion to Canadian Literature* attempted to deal with the question by creating the categories of "Foreign writers on Canada in English" and "Foreign writers on Canada in French" (267-77). Such authors as Ballantyne and Joseph Hatton, for example, were then classified as foreign writers on Canada.

he was designated an English-Canadian author. Also, in this study the texts analysed are not the novels, but their prefaces. As complicated — and inconclusive in present research — as the Canadian readership might have been in the nineteenth century, the argument that the prefaces of Ballantyne concern — by virtue of his books having been published and presumably read in Canada — this Canadian readership and consequently his prefaces belong to the English-Canadian corpus, is acceptable.

There are other, similar cases in the authors' list compiled from the CIHM data. As in many cases in the Canadian literatures, particularly in English-Canadian literature, some authors become Canadian by default rather than by clear criteria, traditional in established, more homogeneous national literatures. The decision to list an author as a Canadian author often occurs because he/she has some link with Canada, but at the same time, for whatever biographical or literary reason, he/she is not classifiable as clearly British, American, German, etc. The following analogous example will serve as a good illustration of this observation. The Australian born Henry Handel Richardson (Ethel Florence Richardson) becomes (or rather "remains"?) "Australian", because she cannot be classified as British, although she spent all of her writing years in Germany and Britain.[38]

Finally, there is the central question: "Why is it important — or interesting *au minimum* — to compile and to analyse the nineteenth-century 'Canadian' novel preface?" This question, whose positioning and answer provide the *raison d'être* of this work, can be reasoned towards on several levels. To begin with, the preface is *there* but it has not been investigated in a comparative Canadian context. The argument that the preface is *there* includes the *a priori* hypothesis while at the same time it is an "empirical" reason.[39] Because the preface is *there* and it has not been investigated, it is justified, indeed, necessary, to pay scholarly attention to it. Next, once its existence was established, its shape, form, type, content, number, etc. — the characteristics and mechanisms of its existence — determine its relative importance for Canadian literature. This argument concerns the prefaces' situation within the context of the Canadian literatures.[40] Further, in the case of the Canadian novel preface there are characteristics which make this text type specifically "Canadian", i.e. English Canadian and Québécois Canadian. These specificities retroactively establish the reason for their compilation and analysis. Consequently, the results of the compilation and the analysis enlarge our literary knowledge of the period. In addition, the present work suggests that there remains a large amount of work to be done to understand better these literatures, specifically in the context of the historical period of the nineteenth century.

---

38 On the "literary nationality" of Richardson see McLeod (227-43).

39 Nothing proves more the originally hypothetical nature of the Canadian novel preface than the fact that at the beginning of the research there was no indication about the number, type, form, content, etc., of these prefaces. There was, however, an assumption — based on a *very* limited number of prefaces written to canonical nineteenth-century Canadian texts, mainly poetry — that there might be a sufficient number of novel prefaces that would warrant further research and subsequently analysis.

40 This is not the place to discuss the misguided and entrenched establishment of the concept of "national literature", a result of Romanticism, the way literary histories are written and the basic scholarly necessity to categorize and to periodize — all of which allow for the handling of the material "literature" as "national" literature.

CHAPTER TWO

A Typology of Nineteenth-Century Canadian Novel Prefaces

Preamble
In this Chapter the typology of the prefaces will be presented. However, it is necessary that before the presentation, some methodological aspects be discussed briefly. First, it should be clear that the preface typology is but one part of the systemic analysis of the prefaces yet it can stand on its own — as a typology.

The systemic analysis, presented in Chapter four, became possible only after sufficient data had been accumulated from and about the prefaces. As mentioned previously, one of the postulates of the *Empirical Theory of Literature* theory is that, where possible, empirical data should be used for the analysis of literature. It is for this reason that a method had to be found that would allow for the extraction of data while at the same time facilitating the construction of a preface typology. The construction of the typology was a result of the finding that the typologies of Lausberg and Genette could not be applied to English-Canadian and French-Canadian prefaces. This was not possible for several reasons. As became clear after a preliminary reading of the prefaces, the English-Canadian prefaces showed a specific structure which would have allowed the application of either the Lausberg or the Genette preface typology only partially. Second, although the French-Canadian prefaces showed a structure that would have allowed for the application of either of these typologies, the application of a typology to only the French-Canadian prefaces and not to the English-Canadian ones would have been methodologically indefensible. Thus, although the Lausberg and Genette typologies have been considered and some of their features implicitly used, a specific typology has been developed. The best method to develop this specific typology was thought to be the use of a "data sheet". Consequently, the data sheet was constructed based on the following: 1. Preface types found in works on the preface, including Lausberg's and Genette's typologies; 2. The concepts of the four *Empirical Theory of Literature* categories; 3. Typological characteristics discovered during a preliminary reading of English-Canadian and French-Canadian prefaces. In the following, the data sheet will be introduced, including a more detailed explanation of the categories designed to extract typological and systemic data from the prefaces.

The following Data Sheet was used:

The Data Sheet:
----
1. *The bibliographical data of the novel (CIHM):* ...
2. *The title and the author of the preface:* ... ...
3. *Typology:*
        Acknowledgement___ Apologetic___ Critical___
        Dedicatory___ Ethical___ Explanatory___Integral___
        Preemptive___ Promotional___ Subversive___ Length
        of the preface___

4. *Systemic data in the preface:*
      Literary Theory ...
      Literary Genre ...
      References to Literary Figures and Texts ...
      Mention of Other Arts ...
      References to or Address of Readership ...
5. *Summary of the preface ... ...*
6. *Theme/Setting of the novel ... ...*
7. *Remarks ... ...*
8. *Scale value of the preface* ___

Categories 1 and 2 are necessary for the order and recognition of the prefaces. The author of the preface is important, if it is not the same person as the author of the novel. These data sheet categories will yield results for the *Empirical Theory of Literature* categories of production (prefacer/author and the text) and processing (the publishing industry).

Category 3: *Typology* is a category which contains information on the various characteristics of the prefaces. The typology of the prefaces pre-supposes a semantic analysis because it is necessary to categorize the contents of the preface. The typological categories became evident and were consequently constructed after a first reading of a large selection (about three-fourths) of the prefaces and of works on prefaces (Lausberg, Riefstahl, Ehrenzeller, Genette, Mitterand, etc.). Thus the specificity of the Canadian prefaces has been taken into consideration while the larger literary context has also been taken into account.

In the designation of the preface's characteristics several analytical decisions had to be made. When a preface is categorized as, for example, an apologetic preface, that does not necessarily mean that the preface is apologetic in its whole, but rather, that it contains that specific characteristic. In reality, most prefaces contain a number of typological characteristics. Naturally, the designation of a preface's characteristics is more often than not potentially ambiguous. In other words, a particular element or aspect may be designated as "ethical" but the same characteristic may also be read as "preemptive". A decision had to be made as to which semantic element is the more prominent one. Thus it often occurred that a particular characteristic allowed the designation of two different categories. This overlapping is possible between some characteristics more than between others. For example, an overlap is possible between the characteristics of "critical" and "explanatory", while it is rare between "subversive" and "ethical". In most cases of the characteristics explained below, further subtypes, termed subgroups, were necessary. The subgroups vary from type to type in the prefaces. It was not deemed necessary to explain the subgroups separately because they are self-evident within the main characteristic. For example, the "acknowledgement" characteristic of English-Canadian prefaces has two subgroups: 1. Secondary sources and 2. Previous publication. Obviously, the acknowledgement in the preface could be in reference to secondary literary, historical, etc., sources. Similarly, the subgroup "previous publication" is an acknowledgement type where the prefacer acknowledges a previous publication of the novel.

It should be noted here again that the typology of the prefaces is intrinsically systemic in nature, not only because its compilation is empirical but also because the typological categories can be a source of information with regard to the four *Empirical Theory of Literature* categories. For example, the typological information of acknowledgement (e.g., the prefacer expresses appreciation for the publication of the novel) is a systemic element because it is an indicator of the interaction between two *Empirical Theory of Literature* categories, the prefacer and the publishing industry. Or, the category of acknowledgement indicates the relationship between the producer (the prefacer) and the receiver (the readership), etc.

The characteristics of the different preface types have been designated as follows:

Acknowledgement: The preface contains acknowledgement(s) to cooperators, helpers, the publisher, the editor, friends, relatives, secondary literature, institutions, etc. The characteristic of acknowledgement in prefaces is often conceptually similar to the characteristic of dedication, although this is often only implied. The acknowledgement in a preface usually appears when the author of the preface feels that some aspect of the novel or the writing of the novel has been assisted by someone or something.

Apologetic: The preface contains some sort of apology directed to an individual or the readership. The apology may also be with reference to some aspect of the novel, or the preface itself.

Critical: In essence, a preface contains a critical characteristic when there is some type of criticism in the preface. The critical characteristic(s) may be in reference to the preface, the novel, or any other literary text, an ideology, a literary figure, the readership, a social group, etc. This category may appear, in some areas, repetitive because the category *Systemic data* includes again the extraction of the areas of genre and literary theory. However, while it is only noted here that the preface has one or more critical characteristics, which may include, for example, criticism of other authors, there it is discussed in more detail and specifically in a theoretical context. Also, the critical characteristic may overlap with an ethical (see below) indicator. The differentiation lies in the fact that the critical indicator is analyzed with regards to its *critical* value, the ethical indicator for its *value judgement*. Thus, this structure of the data extraction creates an overlap of systemic indicators: social critical or an ethical characteristic is a systemic indicator, but at the same time it is a typological indicator. While the overlap in the categories may appear as a repetition, this is not so. The differentiation itself is an important indicator of the preface's function and mechanism.

Dedicatory: The preface or the novel itself is dedicated to someone. As there are many novels with a *bona fide* dedication, i.e., typographically separated and short, the difference between a dedicatory preface and a dedication is that the preface may be titled "dedication" or the preface, titled as such, has a dedicatory paragraph or section in it. In both cases the preface contains usually more than just a dedication.

Ethical: The preface contains explicit or implicit value judgment(s) of a moral (moralizing), ethical, religious, humanistic, social, economic, political, or generally ideological nature.

Explanatory: The preface contains explanations with reference to either the preface or the novel. The explanatory characteristic is recognizable by its semantics, but also by its topic, i.e. the author explains the historical background of the novel or provides a geographical description of the novel's setting.

Integral: The preface is not set apart from the text of the novel. Or, Chapter I is titled "Preface", "Prologue", or "Introduction", although its text is obviously part of the novel.

Preemptive: The preface has a preemptive characteristic when the author of the preface anticipates and therefore attempts to defuse criticism of his work by readers, critics, academics, or his peers, etc.

Promotional: The promotional characteristic of prefaces is one of its most intrinsic features. It is the implicit, or, as in most cases, the explicit intention to promote the novel or some aspect of the novel. A small number of prefaces contain a promotional characteristic with reference to the preface itself.

Subversive: The subversive preface is ironic, satirical, or humorous with regard to either the preface itself or the work. It may also contain ironic, satirical, or humorous characteristics with reference to the readers, critics, the publisher, etc.

Length of the preface: For statistical purposes and for the analysis of the form of the preface, the length of the prefaces is relevant and is therefore noted here.

Category 4: *Systemic Data in the Preface*. This category of data extraction is necessary because some dimensions of the prefaces will yield data that are "naturally" systemic. In other words, prefatorial information about the readership is more immediately systemic than, for example, the integral type of preface. Also, the prefatorial dimensions presented here in some instances tend to be of a more discursive nature. Thus, implicit or explicit references to literary theory, a literary genre, and the mention of specific literary texts and/or authors are indicated. The categories of literary theory and genre include a wide spectrum of aspects ranging from a theoretical and genre perception that a novel must be "founded on facts", to discussions about the function of the preface, or the prefacer's insistence that the work is not a novel. The category of literary figures and texts is useful because it enables us to see — as much as the preface permits this — the author's literary culture and the way the author is positioning himself/herself in the literary canon. The readership is important because the preface may contain information about the intended readership and it could explicitly address specific groups in the readership. It should be noted that the intended readership of the novel is often not clear from the preface. Therefore, only when it is obvious whom the preface or the novel is addressed to, will the readership be indicated. The mention of other arts is important inasmuch as evidence of a connection between, for instance, the visual arts and literature appearing in the preface will tell us about literary life.

Obviously, the above systemic categories are not exhaustive. However, the composition of the English-Canadian and French-Canadian prefaces was such that these were established as the most prevalent and recurring typological characteristics.

Category 5: *Summary of the Preface*. This category is necessary for subsequent recall and selection of prefaces.

Category 6: *Theme and/or Setting of the Novel*. Although the novel itself is not analysed, in the analysis of the prefaces it will be of use to evaluate statistically the relationship between the preface and the novel's theme(s) and/or setting. Although it is perhaps not the most advantageous theoretical approach, to establish the theme of the novel one must adopt a reductionist approach. The theme(s) and/or setting of the novels with prefaces were grouped by geographic or national criteria. In other words, the setting of the novel, e.g., Acadia, determined that the theme of the novel was Canadian. Or, if the protagonists were Torontonians, the theme of the novel was again designated as Canadian.

Category 7: *Remarks*. Special or unusual features were indicated here. Most of the time if the novel had, in addition to the preface, a dedication or a motto, this was noted in this category.

Category 8: *Scale Value of Preface*. This category is used for the purpose of selection of prefaces for close scrutiny in this study. A scale of 1 (most valuable) to 5 (least useful) was used.

1. A Typology of English-Canadian Prefaces[1]

The Acknowledgement
Subgroups: 1. Secondary sources.
                    2. Previous publication.

1. Secondary sources.
Agatha Armour's preface to *Lady Rosamond's Secret: A Romance of Fredericton*
(1898) has two kinds of acknowledgement:

The writer is deeply indebted to several gentlemen of high social position who kindly furnished
many important facts and showed interest in the work, and takes the present opportunity of
returning thanks for such support. And hoping that this may meet the approval of many, the writer
thanks those who have so generously responded to the subscription list.[2]

The first type of acknowledgement is the more common recognition of assistance the
writer has received for the "reality"- or "fact"-bound content of the novel. Since the
novel contains depictions of Fredericton's society during the governorship of Sir Howard
Douglas, the author's assertion that the novel is based on "facts" is strengthened by this
reference to "gentlemen of high social position" who furnished "hard" evidence for the
story.
        The acknowledgement of secondary sources often serves to strengthen the author's
assurance that the novel is "based on facts", as in the case of Douglas Erskine's long
preface to *A Bit of Atlantis* (1900). It is also a common characteristic in the prefaces of
historical novels, for example in Anne Mercier and Violet Watt's *The Red House by the
Rockies* (1896):

Those who desire to read more on the subject will find a full account of the two revolts under Riel
in Major Boulton's "Reminiscences of the North-West Rebellions" (Toronto: Grip Co.); and in
Lord Wolseley's articles on the "Red River Expedition," in Blackwood, 1870, they will find an
admirable résumé of the former of the two risings.

The acknowledgement in a preface may also be in reference to historical events or
figures — but at the same time this may be a "fictional" reference. What I mean is that
a historical event or figure has been described before and it is referred to as an event or
figure that is already known to many. William McLennan's preface to *The Span o'Life:
A Tale of Louisbourg & Quebec* (1899) is a good example:

The reader familiar with the amusing memoirs of the Chevalier Johnstone will recognise in how
far Maxwell was suggested thereby; if he be equally familiar with the detail of Canadian history

---

1   Because of the structure of the preface types and their characteristics, a chronological presentation of the
    corpus was not possible. Where possible, the preface characteristics were chronologically arranged.

2   The sources of preface quotes can be verified with the bibliographical information contained in the *Appendix*
    (A CIHM list of English-Canadian and French-Canadian Novels with Prefaces).

of the period he will have little difficulty in discovering the originals of Sarennes and some of the secondary characters, and in the Epilogue, the legend of the death of the celebrated missionary, le R.P. Jean Baptiste de la Brosse.

A specifically literary acknowledgement occurs when the author acknowledges that he was inspired by a literary text, as in J. Macdonald Oxley's preface to *On the World's Roof* (1896): "The Author desires to express his special obligations in regard to this story to Andrew Wilson's 'Abode of Snow,' and E. F. Knight's 'Where Three Empires Meet'".

2. Previous publication.

This subgroup occurs relatively frequently in English-Canadian prefaces. This is to be expected because many novels were first published in a serialised form. In these cases the author acknowledges the permission to republish after the novel's rights have been sold previously to a magazine. J. Macdonald Oxley, *The Romance of Commerce* (1896): "wishes to make due acknowledgement to Messrs Harper & Bros., and the publisher of the Cosmopolitan magazine of New York, for the privilege of reprinting those of the following chapters which first appeared in their periodicals".

The Apologetic
Subgroups: 1. Genre.
                2. Emerging literature.
                3. Readership.
                4. Autobiographical.

1. Genre.

An example of the apology for the genre of the novel, most frequently in the context of the novel's bad reputation, is to be found in James Russell's *Matilda, or, The Indian's Captive: A Canadian Tale Founded On Fact* (1833); the author combines his claim to narrate facts with an excuse for his lack of art:

I am truly at a loss (Reader) what name to give this little work; to call it a Novel is an appellation which in some measure it does not deserve, as it is founded on fact ... he trusts that the following tale will be perused by the generous reader with a forgiving spirit of the Author's imperfections.

William Stuart Darling, in his *Sketches of Canadian Life* (1849) apologizes for the genre he chose and for his imagination:

The portraiture of Canadian life which is here humbly attempted, has been thrown into the form of a narrative, because a book written in that style appeared to the author not less irksome to write, and more easy to read, but also because he thought, that to trace the fortunes of an imaginary individual would afford an opportunity of describing more correctly the numerous minute details of a settler's experience than a work of higher pretensions and more important character.

The apology for the novel as a genre still occurs as late as 1891 in J. Shinnick's preface for *The Banker's Daughter, or, Her First and Last Ball: A Novel* (1891), who apologizes for his and *all* authors' imagination: "Our object in offering it for publication is that a leisure hour may be agreeably spent, and those who read it, will not have their minds disturbed by descriptive, exciting scenes that only exist in the imagination of authors".

2. Emerging literature.

One of the most common apologies in English-Canadian prefaces occurs in reference to a perception of the uncertain state of Canadian literature, i.e., it is new, it is in a state of birth, it is colonial, etc. A fairly early example among the apologetic prefaces appears in *A Canadian Christmas Tale* ("Grodenk", 1869):

For the Canadian who enters on the field of literature has many obstacles to overcome. All I ask is "nothing extenuate, nor set down aught in malice." I am willing to face public judgment, in the hope that my small effort may be successful, and may help to induce other Canadians to follow in my footsteps, and assist in building up a literature of our own, ...

3. Readership.

The concern with the readership in the context of apology occurs early in English-Canadian novel prefaces. "H.H.B." (J.H. Alway), in his *The Last of the Eries: A Tale of Canada* (1849) addressed in his preface the "Canadian Public" and the "Canadian reader" several times, and the context in which the readership is referred to consists in the readership's potential critical position. For this reason, the prefacer addresses the readership in an apologetic voice:

The writer of the following pages, in presenting his labors to the perusal, and sentence of a discerning Public, does so with some degree of hesitation, not so much from a fear of the subject being devoid of interest to every Canadian, as from a doubt of his having sufficient experience, to clothe it in the most agreeable language.

This apologetic voice is of course at the same time preemptive. Apology to a specific readership group is contained in Ebenezer Clemo's *Canadian Homes; or, The Mystery Solved: A Christmas Tale* (1858):

While apologizing to his lady readers for the little matter of fact that here and there appears, he would at the same time assure them, that he has not therein altogether forgotten them; since he has, in consequence, paid more attention to the interest of the plot, and to the little technicalities of construction that would assist in counteracting certain intrusive horrors, than he might otherwise have done.

The apology, when the author is attempting to appease those readers who might not be among the ones of whose favour she is sure, is another type and it can be found in May Leonard's preface to *Zoe; or, Some Day* (1888): "It is most certainly very difficult to attempt to please every one, when there are so many tastes to please". But an apology may be directed at the general readership as well. Marie Elise T.T. Lauder's temperance novel, *At Last* (1894), has a preface by the author in which she excuses herself for sending the young hero and heroine on a trip to the French and Italian Riviera — presumably because of her own moral convictions and the image of the Riviera.

4. Autobiography.

The apology for inexperience and youth, or other circumstances that the prefacer feels are to blame for whatever the novel is lacking, is often made with reference to the author's autobiography. Because in most cases the prefacer is identical with the author of the novel, this characteristic is best termed autobiographical.

The defence of perceived faults in and of the novel appears early in English-Canadian prefaces. Already in the preface of the novel that is often listed in Canadian literary histories as the first English-Canadian novel, Julia Catherine Beckwith Hart's *St. Ursula's Convent, or, The Nun of Canada: Containing Scenes from Real Life* (1824), we find this preface characteristic:

> Such liberal minds will, it is hoped, approve of whatever is meritorious in the following tale, and candidly excuse the defects a more experienced eye may perceive, in the first production of an author of seventeen, which was the writer's age when *St. Ursula's Convent...* was written.

A somewhat similar apology appears in another early novel of English-Canadian literature, in Joseph Abbott's preface to *Philip Musgrave; or, Memoirs of a Church of England Missionary...* (1846): "There will doubtless be many literary errors in the following pages: living, as I have done, for the last twenty-five years, in the backwoods of this wild country, shut out from the world, it would be extraordinary if there were not". Another type of autobiographical apology, although unique in occurrence, is the appeal to the readers to forgive faulty English, as in Henrietta Skelton's preface to *Grace Morton* (1873): "The merits and demerits of it must express themselves in its being read; but should there be expressions not quite correct in English, I would beg my readers to be lenient in their criticisms, and kindly remember that I am a native of Germany". The similarity of the two prefaces, Abbott's and Skelton's, lies in the prefacers' perception of the quality of writing. In other words, although in Skelton's preface the question is grammar and in Abbott's "literary errors", the apology is in reference to the quality of the text. Another noteworthy dimension of Abbott's apology is that the author uses the harsh physical characteristics of Canada to excuse possible faults in his writing.

Janet C. Conger apologizes for her inexperience in her preface to *A Daughter of St. Peter* (1889): "She can only plead that this the first child of her invention". Georgina Seymour Waitt's preface to her *Three Girls under Canvas* (1900) contains a humorous allusion to her own inexperience as a writer. The author's novel is personified, i.e., the prefacer speaks about the novel as if it were a person. At the same time the author stresses her desire to amuse rather than to educate:

> I stand before you — a tall stripling of a youth, my feet just on the threshold of a world all new to me — and crave your indulgence. ... Now, with this brief apology I come, not as a literary production, not as a book that will make you wiser, but only as a sketch, full of fun. To make hearts merrier, to call forth hearty laughs, is my sole mission, and if I fulfil my purpose, judge me not harshly — I am very young.

An autobiographical apology is to be found in Gilbert Parker's *The Trail of the Sword...* (1896) where the author recounts events of his childhood, the things he did with his father, and apologizes to the latter for not having become a soldier, as his wish had been, but a writer.

The Critical
Subgroups: 1. Readership.
                2. Genre.
                3. Emerging literature.
                4. Morality.
                5. Conventional.
                6. Subversive.
                7. Various.

1. Readership.

Joseph Abbott's *Philip Musgrave...* (1846) has a preface in which the author addresses his readership specifically in England. Other critical characteristics of this preface are implicit and refer to that particularly nineteenth-century phrase "Truth is stranger than fiction". Joseph Abbott also apologizes for "literary errors" but at the same time is confident that criticism cannot affect him because of his situation, i.e., because he lives in the Canadian wilderness. After the previously quoted passage about his "twenty-five years, in the backwoods of this wild country, shut out from the world" he continues: "I do not, however, anticipate the severity of criticism, and shall make no attempt to soften it".

2. Genre.

References to literary genre are often implicitly critical in the wider context of literary theory. Importantly, genre criticism appears very early in English-Canadian prefaces, as in Edward Lane's preface to his *The Fugitives, or, A Trip to Canada...* (1830). While the author questions the genre of his own text — whether it is a novel or not — he discusses the relationship between fact and fiction and ultimately assures the reader that his book is more fact than fiction. Another early example of genre perception in the sense of the configuration of fiction and facts appears in James Russell's preface to *Matilda...* (1833). Interestingly, here the author argues that precisely because the novel is based on facts it is not a novel. The employment of fiction is attributed to the readership, because it "is impossible to narrate such an event, and bring it before the Public in the shape of a book, without having recourse to fiction". R.M. Ballantyne too, writes in his preface to *Snowflakes and Sunbeams...* (1859):

In regard to unimportant matters I have taken the liberty of a novelist, — not to color too highly, or to invent improbabilities, but — to transpose time, place, and circumstance at pleasure; while, at the same time, I have endeavored to convey to the reader's mind a truthful impression of the general effect — to use a painter's language — of the life and country of the Fur Trader.

A more general genre critical assertion, also in a preface by Ballantyne (*Fighting the Whales or Doings and Dangers on a Fishing Cruise*, 1887), is the following:

As all classes, in every age, have proved that tales and stories are the most popular style of literature, each volume of the series (with, perhaps, one or two exceptions) will contain a complete tale, the heroes and actors in which, together with the combination of circumstances in which they move, shall be more or less fictitious.

Vincent E. Briton's preface to *Some Account of Amyot Brough...* (1885) contains a "fact and fiction" perspective:

In treating of the doings and sayings of Captain Brough, I needed to take council of no one; but in dealing with the character and deeds of the hero of Quebec [James Wolfe], I was constrained to seek aid from other writers. I trust they have not misled me.

The preface to Catherine Traill's *Canadian Crusoes: A Tale of the Rice Lake Plains* (1881) argues also for truth and facts. This is particularly important in this case, because the preface was obviously not written by Traill, but by her sister, Agnes Strickland. Since the novel was first published in London, England, one can safely assume that the readership addressed in the preface was largely the British readership.

John Carroll's *The School of the Prophets, or, Father McRorey's Class, and 'Squire Firstman's Kitchen Fire: A Fiction Founded on Facts* (1876) contains two prefaces, one by Enoch Wood[3] and one by the author. The preface by the author discusses the configuration of truth and fiction and is specifically addressed to a general readership. In essence, Carroll provides for the reader his own critical understanding of fiction. At the same time, he outlines the objectives he had in mind when writing his book — in itself a critical characteristic as soon as he wrote and placed it in front of the novel, i.e., in the preface. Lastly, he speaks to the critics in an attempt to justify the designation of his book as a novel by referring to his knowledge of contemporary criticism on the novel.

Although other examples reinforce this particularity of nineteenth-century English-Canadian novels, namely that "truth is stranger than fiction" and that the author wrote the novel based on "fact and fiction", there are sometimes interesting deviations from this general rule. The preface to Richard Lanigan's *They Two, or, Phases of Life in Eastern Canada Fifty Years Ago* (1888), written by the editor of the novel, expressly maintains the contrary position. In this context, the general critical attitude was that the novel based on "facts" belongs to the canon. In this preface this is implicitly negated: "It is no commendation of a novel now-a-days to assure the reader that the incidents are all actualities; for the more absurdly false they are, so long as they are sensational, the more popular are such stories with a certain class of readers". Paradoxically, the editor appeals to his readership, which is not the same one he attacks, and maintains that the novel at hand still conforms to the "fiction based on truth" concept: "What influence the perusal of such 'Munchausenisms' will have on the literary taste of the age, and on the morality of the rising generation, the future alone will solve. This book has neither falsehood nor sensation to recommend it".

---

3   Enoch Wood was a Methodist minister of note (cf. *Dictionary of Canadian Biography* XI 935-36).

Implied genre criticism can be found in several prefaces in which the author explains the publication of a novel based on the success of a previous novel. A noteworthy example is Catherine Parr Traill's novel *Lost in the Backwoods: A Tale of the Canadian Forest* (1882). The preface of Sir Robert Baden-Powell, the founder of the Scout movement, to William F. Butler's *Red Cloud: A Tale of the Great Prairie* (1888) has the same kind of genre critical dimension. The prefacer praises this novel based on his experience with another, *The Story of a Failure*, by the same author. The experience, a curious enough example in literature, pertains to Baden-Powell's ability to use the novel as a "manual of war": "That is what *The Story of a Failure* did in my case: after reading that book I knew what to avoid in Ashanti, and so was able to make my work successful". In his appraisal of the new novel, *Red Cloud...*, Baden-Powell relates the novel to its usefulness to scouting, and the movement's basic ideology, male camaraderie.

J. Shinnick, in the preface to *The Banker's Daughter, or, Her First and Last Ball: A Novel* (1891), presents genre perception of his own novel:

In offering this little volume to the public we do not claim for it any literary merit. ... Our object in offering it for publication is that a leisure hour may be agreeably spent, and those who will read it, will not have their minds disturbed by descriptive, exciting scenes that only exist in the imagination of authors.

The curious part in this preface is the assertion that "exciting scenes" exist in the imagination of authors — when the author of the preface is the author of the novel! Imagination, the source of fiction, is negated as a subversive force.

An exceptional type of genre-critical perspective appears in John Richardson's preface to *The Canadian Brothers; or, The Prophecy Fulfilled: A Tale of the Late American War* (1840). The preface quotes correspondence between the author and the royal court in which the court's decision is given prominence because it apparently decided to grant Richardson permission to dedicate his novel to the king, when this is usually not done with fiction. The reason for the permission is the court's decision to read the novel not as a novel, i.e., not as fiction:

Dear Sir, — I have to acknowledge your letter of the 1st instant, together with its enclosure, and beg to express the deep gratification I have felt in the perusal of that chapter of your new work which treats of the policy of employing the Indians in any future war we may have with the United States. Should you be desirous of dedicating it to His Majesty I can foresee no difficulty.

Criticism of a genre other than the novel, in this case travel literature, appears in John Mackie's preface to his *The Heart of the Prairie* (1876):

Not so many years ago, when the facilities for travel were different from what they are now, a great deal of rubbish and erroneous impressions were disseminated by so called literature purporting to deal with adventures and phases of life in certain little-known places of the earth.

The strong criticism of travel literature, if indeed it is what Mackie intended here, is curious if for no other reason than that in the eighteenth and early nineteenth centuries travel literature was a dominant and well-published genre in Canada. The important critical aspect of Mackie's preface is again the conviction that fiction must be built on facts: "I can, at least, claim truthfulness of detail for this story". Another, earlier critical aside about travel literature, in reference to Boswell, is to be found in Thomas Chandler Haliburton's "Valedictory Address" in his *The Attaché, or, Sam Slick in England* (1843). Here, a critical perception of travel literature, an important and voluminous genre of the time, and the factual orientation of the period, are connected: "Neither the 'Clockmaker' nor the 'Attaché' were ever designed as books of travels but to portray character — to give practical lessons in morals and politics". Haliburton's "Valedictory Address" contains further critical characteristics with reference to choices in the construction of the novel, i.e., the inclusion of humour, the use of language, etc.

In the preface to *The Mysteries of Montreal: A Novel Founded on Facts* (1846), the anonymous author writes about the genre "light literature". The author argues for fiction that depicts the good and avoids the depiction of evil in detail. He feels that in his time light literature degenerated, in that it does depict the bad. This "degeneration" he balances with the observation that "Now, it [literature] has assumed a far superior tone by confining itself to localities, or individual classes of people". This prefacer's genre perception is interesting because it conceptually predates Howells's interpretation of American literature as focussing on regionalism.[4]

Criticism in reference to the preface itself appears in Julia Catherine Beckwith's *Tonnewonte, or, The Adopted Son of America: A Tale Containing Scenes from Real Life* (1825). The author discusses the preface as a prerequisite of publication using the device of a fictional character: "Oh, your servant, Mr. Noxbury; I beg pardon, but my mind was indeed much occupied. My publisher has sent to me for a preface. ... A preface! Why, then, you really intend publishing your manuscript?" The reference to prefaces appears also later, as in Bruce Weston Munro's preface to *A Blundering Boy: A Humorous Story* (1886):

Of course, no boy will read this preface; it would, therefore, be a waste of time to address a discourse to boys in it. Reader, did you ever observe the manner in which a boy ignores the preface in his school-books? If not, you do not know how much scorn a boy's face is capable of displaying.

J.J. Procter's *The Philosopher in the Clearing* (1897) contains a similar perception of the preface. He placed his "Pausing at the Gate. The Preface" within the text of the novel, in what is called Chapter II, because "Any way, interesting or not, prefaces are never read".

3. Emerging Literature.

The subgroup of prefaces with critical characteristics related to the notion of "emerging literature" can be exemplified already in the preface of the first Canadian novel. Julia Catherine Beckwith Hart's *St. Ursula's Convent...* (1824) offers implicit criticism of English-Canadian letters:

---

4 Cf. Perosa 139-71.

Our country is gradually rising into notice. Our physical resources are great. Our population is increasing; and the time may come, when British America will be as noted in "song" or "deeds," as any kingdom of Europe: but, to attain that eminence, she must cherish native genius in its humblest beginnings.

The propagation of and belief in "native", i.e. Canadian and American literature, in the context of an emerging literature, is the main concern of Julia Catherine Beckwith not only in her above-quoted preface to the "Canadian" novel *St. Ursula's Convent...* (1824) but also in the "American" *Tonnewonte...* (1825). The author ("Grodenk") of *My Own Story: A Canadian Christmas Tale* (1869), speaks also about the Canadian author of the emerging literature: "I am aware that in publishing this story I shall encounter much criticism, and some rebuke; for the Canadian who enters on the field of literature has many obstacles to overcome".

John R. Gair in his "The Author's Preface" to *Fun on the Road* (1886) argues that the author of a book is more important, all things being equal, than the critic of the same book — all in reference to the readers. The key critical thought here, of course, is not the author's anticipation of criticism. Rather, it is his acute awareness of his situation as a *Canadian* author in the context of an emerging literature.

A particular aspect of the emerging Canadian literatures as compared to that of Britain, and, in the mind of this author, the United States — also perceived as having an established literature — is the reference to publishing opportunities. J. Macdonald Oxley, in his preface to *Bert Lloyd's Boyhood: A Story from Nova Scotia* (1892), discusses the opportunities for publication and readership in Britain and the U.S. *versus* Canada.

4. Morality.

Another subgroup of criticism is a form of the ethical perspective. Enoch Wood, the Methodist minister of note (see above note 3), wrote the preface to John Carroll's *The School of the Prophets...* (1876). The minister's preface combines a definition of genre (fiction) with the history of early Canada in the context of religious life.

5. Conventional.

Criticism in its conventional sense occurs when the preface is written by other than the author of the novel and when this is done in the context of an appraisal. Examples are the preface "Mrs. Brooke", in the 1810 edition of Frances Brooke's *The History of Lady Julia Mandeville*, or several prefaces to the *Sam Slick...* (1854, 1859) novels of Thomas Chandler Haliburton. Similar criticism is contained in the preface of John Campbell's *Two Knapsacks: A Novel of Canadian Summer Life* (1892) where the author of the preface not only appraises the novel in its appeal to regional readers (Torontonians) and to readers of various Canadian ethnic groups of the time, but consciously calls attention to the author's native Canadianness. The connection to the literature of the "mother country" is not forgotten either: "The literary flavour is all that can be desired; the author evidencing a quite remarkable acquaintance with English literature, especially with Wordsworth, the Poet of the Lake Country".

6. Subversive.

An example of the subversive critical subgroup is Bruce Weston Munro's preface to *A Blundering Boy, a Humorous Story* (1886):

The writer, disgusted with books in which the heroes are treated with much respect, endeavours to heap every indignity upon these foolish boys. ... The writer respectfully observes that this maniac is not drawn from nature, but from romance. ... The writer seems most at home when attempting to poke fun at romance; yet he is tormented night and day, so much so that he has no peace, with romance.

7. Various.

Other critical perspectives include Frank Johnson's preface to *The Village of Merrow; Its Past and Present* (1876), which contains a critical perspective in connection with the publication of his novel. In his "Dedication" to William Chambers he praises the Chambers brothers' publications because they advance the cause of education.[5] At the same time, Johnson connects the situation of the English agricultural labourer with the history of not only Canada but, obviously in the context of immigration, also of America in general. It is not surprising, then, that the novel contains a second preface, an "Introduction to the American Edition", although the novel was, in fact, published in Montréal by Lovell. The "Introduction to the American Edition" interestingly contains a long discussion on the advantage of an educated lower class for British society. The education of the lower classes in Britain would not only be an advantage for that society, but it would eliminate the problem of emigration to Canada and the States composed of "the coarsest clay of human life". A unique case is William Kirby's preface to the 1897 edition of *The Golden Dog (Le Chien d'Or): A Romance of the Days of Louis Quinze in Quebec*. Kirby's misfortunes due to the machinations of Lovell are well known and Kirby's preface is a published confirmation of the pirating of his work. This preface is critical in the sense that the author is questioning the copyright situation existing at that time.

The Dedicatory
Subgroups: 1. Readership groups.
                    2. Individuals.
                    3. Thematic.

1. Readership groups.

Specific prefatory dedications are rare, although prefaces do address specific readership groups. Robert Wilson's preface to his novel *Never Give up, or, Life in the Lower Provinces* (1878) dedicates it to young men. The long preface to *A Blundering Boy: A Humorous Story* (1886) by Bruce Weston Munro dedicates the novel to young boys. Alexander Begg's preface to his *Dot It Down: A Story of Life in the North-West*

---

5 The Chambers brothers of Edinburgh published several important works of the time, such as Chambers' Encyclopædia and the *Chambers' Edinburgh Journal*.

(1871) is titled "Dedication" and he addresses and dedicates his novel to "My Dear Friends" — these being, as it becomes obvious from the preface, a general readership. An interesting dedicatory preface is Alfred A. Glasier's to his *The Irving Club among the White Hills* (1877) because of its implication of genre perception. His dedication is directed at, it seems, writers in general, although he addresses "amateur journalists": "In recognition of their successful efforts to secure for Amateur Journalism an acknowledged place in the literature of Canada, this volume is dedicated by The Author". Another dedication of interest is Isabel Garison's to her novel *Looking Forward* (1890), because she dedicates it to French Canadians.

2. Individuals.

As mentioned before, many novels were dedicated to individuals with a few lines on a separate page. These types of dedications were not included as prefaces in this study. However, there are examples of dedications which are really prefaces addressed to specific individuals. Thomas Chandler Haliburton's *The Clockmaker; or, The Sayings and Doings of Samuel Slick, of Slickville* (1838) has a preface which is dedicated to Lieutenant-Colonel C.W. Fox. In the preface Haliburton justifies the dedication to the LieutenantColonel by referring to Fox's favourable opinion of the writer's work. John Richardson's preface to *The Canadian Brothers...* (1840) evokes the earlier custom of dedications to monarchs, which are now "regulated". The reference pertains to an apparent custom of the royal court in London of making a distinction of genres, fiction not being worthy of dedication to the monarch. The following quotation is part of the preface, a letter addressed to the author, Richardson, by an official of the court: "I do not presume you wish to apply for permission to dedicate the work to His Majesty, which is not usually given for works of fiction". In the case of Richardson, as the subsequent correspondence shows, the permission was granted for reasons explained above, in the *critical* category. Gilbert Parker dedicates his novel *The Trail of the Sword...* (1896), in a longer than usual preface, to his father and makes autobiographical references.

3. Thematic.

An example of the thematic dedicatory preface occurs in *Fables of the Nechaco: A Complete Novel of One of the Most Remarkable and Romantic Districts on the American Continent* (18--), by "Slivers", in which the novel is dedicated to those who find Canada's geographical space attractive: "To those who love the open, who are ambitious to know the truth and aid and profit in the development of the last and best great west, this book is dedicated".

The Ethical
Subgroups: 1. Morality.
              2. Social consciousness/patriotism.
              3. Political.
                    a. Historical.
                    b. Social conditions.
              4. Various.

1. Morality.

An early example of the writer's concern with morality can be found in James Russell's preface to his *Matilda...* (1833):

> The Author flatters himself there is not an expression throughout the narrative that cannot appear before the most delicate eye, neither will it taint the mind, but more probably lead it to the fountain of good. As a first essay it pleads many excuses. — It was written with the intention of pointing out the interposition of Divine Providence in support of persecuted innocence.

The preface of Thomas Chandler Haliburton to the new 1859 edition of *Sam Slick's Wise Saws and Modern Instances; or, What He Said, Did, or Invented* explicitly promotes the moral issues the author consciously incorporates in his work. In addition, Haliburton employs, as he explains in his preface, humour to promote his views of morality:

> The original design in writing the sketches known as the "Sayings and Doings of the Clock-Maker," which has never since been lost sight of, was to awaken Nova Scotians to the vast resources and capabilities of their native land, to stimulate their energy and enterprise, to strengthen the bond of union between the colonies and the parent State, and by occasional reference to the institutions and governments of other countries, to induce them to form a just estimate and place a proper value on their own.

The most frequent ethical preface is the type in which the author assures the reader that the novel is morally acceptable. Charles Shrimpton's preface to his *The Black Phantom, or, Woman's Endurance: A Narrative Connected with the Early History of Canada and the American Revolution* (1867) assures the reader that the novel is written on moral principles and that these principles are even more important than "literary excellence". The anonymously published novel *The Adopted Daughter, or, The Trials of Sabra: A Tale of Real Life* (1873) illustrates this perspective again in its preface to the second edition: "[the novel] will have a moral and religious influence upon the minds of those who may peruse it". David Hickey, in the preface to his *William and Mary: A Tale of the Siege of Louisburg, 1745* (1884) defends his novel on moral grounds: "Of course the customary sneer towards the religious novel is expected, yet I do not know whether 'William and Mary' is entitled to the distinction. It is, however, strictly moral".

The invocation of God's assistance for the success of the publication or the writing of the text is another example of the moral-ethical preface, as in *Tim Doolan, the Irish Emigrant: Being a Full and Particular Account of His Reasons for Emigrating...* (1869) by the "Author of *Mick Tracy*": "Whether seaworthy or otherwise, he again launches this little barque, with the prayer, that He who rules the raging of the sea, may guide her to whatever result will most glorify Himself". James Mann's preface to *The Victorious King: An Allegory* (1878) is written with reference to the Bible and the Bible's importance for morality. In a sense, this perspective can be understood as drawing on God's assistance. The prolific R.M. Ballantyne provides a moral-ethical perspective in the context of the invocation of God's assistance and a humanistic *Weltanschauung* in the preface for several of his novels (e.g. *Fighting the Whales...* [186-], *Over the Rocky Mountains...* [1879], *Away in the Wilderness...* [between 1894 and 1905]): "In writing these volumes, the author has earnestly endeavoured to keep in view the glory of God and the good of man".

The assessment that contemporary literature is not in compliance with moral standards is the concern of several authors of prefaces. For example, James Mann in his *The Victorious King: An Allegory* (1878) has an introduction by John Potts. In the introduction Potts writes: "The world is flooded with pernicious papers, tracts, magazines, pamphlets, and books. There is nothing more calculated to enervate and defile the mind of the community than the reading of frivolous and impure literature".

The advocacy of joy in Christianity as opposed to the perception of melancholy in religion is the subject of Amelia Panton Stroud's *Daisy Dalton's Decision* (1894). Her preface is a short synopsis of this theme.

A moral-ethical preface is more obviously to be expected when written for a novel with a moralistic theme. John Carroll's *The School of the Prophets...* (1876) is prefaced in this way: "An author ... whose literary productions have been of essential service to the Church in Canada...". The moralistic-religious rhetoric is also frequent in other English-Canadian prefaces as in Ralph Connor's to *Black Rock: A Tale of the Selkirks* (1900): "There is a warfare appointed unto man upon earth, and its struggles are nowhere more intense, nor the victories of the strong, nor the succors brought to the fallen, more heroic, than on the fields described in this volume". In the same vein are the moral-ethical prefaces which assert that the novel is for the edification of the soul. An example is Marie Elise Lauder's *At Last* (1894):

If my boy-hero and my heroine travel somewhat in France and the Riviera of Italy, they have ever the one great aim — to bring God a consecrated service.... If the golden promises, and the resulting peace born of them to my heroine and her laddie, should bring comfort, healing strength to rise and conquer, to any troubled and tempted soul, the writer will have her reward.

A more general sense of morality is expressed by Kate Bottomley *alias* "Vera", who argues in her preface to *Honor Edgeworth, or, Ottawa's Present Tense* (1882) in favour of a general sense of ethical concern: "The predominant feeling throughout the entire composition has been one of pure philanthropy, as the author desires to benefit her fellow-creatures, in as far as it lies in her very limited power". A similar concern underlies her preface to a second novel, *The Doctor's Daughter* (1885). Thomas Barlow Smith's preface to his *A Seraph on the Sea, or, The Career of a Highland Drummer Boy* (1891) is another example of a general perspective on morality. Smith dedicates his novel to "that class of his fellow beings who have been unfortunate in their lives". Again, morality in a general sense is the topic of Margaret E. Tennant's *The Golden Chord: A*

Story of Trial and Conquest (1899) and she voices her conviction in her preface: "that anything I might be enabled to write might bear forth an influence that would be for the moral uplift of humanity". R.M. Ballantyne, differently from the example above, addresses morality with a more general perspective in his preface to *The Walrus Hunters: A Romance of the Realms of Ice* (1893): "That this tale may, in some small degree, advance the cause of right, and tend to demolish wrong, is the height of my ambition".

2. Social consciousness/patriotism.

Prefaces expressing social consciousness, including awareness of women's social position, democracy, and patriotism, etc., form another subgroup of the ethical preface. J. Abbott, in his preface to *Philip Musgrave, or, Memoirs of a Church of England Missionary in the North American Colonies* (1846) complains about the ignorance of the Canadian "social, political, or religious condition" in the "mother country", England. Frank Johnson's preface to *The Village of Merrow; Its Past and Present* (1876) expresses social consciousness by a concern with the lot of the "Scottish ploughman" and his subsequent emigration. An ethical preface that has several dimensions connecting morality, patriotism, and history, is William Henry Withrow's preface to his *The King's Messenger, or, Lawrence Temple's Probation: A Story of Canadian Life* (1879, 1897). The preface to the anonymous *The Hunted Outlaw, or, Donald Morrison, the Canadian Rob Roy* (1889) is socially and ethically sensitive in the sense that it treats the criminal act as an *inexplicable* human characteristic. An expression of social consciousness is the preface of L.S. Huntington's *Professor Conant: A Story of English and American Social and Political Life* (1884), in which the author curiously connects the notion of democracy with love:

Carlyle says: "Universal Democracy, whatever we may think of it, has declared itself, as an inevitable fact of the days in which we live," and a greater than Carlyle has ordained that to study the loves of men and women is to court enchantment and infatuation.

The preface to Edmund E. Sheppard's *Dolly, the Young Widder Up to Felder's* (1886) is an example of social consciousness with regards to women:

Good stories are said to have a moral, and clever ones must have a great idea running through their pages. I believe in the goodness, fidelity, and truth of women, and comprehending the suspicion and pride of the ordinary man, have tried to point out how trifles in the jealous or even watchful mind build up awful images of perfidy and distrust.

A specific dimension of social consciousness is the concern with family life and youth. Wallace Lloyd (James Algie) discusses family life and his perception of the problem of divorce. In his preface to *Houses of Glass: A Romance* (1899) Algie explains his concern, based on his religious convictions, which, in turn, he believes to be grounded in nature: "A union based on the moral, physical and spiritual affinity of man and woman, is the only one which nature stamps as genuine, and any violation of this principle brings with it its own punishment". Edmund E. Sheppard, the author of *Widower Jones: A Faithful*

History of His "Loss" and Adventures in Search of a "Companion": A Realistic Story of Rural Life (1888) wrote a preface in which he dedicates his novel

To those who fear "father will marry again"; to the wife who thinks her husband may sometime give her children a stepmother; to the husband who wonders how his wife would act if he were dead; to those who care for pictures of real life with its sorrows and joys, its peculiarities and pretensions, its heartaches and laughter....

Youth and morality are the concern in the preface of Hannah Maynard Pickard's *The Widow's Jewels* (1848):

To aid in strengthening upon your young minds impressions of this important duty, the writer has collected from memory, and placed in contrast, the incidents of the following pages, knowing that every lesson, however simple, which you treasure up and profit by, will be imparting another ray of beauty to "jewels" which are to shine for ever and ever in the praise of God.

The concern with morality and youth is most obvious when the author is a man of the cloth. Among the several examples of this kind of text, Robert Wilson's preface to his *Never Give Up, or, Life in the Lower Provinces* (1878) is an interesting one: "The hope is cherished that some good may result from its perusal, and that some young man into whose hands it may fall, may find it an encouragement and strength in the struggle of life".

The novel *Jessie Grey, or, The Discipline of Life: A Canadian Tale* (1870) by "L.G." has a preface addressed to a specific readership, children. The author outlines his opinion of what will make these children good citizens of a future Canada: the belief in God. Similarly, "Grodenk"'s *My Own Story: A Canadian Christmas Tale* (1869) contains a patriotic preface in which the author hopes that his novel is "less injurious to the young readers of our country than the great bulk of the novels annually imported from other lands". Kate Murray's preface to *The Guiding Angels* (1871) can also be classified as having characteristics related to youth and morality:

But it has been written for the young, and it is hoped it may be used by them with pleasure and with profit. Whether or not it will fail of its desired end is known only to Him who hath said, "My word shall not return unto me void, but shall accomplish that whereunto I have sent it." If by its perusal the path of religion is rendered more attractive to one youthful traveller, or one young heart be cheered in its onward journey, it will not have been written in vain.

3. Political.
Subgroups: a. Historical.
              b. Social conditions.

A particular type of the ethical preface is the kind where the prefacer is concerned with political issues. These prefaces may be subgrouped into "historical" and "social conditions" kinds of prefaces.

a. Historical.

John Richardson in his preface to *Wacousta, or, The Prophecy: An Indian Tale* (1832) clearly takes sides in the history of French Canada *versus* English Canada:

Still, though conquered as a people, many of the leading men in the country, actuated by that jealousy for which they were remarkable, contrived to oppose obstacles to the quiet possession of a conquest by those whom they seemed to look upon as their hereditary enemies....

Further on in his preface, Richardson strongly disclaims any responsibility by Britain or English Canada, and he blames, on several points, French Canada. At the same time, speaking of the contemporary political and social situation, he believes that the hostility of French Canadians has died away, albeit due to the "genius and power of England".[6] His preface to *The Canadian Brothers...* (1840) contains also several political characteristics. The cited correspondence between Richardson and the royal court in London, for example, contains references to the possibility of a future war with the United States. Richardson's summary of his objectives when writing the novel also has a political tone:

Since in eschewing the ungenerous desire of most English writers on America, to convey a debasing impression of her people, and seeking, on the contrary, to do justice to their character, as far as the limited field afforded by a work, pre-eminently of fiction, will admit, no interested motive can be ascribed to him. Should these pages prove a means of dissipating the slightest portion of that irritation which has — and naturally — been engendered in every American heart, by the perverted and prejudiced statements of disappointed tourists, whose acerbity of stricture, not even a recollection of much hospitality could repress....

This subgroup may be further exemplified by the preface to *Two and Twenty Years Ago: A Tale of the Canadian Rebellion* (1859) by "Backwoodsman". The preface refers to the treatment of the Upper Canadian Mackenzie Rebellion in 1837. The author shows political awareness when he says in his preface:

It is a subject which must be touched gently, not to wound the sensibilities of many who were actors therein, and some of whom from the generosity of our government are high lights among us. The following Story will be found to be as impartial as is consistent with the moral it incalculates, loyalty and filial piety....

The Mackenzie Rebellion appears as a political indicator also in William George McKinnon's preface to *Saint George: or, The Canadian League* (1852): "the author has not allied himself to any party or taken the view of any particular faction with regard to the insurrection". The long preface (8 pages) gives detailed historical background (an explanatory characteristic) for the novel with letters written by participants in the rebellion. Further examples include Mrs. Jerome Mercier, *The Red House by the Rockies: A Tale of Riel's Rebellion* (1896). In this case, the theme of the novel determines the preface's political undertones. Perhaps the most obvious political statement

---

6   Cf. Duffy 3-5.

in her preface is the justification for using historical documents, letters and diaries, in the novel. The point here is not the assurance that the novel is based on "facts", but the suggestion that Riel is a politically sensitive issue: "The letters and diaries here given are all genuine. Were it not so, they would detract from any interest the little tale may have as a mere narrative; and, being matters of fact, it seems best to insert them, since this page of history is one not open to many". The author's statement that the Riel Rebellion is a chapter in Canadian history not discussed is of course true in the sense that English Canada viewed the Rebellion with hostility. A similar political tone can be found in Mme Morel de la Durantaye's preface to *A Visit to the Home of Evangeline: Historical Romance of the Acadians* (1898). The author deplores the fact that the Acadians were expelled, but even more that their history seems to have been forgotten — in French Canada. The author was sent to Acadia by the Mayor of Montreal "in a charitable cause" and during her work she discovered the history of Acadia, which, she feels, has been neglected. Her own interest in Acadians was originally triggered by her interest in her Acadian ancestry.

The historical theme of 1812 determines the political undertone of W.H. Withrow's preface to his novel *Neville Trueman, the Pioneer Preacher: A Tale of the War of 1812* (1880):

To present certain phases of Canadian life during the heroic struggle against foreign invasion, which first stirred in our country the pulses of that common national life which has at length attained a sturdier strength in the confederation of the several provinces of the Dominion of Canada.

b. Social conditions.

The second subgroup of political prefaces, the "social conditions" type, may be illustrated through the following prefaces. Ebenezer Clemo's preface to *Canadian Homes, or, The Mystery Solved: A Christmas Tale* (1858) contains information about the economic, political, and social condition of Canada at the time. Frank Johnson's preface to the *The Village of Merrow: Its Past and Present* (1876) contains a political dimension in that it discusses the history and repercussions of emigration from the British Isles and of immigration to North America (Canada *and* the United States). A contrary view is expressed in Thomas B. Smith's preface to *Young Lion of the Woods, or, A Story of Early Colonial Days* (1889), in which the author promotes the virtues of colonization. The preface to Isaac Broome's *"The Brother": Splendor and Woe* (1890), a novel with elements of science-fiction — probably a unique example of this genre in the nineteenth-century Canadian literatures — is wholly of a social conditions type. The author gives a contemporary account of the activities of socialists in the United States and Great Britain, with some references to Germany. A political statement with interesting dimensions is Isabel Garison's preface to her *Looking Forward* (1890). The author addresses the "brave sons" and "fair daughters" of "La Nouvelle France", praises their sense of history and calls them to "become one with the great Republic whose doors stand open to receive you!" (The "great republic" is of course the United States.)

4. Various.

The ethical preface, as the following examples show, could also stretch into less obvious areas of life. Here are two examples of ethics connected to animals: Margaret Marshall Saunders's *Beautiful Joe: The Autobiography of a Dog* (1895) is prefaced by Hezekiah Butterworth, who expounds on the value of compassion towards animals and how this compassion will benefit humanity. Annie G. Savigny, who wrote *Lion, the Mastiff: From Life* (1895), a topic similar to Saunders' *Beautiful Joe...* (1895), attached a similar preface by William Caven to her book.

There are a few examples of temperance novels that contain prefaces with characteristics of both the social consciousness and the moralistic types. Examples of temperance prefaces include Henrietta Skelton's preface to *A Man Trap, and, The Fatal Inheritance: Two Temperance Tales* (1876) in which she proposes the establishment of "coffee houses", analogous to the custom in Germany, where workers could go instead of drinking in pubs. Similarly engaged is Austin Potter's preface to his *From Wealth to Poverty, or, The Tricks of the Traffic: A Story of the Drink Curse* (1884). Another example of the temperance preface is in Cornelius Wilson's *Rescued in Time: a Tale* (1894): "And while we have endeavored to present the evils of the "drink traffic", we have, at the same time, tried to show that there is an all-wise Providence guiding the affairs of men".

The Explanatory
Subgroups: 1. Genesis.
               2. Thematic.
               3. Background (History/Geography).
               4. Intention.

1. Genesis.

In Carroll's preface to *The School of the Prophets...* (1876), the explanatory character consists of the prefacer's description of his novel's genesis. A similar explanation with reference to the genre and the genesis of the novel in the mind of its author occurs in the preface to Briton's *Amyot Brough, Captain in His Majesty's 20th Regiment of Foot who fought...* (1886):

In relating, at some unnecessary length, perhaps, the plain and unvarnished history of Captain Amyot Brough, my mind has been entirely at ease on one important point — none will ask whether it be true or false. It is a pleasing reflection, and my pen has much enjoyed the liberty thereby secured.

A genesis explanation may also pertain to the publication history of the novel. An example of this type appears in Louie Barron's preface in which he discusses the first publication of his novel *Zerola of Nazareth* (1895) in the American *Christian Herald*. The same author goes to great lengths to discuss the type of novel he intended to write and thus explains, in addition to the publication history of the novel, the genre and genesis of his novel.

The preface to Richard Lanigan's *They Two...* (1888) was written by the editor with the purpose of explaining the background of the book and the circumstances of its publication.

2. Thematic.

The second subgroup of the explanatory preface is the thematic-explanatory preface. In general, this type is characterized by explanations about the theme of the novel. An example of the author's explanation as to why he wrote the novel and how the theme of the novel relates to the author's life as he perceives it is Joseph Abbott's preface to *Philip Musgrave...* (1846). Another early example of the thematic-explanatory aspect and of the survival theme in Canadian literature appears in Agnes Strickland's preface to Catherine Parr Strickland Traill's *Canadian Crusoes: A Tale of the Rice Lake Plains* (1852).

A thematic-explanatory characteristic occurs also when the author connects the theme of his novel with personal observations of life and proceeds to explain it in that light. For example, Kate Madeline Bottomley ("Vera") decribes her observations of contemporary society in Ottawa with reference to the same topic in her novel, *Honor Edgeworth, or, Ottawa's Present Tense* (1882). Similarly, the moralistic reason of the author for writing a temperance novel is at length explained in Austin Potter's preface to his *From Wealth to Poverty...* (1884). David Hickey's preface to the novel *A Tale of the Siege of Louisburg, 1745* (1884) is also a good example: "It was long a matter of surprise to me, why the story of the remarkable siege of 1745 had never been presented to the public in popular form. The present work is an attempt to do this". Egerton Ryerson Young's preface to his *Winter Adventures of Three Boys in the Great Lone Land* (1899) is also thematic-explanatory, because he attempts to explain Canada's national "Indian" image. Young recounts that in his view the image of the Indian has been falsely presented and that he wishes to rectify this with his novel. Edmund William Forrest's preface to the novel *Ned Fortescue, or, Roughing It through Life: A Story Founded on Fact* (1871) contains a thematic-explanatory discussion:

In the following pages I have endeavored to portray a phase of life upon which many romances have been founded, and it has been my object to give the reader, who may be unacquainted with the Vie Bohemienne of the Army, a true idea of the feelings and circumstances as felt and seen by a soldier in the "ranks," who gradually wins his way from the first step of the ladder to that position from whence most other story-tellers start when they adopt a military hero.

The thematic-explanatory aspect of a preface may extend into a political statement, as in the case of Frank Johnson's preface to *The Village of Merrow: Its Past and Present* (1876), where the author explains not only his reasons for writing the novel, but also the social, political, and economic background of his theme, which is emigration from the British Isles.

3. Background (History/Geography).

A further subgroup, the explanation of the historical or geographical background of the novel, is a frequent feature of the explanatory preface. The background-explanatory aspect is most obvious when the preface is explicitly constructed for a readership that is, in the mind of the author, unfamiliar with some aspect of the novel. This is most obvious in the case where a specific readership is addressed. John Richardson, in his *Wacousta...* (1839), begins his "Chapter I Introductory" thus:

As we are about to introduce our readers to scenes with which the European is little familiarised, some few cursory remarks, illustrative of the general features of the country into which we have shifted our labours, may not be deemed misplaced at the opening of this volume.

After this, Richardson explains the historical and geographical background of his novel. One must, however, differentiate this type of "contemporary" explanatory preface from the ones where the historical background is indeed "historical", that is, provided for a period far back from the time of the author. Agatha Armour's preface to *Lady Rosamund's Secret: A Romance of Fredericton* (1898) contains the statement that "the object of the following story has been to weave simple facts into form dependent upon usages of society during the administration of Sir Howard Douglas, 1824-30". Birger Bech explains in his preface to *The Unknown* (1887) that "During my stay in Germany some years ago, I gathered certain facts which I now have tried to make use of".

For the purpose of delineating the components of fiction and "historical facts", authors often explain the historical background of the novel in the preface, sometimes in great detail. For example, Blanche Lucile Macdonnell in her preface to *Diane of Ville Marie: A Romance of French Canada* (1898) gives an account of the history of the Le Ber family. Mme Morel de la Durantaye writes an epistolary preface to her *A Visit to the Home of Evangeline...* (1898) in which, by explaining her own contact with Acadian history, she hopes to arouse interest in her novel. Maud Ogilvy's preface to her *Marie Gourdon: A Romance of the Lower St. Lawrence* (1890) contains almost exactly the same type of background-explanatory characteristic as the one by Mme Morel quoted above: the personal experience of a historical theme upon which the novel is built. The background-explanatory character is included in the preface because the authors apparently intend to draw attention to their experience, so as to strengthen the immediacy of the historical theme. Overall, one of the best examples of the background-explanatory preface is Stephen Cureton's to his *Perseverance Wins: The Career of a Travelling Correspondent: England, Canada, United States, Hawaiian Islands, New Zealand, Australia, Egypt, Italy* (1880):

To the Reader.
—

During a trip through that extensive range of country from the Red River to the Rocky Mountains, more familiarly known as Manitoba, and the Northwest Territory of Canada, the author made copious notes of his experiences, embracing facts of incidents, adventures, and observation. Circumstances, which a perusal of this volume may suggest, made it advisable to destroy the bulky book of notes. Any political or social opinions are simply the individual thoughts of the author obtruded as the occasion under illustration occurred. At the end of this book will be found a glossary containing an interpretation of words and phrases not in common use; also the key to cipher dispatch, and extract of log taken during the voyage from Australia to England. The latest letters are not overdrawn. The writer has seen a belt of valuable walnut timber in a section of the Northwest Territory, which the Government maps indicate to be a treeless region.

An exceptional historical characteristic can be found in Achilles Daunt's preface to his *The Three Trappers: A Story of Adventure in the Wilds of Canada* (1882). This preface is exceptional because in it its author shows concern for the environment in Canada and a "Greenpeace" attitude towards its use:

A few scattered herds still survive among the foothills and parks of the Rocky Mountains, but such scenes as that on page 99 are things of the past. Ceaseless, senseless slaughter has at last reduced the once innumerable herds of buffaloes to a straggling handful.

4. Intention.

An important subgroup of the explanatory prefaces is the type that contains the prefacer's explanations of his intention(s) in writing the novel. For example, John Galt's preface to his *Lawrie Todd, or, The Settlers in the Woods* (1830) contains at least two explanations of his intentions, one aimed at immigrants and the usefulness of the novel to them and the other an essentially moralistic conviction that the novel has a higher value than that of "amusement":

A description, which may be considered authentic, of the rise and progress of a successful American settlement, cannot but be useful to the immigrant who is driven to seek a home in the unknown wilderness of the woods. The privations are not exaggerated, nor is the rapidity with which they may be overcome. The book, therefore, though written to amuse, was not altogether undertaken without a higher object.

The explanatory characteristic of the preface often implicitly expresses the author's intention, i.e., a clarification of what the novel is supposed to be in the mind of its author: "The following story is intended to illustrate one of the many phases of the fur-trader's life in those wild regions of North America which surround Hudson's Bay" — as R.M. Ballantyne writes in the preface of his *Ungava: A Tale of Esquimau Land* (18--, 1858, 1893). This more general intention is expressed already in Thomas Chandler Haliburton's preface to his *The Attaché, or, Sam Slick in England* (1843). Haliburton's preface is a rarity among English-Canadian prefaces by its typographical position in relation to the text of the novel: it is a post-face rather than a preface. It is placed at the end of the novel, as Chapter LXVI, titled "Valedictory Address". Its typological function, however, is that of a *bona fide* preface. Its explanatory character lies in the fact that Haliburton gives a fairly lengthy explanation as to why he wrote the novel. It also contains explanations that refer to the text as genre: why he constructed the novel with humour. In both cases the author's intentions are being clarified.

The justification for "romancing" the novel, which actually is supposed to be based on "facts", is another aspect of the intention-explanatory preface, although it is an extension of the above-mentioned "fiction founded on facts" explanation, as in the preface of Douglas Erskine's *A Bit of Atlantis* (1900):

The object of this work is suggestive, rather than intended to uphold a theory. While the subject may not be of equal interest to all, from a purely historical or scientific point of view, an element of romance may tend to popularize it, and induce a wider study.

The intention-explanatory characteristic may be explicitly ideological. In the case of Joseph Edmund Collins's preface to his *The Four Canadian Highwaymen, or, The Robbers of Markham Swamp* (1886) the author explains his writing with reference to the Canadian readership:

I have no doubt that some of my friends who are in the habit of considering themselves "literary," will speak with despair and disparagement of myself when they read the title of this book. They will call it "blood and thunder," and will see that I am on my way to the dogs. Well, these people are my friends after all, and I shall not open a quarrel with them. For they themselves have tempted the public with stupid books and essays; and they failed in finding buyers. Therefore they have demonstrated for me that a stupid book doesn't pay; and I will not, even for my best friend, write anything but what the people will buy from me.

Lucius Seth Huntington, in the preface to his *Professor Conant: A Story of English and American Social and Political Life* (1884), connects democracy, the ideological base, to romance, which he terms "the study of the loves of men and women" and thus explains his intentions in the novel.

The justification for the writing of the novel also presents the characteristic of an intention-explanatory preface. For example, James B. Kennedy's preface to *Afloat for Eternity, or, A Pilgrim's Progress for the Times* (1893):

Why write another book? when the Earth already groans beneath the ponderous productions of the pen? Because each generation, in its voyage on the sea of time, splits on the shelved book rock that has been thrown up by the upheavals of the past. One half revels in the old; the other half says, "Give us something new."

"A few explanatory words are necessary", writes the author of *The Victorious King: An Allegory* (1878), James Mann, and provides a list in his preface of characters in his novels whose names allude to biblical figures. This type of explanation serves two purposes: it shows the author's intention of involving the reader in the theme of the novel (Bible) and at the same time, he wants to facilitate the reading of the novel.

A rarity among prefaces to English-Canadian novels of the intention-explanatory type is Ballantyne's formula preface, which he wrote for a number of his novels (1880, between 1894 and 1905, 1879, 1887, etc.). In these formulaic prefaces he explains the reason for writing his novels:

There is a vast amount of interesting information on almost all subjects, which many people, especially the young, cannot attain to because of the expense, and, in some instances, the rarity of the books in which it is contained. To place some of this information, in an attractive form, within the reach of those who cannot afford to purchase expensive books, is the principal object of this miscellany.

The Integral
John Richardson's preface to *Wacousta...* (1832) is titled Chapter I, although it is clearly a preface. A similar preface is that of Charles G.D. Roberts to his *The Forge in the*

Forest... (1896). Roberts titled his preface "A Foreword" and the information he conveys in it is written in the same narrative mode as the rest of the novel.

A specific type of the integral preface occurs when its title is combined with its placement in relation to the main text of the novel. The title "Prologue", borrowed from the usage in drama, is in most cases employed by the prefacer when the text conveyed is, similarly to the two examples above, an integral part of the narrative. J. Kerr Lawson's *Dr. Bruno's Wife: A Toronto Society Story* (1893) is a good example of this type of preface. But other terms too are used in this sense. For example, Leslie Vaughan titled her first Chapter "Introduction" (*Charlie Ogilvie: A Romance of Scotland and New Brunswick*, 1889). Thomas Chandler Haliburton's several *Sam Slick...* (e.g. 1853) novels have an "Introductory letter" placed before the first chapter. These are, nevertheless, integral prefaces because they are in reality part of the novel, although their typographical placing and their title show some prefatorial features.

The Preemptive
Subgroups: 1. Inexperience.
             2. Readership.
             3. Depreciation.
             4. Morality.
             5. Subversive.

1. Inexperience.

The relatively frequent apology of women authors for being young and inexperienced and for the fact that the publication is the first one, can be collectively classified as preemptive characteristics. For example, Beckwith (Hart)'s preface to her *St. Ursula's Convent...* (1824) has several preemptive characteristics of this type: "The author does not, indeed, flatter herself, that this juvenile performance will add to the celebrity of the country; but the fostering hand of public patronage if kindly extended to such a production, may elicit others of real and intrinsic merit".

The reference to "the first literary effort" is a frequent inexperience-preemptive device. Examples of this preemptive characteristic are numerous: Edward Lane, *The Fugitive...* (1830), Alexander Begg, *Dot It Down: A Story of Life in the North-West* (1871), John R. Gair, *Fun on the Road* (1886). Agatha Armour's preface to her *Lady Rosamund's Secret: A Romance of Fredericton* (1898) contains the following inexperience-preemptive statement: "In producing this little work the public are aware that too much cannot be expected from an amateur. Hoping that this may meet the approval of many". As a late example of this type, here is an excerpt from Georgina Seymour Waitt's preface to *Three Girls under Canvas* (1900), who points out her youth: "To make hearts merrier, to call forth hearty laughs, is my sole mission, and if I fulfil my purpose, judge me not harshly — I am very young".

2. Readership.

From among the readership-specific preemptive prefaces perhaps the critics' group should be singled out as an example. Louie Barron's preface to *Zerola of Nazareth* (1895) contains the following passage: "As to the critics. I ask them to be merciful, though not patronizing. I acknowledge that this is my first effort in fiction and promise that I shall try to do better in the future". Earlier readership preemptive characteristics appear in the preface of Julia Catherine Beckwith's novel, *St. Ursula's Convent.*... The author's lengthy explanation of the nature of Canada's emerging literature, her references to her age and to the fact that the novel is her first attempt at writing literature, and her references to "native" Canadian literature, all have the implicit function of preempting criticism. Because her novel is often named as the first Canadian novel, one preemptive characteristic, the preemptive device with reference to Canada being an emerging nation with an emerging literature, must be especially pointed out.

The preemptive device based on the presumption that a novel "founded on facts" is less prone to criticism appears early in English-Canadian prefaces. This aspect is obviously directed at both the critics and the readership. An early example of this preemptive characteristic is Edward Lane (*The Fugitives...*, 1830), who argues thus against possible criticism: "But be it remembered, this is not altogether a work of fancy; inasmuch, as the few chapters attributed to the pen of the 'Cabin Boy,' contain real facts, and are correctly copied from his own manuscript, now in my possession". Here, the address of a general readership is only implied and Lane's assertion of "facts" must be understood as a requirement of the contemporary literary environment, which he obviously sees manifested in the readership. James Russell's preface to his *Matilda...* (1833) contains preemptive devices that aim specifically at the readership. The author explains that his work was written in totally uncivilized circumstances, "among Indian tribes, wilds and woods, where nothing is heard". The Canadian environment, which, as shown above, is used as an explanation or excuse to neutralize critical value judgements, i.e., the state of the emerging literature in Canada, is here further developed: the creation of a literary work in such an environment deserves the benevolence of the readership. Russell employs a second, preemptive device of depreciation: "he trusts that the following tale will be perused by the generous Reader with a forgiving spirit for the Author's imperfections."

3. Depreciation.

The characteristic of depreciation occurs in various forms, such as the preemptive. Depreciation may be varied, referring to the author himself/herself, Canadian literature, writing itself, etc. John R. Gair, in his preface to *Fun on the Road* (1886), writes the following: "I have tried my best in a plain Scotch way to put this volume together, and not claiming it to be intellectual or refined". Another example of this preemptive device is the preface in Kate Murray's *The Guiding Angels* (1871): "No literary merit is claimed for the following work". An example of the device of preemptive depreciation, in the context of Canadian literature, appears in "Grodenk"'s preface to *My Own Story: A Canadian Christmas Tale* (1869): "I am aware that in publishing this story I shall encounter much criticism, and some rebuke; for the Canadian who enters on the field of literature has many obstacles to overcome. All I ask is 'nothing extenuate, nor set down aught in malice'".

The depreciative comparison of Canadian authorship to European writers, as in the case of Beckwith, occurs in other prefaces. An example is Kate Madeline Bottomley ("Vera"), who, in her preface to her novel *The Doctor's Daughter* (1885), is preemptive with regard to her preface when she compares her own to the prefaces of Dickens. The preemptive characteristic of self-depreciation in a preface may also be based on the economic returns of a bestseller; the author hopes to neutralize value judgements reserved for canonized literature. This is the attitude of Edmund Collins, in *The Four Canadian Highwaymen...* (1886):

By-and-by, when I drive a gilded chariot, and can afford to wait for books with quieter titles and more dramatic worth to bring me their slow earnings, I shall be presumptuous enough to set such a star before my ambition as the masters of English fiction followed.

4. Morality.

The concern with morality is a generally ubiquitous characteristic of English-Canadian prefaces. Usually, the prefacer assures the reader that the work is on safe moral ground. The example of "Malcolm"'s[7] preface to *The Dear Old Farm: A Canadian Story* (1897) is such a type. At the same time, the moral dimension is reinforced with a patriotic rhetoric:

Strange to say, too, in these days of books "with a purpose," the author makes no such claim for this volume, nor will the reader find therein a mystical and often disgusting study on the relation of the sexes. If he had had the first named in mind when writing he would have labelled this book "Essays," and if the second "Medical Talks." This volume, however, is sent forth just as it is, a plain, homely, Canadian story.

A combination of advocating "light literature", the use of "facts", and the moral value of the work in attacking "defects in the social system" — all of which will supposedly render the work immune to criticism — is found in the ethical-preemptive preface of the fragment *The Mysteries of Montreal...* (1846). William McDonnell's preface to his *The Heathens of the Heath: A Romance...* (1874) is preemptive in that "whatever criticism may be bestowed upon it shall be in a spirit as generous as it is "just" because "the disenthrallment of his fellow men from degrading usages, prejudices and beliefs has been the sole object of the author". Thus, the prefacer maintains that the novel has been written for the moral good of men and therefore criticism ought to be expressed in that context.

5. Subversive.

A subversive-preemptive characteristic is to be found in Lucius Seth Huntington's preface to *Professor Conant...* (1884): "The author assumes only the rôle of a reporter, and the public will judge if he does his work well. He is not responsible for what his characters say, but only for giving them the opportunity to say it".

---

7   "Malcolm" is MacLean Sinclair (cf. Klinck I 309).

The Promotional
Subgroups: 1. Thematic.
                2. Previous publication.
                3. Genre.
                4. Other than author prefacer's promotion.
                        a. General.
                        b. Emerging literature.
                        c. Morality.
                        d. Biographical.
                5. Morality.
                6. Various.

1. Thematic.

The promotion of the novel's theme can be short but at the same time the most prevalent aspect of the preface. For example, the novel *Agnes Harcourt, or, "For His Sake": A Canadian Story Illustrative of the Power of a Child's Life* (1879), is prefaced as follows:

This story has been written and published in the hope of increasing the interest already taken in the little English emigrants brought out to Canada under Christian supervision. This story, though fictitious, is representative of the life and influence of many a little girl adopted into the families of our Canadian homes.

Joseph Abbott, in the preface to his novel *Philip Musgrave...* (1849), promotes his novel and the novel's theme, at the same time discussing the genre of his text:

Now my object is to disabuse the mind of the English reader on this point[8]; and, to do so, I shall have recourse to no other means, because I know of none more likely to be effectual, than to give him a simple memoir of missionary life in these colonies.

In another early English-Canadian preface, H.H.B. (J.H. Alway), in his *The Last of the Eries: A Tale of Canada*, promotes his novel for its content of "useful information" and its "fictitious and real portions", as well as for its value as "amusement for an idle hour".

Another aspect of the thematic-promotional preface is when the prefacer advocates the "usefulness" of his work. John Galt wrote in his preface to *Lawrie Todd, or, The Settlers in the Woods* (1830): "A description, which may be considered authentic, of the rise and progress of a successful American settlement, cannot but be useful to the emigrant who is driven to seek a home in the unknown wilderness of the woods".

John Richardson's preface to *The Canadian Brothers...* (1840) contains an interesting aspect of the thematic-promotional characteristic. As mentioned before, several letters from the correspondence between Richardson and the royal court in London are included in the preface. These letters pertain to the matter of dedication and the fact that Richard-

---

8   I.e., to enlighten the uninformed English public about colonial life.

son was granted permission to dedicate his novel to the king because of the novel's theme, North-American Indians in war. Thus the implicit promotion of the novel is a result of its theme.

2. Previous publication.

The promotion of a work based on the success of a previous publication is another promotional device, as in the preface by the "Author of 'Mick Tracy'", *Tim Doolan, the Irish Immigrant...* (1869): "The Author of the following pages, feeling somewhat encouraged by the success of a former publication, ventures again before the public, with the hope that the narrative here presented may not be without its use".

3. Genre.

The context of promotion can also be determined by the author's literary perception and, consequently, by the genre (the novel or fiction in general) the author wishes to advocate. This subgroup may be termed genre-promotional. Louie Barron's preface to *Zerola of Nazareth* (1895) contains the following paragraph:

In offering this oriental story in book form to the reading public I do so in the hope that it may entertain and help to make leisure hours pass pleasantly. This was my purpose when it appeared as a serial. I confess I had no other in writing the tale. To entertain is the mission of fiction.

The preface to Ralph Connor's *Beyond the Marshes*[9] (1898), written by the Countess Ishbel Aberdeen, is perhaps the most lyrical preface I have come across; in it she advocates the importance of reading. This characteristic, although the prefacer intended it to be understood in a general context, is here genre-promotional with reference to this short "novel".

The promotion of a fictional narrative, by the assurance that the novel is not too fictitious, is by implication another genre-promotional device. John Mackie's preface to *The Heart of the Prairie* (1876) is devoted in its entirety to this view. Another genre-promotional device is to contextualize and compress the theme of the novel in the preface as in J. Macdonald Oxley's preface to *The Romance of Commerce* (1896):

There has been a romance of commerce no less than a romance of war. Men have shown an equal enterprise and daring in the pursuit of wealth as in extending the bounds of empire, and gold has run close rivalry with glory in adding brilliant pages to the world's history.

Richard Lanigan's novel, *They Two...* (1888), contains a preface by the editor with this promotional characteristic:

It is no commendation of a novel now-a-days to assure the reader that the incidents are all actualities; for the more absurdly false they are, so long as they are sensational, the more popular are such stories with a certain class of readers. What influence the perusal of such "Munchausen-

---

9   Here, *Beyond the Marshes* is classified as a short novel.

isms" will have on the literary taste of the age, and on the morality of the rising generation, the future alone will solve. This book has neither falsehood nor sensation to recommend it.

A similar kind of promotion is used by James Thomas Jones (Mary Leslie) in the earlier preface to *The Cromaboo Mail Carrier: A Canadian Love Story* (1878) where the author assures the readers of the value of the novel in contrast to the often prevalent negative perception of novels in general.

The discussion of the role of the preface is relatively rare in the prefaces. However, when the author embarks on this subject, the matter of the preface is usually discussed in a genre-promotional tone. Kate Bottomley ("Vera") discusses the importance of the preface in her preface to *The Doctor's Daughter* (1885):

Charles Dickens observes with much truth, that "though seldom read, prefaces are continually written." It may be asked and even wondered, why? I cannot say that I know the exact reason, but it seems to me that they may carry the same weight, in the literary world, that certain sotto voce explanations, which oftentimes accompany the introduction of one person to another, do in the social world.

Much earlier, Edward Lane prefaces his *The Fugitives...* (1830) with a discussion of the uselessness of prefaces, underlining his position with a moral-ethical dimension ("we mortals can make nothing"), but nevertheless proceeding to write a preface. A second genre-promotional characteristic in this preface is the author's promotion of the "Romance of real life" as opposed to "a Novel, full of hair-breadth escapes, and lover's sighs; or a Romance, in each of whose awfully sublime and soul-harrowing pages, a gaunt spectre meets the astonished eye".

4. Other than author prefacer's promotion.
　　　Subgroups:　　a. General.
　　　　　　　　　　b. Emerging literature.
　　　　　　　　　　c. Morality.
　　　　　　　　　　d. Biographical.

a. General.

When the author of the preface is not the author of the novel, but, for example, the publisher, the promotional character of the preface is most obvious. Although prefaces by the publisher are not frequent, a few will sufficiently illustrate this type. A good example of promotional prefaces written by a friend or colleague of the author occurs in John Carroll's *My Boy Life, Presented in a Succession of True Stories* (1882) by "W.H.W."

In one case, the novel is promoted as a genre with reference to an earlier publication, another novel, by the prefacer. Although a unique case, this example's listing in this category may seem arbitrary. The deciding factor to list it here was the fact that the prefacer was other than the author of the novel. William F. Butler's *Red Cloud: A Tale of the Great Prairie* (1888) is promoted by Sir Robert Baden-Powell, because he liked a former novel by Butler, *The Story of a Failure*.

b. Emerging literature.

This characteristic occurs when the promoter draws attention to the author's native Canadian birth. John Campbell's novel, *Two Knapsacks...* (1892), contains a preface by the publisher in which the native birth of the author is specially promoted. An exception to the rule is Mme Morel de la Durantaye's preface to *A Visit to the Home of Evangeline...* (1898) in which the author promotes her own Canadianness.

c. Morality.

A variation of prefaces written by the editor, combined with the promotional characteristic based on the moral affinity between the author, his work, and the readership, appears in James B. Kennedy's *Afloat for Eternity...* (1893): "Christians of all Churches will find in the book that which will amuse, encourage, instruct, and inspire them". Enoch Wood, cited above, represents one kind, that of the fairly frequent clerical advocate.

d. Biographical.

The promotional character of the preface is obvious also when a critic, scholar, or someone knowledgeable, writes the preface. In these cases the preface is more often than not written with descriptive and/or factual biographical components. This type of preface is more frequent in new editions and usually when the author of the work is no longer living. The history of Canadian literature and publishing being short, this type of preface is rare in the nineteenth century. Several prefaces to novels by Thomas Chandler Haliburton are early exceptions, explained by their popularity in Canada, Britain, and the U.S. The prefaces to different editions of *The Clockmaker...* (e.g. 1872) are of this type. The authors of these prefaces are promoting the work, but at the same time they also evaluate and analyse the literary text, and present biographical data about Haliburton's life.

5. Morality.

The promotional characteristic of the preface, as in so many other aspects of nineteenth-century English-Canadian literature, is often based on moralistic or religious assumptions. Kate Murray's preface to her *The Guiding Angel* (1871) is perhaps the best prototype for the promotion based on morality: "If by its perusal the path of religion is rendered more attractive to one youthful traveller, or one young heart be cheered in its onward journey, it will not have been written in vain". Another example of such promotion based on morality is Janet C. Conger's preface to her *A Daughter of St. Peter's* (1889). "L.G.", in the preface to *Jessie Grey, or, The Discipline of Life: A Canadian Tale* (1870) is promotional on the grounds of morality, while at the same time advocating his native Canadianness. John Carroll, the author of the historically important *Case and His Contemporaries; or, The Canadian Itinerant's Memorial Consisting of a Biographical History of Methodism in Canada* (5 vols., 1867-77), wrote the novel titled *The School of the Prophets...* (1876), whose introduction by Enoch Wood (see above) specifically advocates the Methodist ideology of the work. At the same time both the author of the introduction, Enoch Wood, and Carroll, the author of the preface, endorse the fictionality of the novel. Thus, these two prefaces are a good example of the overlap between the genre and the morality-promotional aspects.

The appeal to the reader's moral and religious beliefs, the acknowledged common ground of the reader, the author, and his work, results in a promotional attitude in the two prefaces to Ralph Connor's *Black Rock...* (1900). This morality-based promotional device is often reinforced by the simultaneous advocacy by the author and the editor, or another prefacer. In James Mann's *The Victorious King: An Allegory* (1878) the preface by the author promotes the novel on the grounds of morality and the reading of the Bible, and the "Introduction" by John Potts is by and large a repetition of Mann's premise, but with the addition of a discussion of "bad books". A total identification of Canada (English Canada) with morality and religiousness, and thus the promotion of a novel which thematically and ideologically upholds that image, is to be found in the preface of *The King's Messenger; or, Lawrence Temple's Probation: A Story of Canadian Life* by William Henry Withrow (1879):

The following Story is an attempt to depict, from personal observation, phases of Canadian life with which the writer is somewhat familiar — with what success others must decide. If it shall inspire in our readers a stronger love of that noble country, and a desire to live for its moral and religious progress, it will not have been written in vain.

6. Various.

Although the editor or the publisher are the most frequent promoters other than the author, there are several examples of other kinds of supporters, who wrote promotional prefaces. The Marchioness of Aberdeen, is one notable example. A person of some importance and an author in her own right, Ishbel Aberdeen contributed several promotional prefaces to English-Canadian works.[10] Considering her involvement in social matters and in feminist issues, it is of note that she wrote a preface promoting Marshall Saunders's animal story, *Beautiful Joe: The Autobiography of a Dog* (1895). The theme of the work lying outside of her sphere of interest, it is more likely that her support stems from her interest in matters Canadian in general, i.e., the importance of native Canadian writing: "It is with great pleasure that I learn you are about to publish a Canadian edition of 'Beautiful Joe'". An interesting exception to the standard promotional traits of prefaces is the allegory of the messenger dove to "send it [the novel] forth", used by Mrs. Flewellyn in her preface to *Hill-Crest* (1894).

Another promotional device is found when the prefacer manages to use some connection to a prominent personality. For example, May Leonard, in her preface to her *Zoe, or, Some Day, a Novel* (1888), makes reference to a letter sent by Queen Victoria in acknowledgement of receipt of her novel. Major Richardson's similar technique has been remarked upon.

The often apologetic and preemptive characteristic of using youth and first publication as criteria for a positive evaluation is at least in one case reversed and used to promote. Bruce Weston Munro's "Note" and long "Preface" to *A Blundering Boy...* (1886) both

---

10 Cf. *The Canadian Encyclopedia* (I 2) and Gwyn (273-92).

contain explicit and implicit references to the value, and therefore worth of promotion, of the novel as a first attempt by a young author: "Such as it is, the book was written while I was twenty years of age, being finished before I completed my twenty-first year. The exuberance of twenty is stamped on every page. Some day I shall not be sorry that I left the book just as it was originally written".

The Subversive

Thomas Chandler Haliburton's "Valedictory Address" to *The Attaché, or, Sam Slick ...* (1856) has humorous and ironical characteristics. The author "personifies" the main character of his novels, Sam Slick, and, in a self-deprecatory manner, he places himself below the imaginary character:

In all cases but two he has exceeded his own anticipations of advancing me. He has not procured for me the situation of Governor-General of Canada, which, as an ambitious man, it was natural he should desire, whilst as a friend it was equally natural that he should overlook my entire unfitness for the office; nor has he procured for me a peerage, which, as an American, it is surprizing he should prize so highly....

Joseph Edmund Collins's preface to his *The Four Canadian Highwaymen...* (1886) is subversive by using preemptive aggression underlined with irony. Under the preemptive typological category, this characteristic of his preface was explained above; here it should be added that the preemptive characteristic is presented in an ironical tone. For example, the text is opened thus: "The following story is founded on fact, everybody about this part of Canada who is not deaf having heard of the gang at Markham Swamp". Further on in the preface, Collins makes some biting remarks about "high brow" literature and "littérateurs". George W. Hanna, under the pseudonym Gentil Spirito, wrote the novel *Earthborn!* (1889), in which the preface may be attributed to the editor. It is the type of preface which pretends that the work was written by someone else and that under adventurous circumstances it became the property of the publishing "author".

R.M. Ballantyne, the prolific author of adventure novels, wrote for two of his novels two different types of humorous preface. To his *The World of Ice, or, The Whaling Cruise of "The Dolphin" and the Adventures of Her Crew in the Polar Regions* (1894) he wrote: "Dear Reader, most people prefer a short to a long preface. Permit me, therefore, to cut this one short, by simply expressing an earnest hope that my book may afford you much profit and amusement". And to *Charlie to the Rescue: A Tale of the Sea and the Rockies* (1890) he wrote: "Having got nothing prefatorial to say, I avail myself of this blank page to say so".

Frederick C. Emberson's preface to *The Yarn of the Love Sick Parsee* (1897) is humorous throughout — and so is the whole novel, with humorous advertisements and table of contents.

Cy Warman's preface to *Snow on the Headlight: A Story of the Great Burlington Strike* (1899) is a personification of the text in humorous context, where the readership is also included:

Here is a Decoy Duck stuffed with Oysters. The Duck is mere Fiction: The Oysters are Facts. If you find the Duck wholesome, and the Oysters hurt you, it is probably because you had a hand in the making of this bit of History, and in the creation of these Facts.

Georgina Seymour Waitt's preface to *Three Girls under Canvas* (1900) is humorous because the narrator of the preface assumes the identity of the novel, i.e., the novel is personified. The personified novel is a child whose parent, then, is the author and they engage in a dialogue. While the prefacer may have used this device to make the preface more palatable and thus her intention is more rhetorical than humorous, the tone of the preface is, nevertheless, humorous.

2. A Typology of French-Canadian Prefaces

The Acknowledgement

Acknowledgement characteristics were not found in French-Canadian prefaces. However, acknowledgements did occur in dedications. These were short and without elaboration. Since they occurred in dedications and dedications were not considered as prefaces in this study, this prefatorial characteristic is not exemplified here.

The Apologetic

An exception to the usual prose format of prefaces is Benjamin Sulte's preface to *Au Coin du feu, histoire et fantaisie* (1877) because it is written in verse. The last quatrain has an apologetic character:

> Peut-être dira-t-on que, trompant la rubrique,
> J'aborde à tout propos un thème trop ancien:
> Qui donc ne voudrait plus se sentir Canadien
> Et verrait sans amour une étude historique?

The preface of Charles L'Epine's *Le Secrétaire d'ambassade* (1878) is largely apologetic. The author first explains that the publication of the novel occurs in Canada because, for reasons beyond his power, the already accepted manuscript could not appear in Paris. Next he apologizes for the novel with regard to the now different readership, which requires a "tamed" text:

D'ailleurs, si nous avions pu prévoir que notre petit livre parût jamais sous un autre ciel que celui qui nous l'inspira, dût être offert à une société différente de celle qui nous fournit et nos caractères et nos tableaux, sans nul doute que nous n'y aurions pas introduit certaines des scènes qu'on y trouvera; ou si nous l'eussions fait, nous en aurions pour le moins, en le composant, adouci ou atténué les couleurs.

The second apologetic characteristic gives the apology more substance by adding a quotation from a canonical literary text:

C'est surtout en cela que nous sentons, que nous reconnaissons avoir besoin de toute l'indulgence de nos lecteurs et lectrices. Volontiers, nous dirions avec le Philinte du LaFontaine de la comédie:
Ne l'examinons point dans la grande rigueur,
Et voyons ses défauts avec quelque douceur.[1]
[1]Molière, *Le Misanthrope*, act.1, sc.1ère, v.147 et 148.

The preface to *L'Enfant perdu et retrouvé, ou, Pierre Cholet* (1887) by Jean-Baptiste Proulx contains a general apology, although implicit rather than explicit. He asks the readers for indulgence and asserts that he has been conscientious and has worked hard. Thus he excuses himself for any faults. Paul-Emile Prévost's preface to his *L'Epreuve* (1900) contains an apologetic element interestingly connecting the preface and certain aspects of the novel:

Ce que je viens d'écrire semble à première vue, peu en rapport avec le petit roman que je livre au public. D'abord, parce qu'on peut penser que je pousse le pédantisme jusqu'à croire à la nécessité d'une longue préface pour mon premier-né, dont je reconnais, je vous l'avoue, la constitution rachitique; ensuite, parce que je fais si peu de psychologie dans mon livre, qu'il est tout-à-fait hors de propos d'en causer autant dans ma préface — je m'arrêterai bientôt afin d'éviter d'être si long en chiffres romains que vous n'abordiez ensuite les chiffres arabes — ....

The Critical
Subgroups: 1. Genre.
              2. Other than author prefacer's criticism.
              3. Conventional.
              4. Emerging literature.

1. Genre.

Philippe-Ignace-François Aubert de Gaspé (fils), the author of what was until recently considered the first French-Canadian novel, begins his preface to *L'Influence d'un livre* (1837) with a critical assessment of novel literature:

Les romanciers du dix-neuvième siècle ne font plus consister le mérite d'un roman en belles phrases fleuries ou en incidents multipliés; c'est la nature humaine qu'il faut exploiter pour ce siècle positif, qui ne veut plus se contenter de Bucoliques, de tête-à-tête sous l'ormeau, ou de promenades solitaires dans les bosquets....

Aubert de Gaspé also refers to La Harpe, the important French literary historian and to Shakespeare and Voltaire. Charles Marcil's preface to *L'Héritière d'un millionnaire: roman historique* (1867) is genre-critical as shown in the following:

Dans les pages que nous avons écrites, nous ne nous sommes guères soucié des proportions symétriques. On y trouvera trois espèces de choses: de faits réels, de l'imagination dans une certaine mesure, et beaucoup de liberté d'allure. N'écrivant pas un poème, nous n'avons pas cru devoir nous soumettre passivement à une discipline littéraire rigoureuse. Nous avons laissé courir notre plume librement, plus anxieux de plaire par les détails que par les combinaisons de l'ensemble. On sera assez bienveillant pour nous tolérer cet acte d'émancipation.

Another version of genre-critical characteristic is to be found in Antoine Gérin-Lajoie's preface to his *Jean Rivard, le défricheur: récit de la vie réelle* (1874). The author says forcefully in his preface that "L'intention de l'auteur toutefois n'a jamais été de faire un roman...". The same critical position is reinforced in the author's "avant-propos". Another critical characteristic, but which may be understood as corollary to genre criticism, is an evaluation of the principal character of the novel, Jean Rivard. A unique feature of this preface is that after the prefatorial discussion the text of the preface flows into the story. The preface to Charles L'Epine's *Le Secrétaire d'ambassade* (1878) contains genre-critical characteristics, but in the form of the author's evaluation of his own novel. Here is an example, in which the author is at the same time subversive (humorous):

Quant au style, nous prenons sur nous d'assurer au public que nous nous sommes rigoureusement piqués de rester en tout et partout fidèle à notre nom; tout en nous efforçant également, sous cet aspect, de donner à notre faible production le plus de relief et de piquant qu'il nous était possible.

Henri-Emile Chevalier in his preface to his *L'Ile de Sable* (1878) assesses Garneau's *Histoire du Canada* and relates it to his own work in a context of genre: "Il y a dans votre narration le canevas d'un beau roman historique: je suis heureux d'avoir répondu à l'appel que la littérature sérieuse fait à la littérature légère". Thus Chevalier not only praises Garneau's work but connecting that work and his own, he relates canonical and non-canonical literature and, at the same time, positions the two, the historical text and his novel, in two types of literature. Jean-Baptiste Proulx's preface to *L'Enfant perdu et retrouvé, ou, Pierre Cholet* (1887) is critical in the sense of the author's self-evaluation with reference to the genre of the work and his apology for local colour in the text. Edmond Rousseau's preface to *Les Exploits d'Iberville* (1888) has genre-critical characteristics in that it defends the genre of the novel in general and the historical novel in particular. Jules-Paul Tardivel's preface to *Pour la patrie: roman du XXe siècle* (1895) includes a refernce to other critical perceptions that is similar to Aubert de Gaspé's use of La Harpe, although Tardivel's authority is religious rather than literary:

Le R.P. Caussette, que cite le R.P. Fayollat dans son livre sur l'Apostolat de la Presse, appelle les romans une invention diabolique. Je ne suis pas éloigné de croire que le digne religieux a parfaitement raison. Le roman, surtout le moderne, et plus particulièrement encore le roman français me paraît être une arme forgée par Satan lui-même pour la destruction du genre humain.

Tardivel then continues to defend the "proper" novel, mainly because of its influence on society. At the same time, he reasserts his beliefs about the contemporary state of the genre in general and in French Canada in particular: "Le roman est donc, de nos jours, une puissance formidable entre les mains du malfaiteur littéraire".

Another version of the genre-critical preface is Paul-Emile Prévost's to *L'Epreuve* (1900). Essentially, Prévost advocates special characteristics of women as distinct from those of men and then relates literary expressions of this conviction to the novel as a genre. The author underlines his position with references to Balzac, Dumas père and Dumas fils, and Hugo, who exemplified the positive in women in their writing. The position of women as presented in the works of these authors provides the grounds for Prévost's statement that "Ce genre de roman est moral". Another critical aspect, although perhaps more removed from a clearly genre-oriented criticism is Prévost's analysis of "le romantisme" and its relation with psychology. The feature of genre criticism appears in the author's discussion of the treatment of women in novels. Prévost's preface and its aspects here categorized could also be listed under the ethical prefaces in the subgroup of political/social conditions.

2. Other than author prefacer's criticism.

From among the prefaces which were not written by the author of the novel, Charles Marcil's *L'Héritière d'un millionnaire...* (1867) contains two prefaces. In addition to the above cited preface by Marcil, the "avis au lecteur" was written by the editor, J.A. David. He discusses the novel in the context of genre criticism:

Indépendamment de l'intérêt qui se rattache à une intrigue dramatique, les patrons de notre enterprise ne pourront que féliciter M. Marcil sur l'élégance et l'exactitude de son style. Du reste, nous aimons à constater, sans aucune adulation, que la plume de l'auteur, comme plume littéraire et politique, est déjà favorablement connue dans les lettres canadiennes.

Alphonse Thomas's *Gustave ou un héros canadien: roman historique et polémique* (1882) contains a preface signed "Les éditeurs". The "editors", presumably C.-O. Beauchemin alone, assesses the novel based on their perception of Canada as a country with two religions. He praises the novel because it serves "la cause catholique en présentant sous forme de roman les questions de controverse qui surgissent le plus ordinairement et qui peuvent offrir quelque danger pour la foi". The novel contains a separate page where the Archbishop of Montréal gives permission for the publication of the novel and the editor(s) reinforce(s) the permission by the church by assuring the readers that the novel is *nihil obstat*.[11]

Firmin Picard's preface to Rodolphe Girard's *Florence: légende historique, patriotique et nationale* (1900) shows a sense of genre definition and a perception of contemporary fiction:

Son roman est la glorification des plus belles vertus: ce n'est pas un roman à la mode, commençant par des roucoulements quelconques pour se terminer par le mariage. Son roman est original, bien conçu, bien écrit: il a mis son coeur partout. Il a évité le banal, les expressions fautives trop en vogue encore, hélas! et qui défigurent un ouvrage, quelque bien agencée qu'en soit la trame.

3.Conventional.

Joseph Marmette's prefaces to *François de Bienville: Scènes de la vie canadienne au XVIIe siècle* (1870, 1883) contain critical aspects in a general sense. The first preface (1870) contains critical elements in a general context of evaluating fiction, particularly in Canada:

Le récit qui va suivre n'est pas le fruit ni du caprice, ni du hasard, contrairement au grand nombre de ces oeuvres légères dont notre siècle est ahuri. Et, comme il n'est guère probable qu'on mette le motif qui me l'a fait écrire au compte de l'intérêt pécuniaire — il est bien établi que les lettres ne sauraient, en Canada, faire vivre, même médiocrement, le plus frugal comme le plus fécond des écrivains — je puis dire avec Montaigne, dès le début: "Cecy, lecteurs, est un livre de bonne foy."

The second preface, in the 1883 edition of the novel, contains a critical characteristic with reference to stylistic changes Marmette undertook for the publication of his collected works, i.e. *Le Chevalier de Mornac* (1873), *François de Bienville* (1883), *L'Intendant Bigot* (1871, 1872, 1875), and *La Fiancée du Rebelle* (1875).

---

11 This strategy is of note because normally the *nihil obstat* stands on its own, without any explanation.

4. Emerging literature.

J. Doutre's preface to *Les Fiancés de 1812: Essai de littérature canadienne* (1844) has a strong perspective on the emerging French-Canadian literature. The author first assesses the situation of native literature and compares it to the situation of other arts. He decries the lack of appreciation of native authors by the Canadian public while the same public always applauds "les écrivains étrangers [qui] ont toujours joui parmi nous d'une célébrité qui commandait une respectueuse admiration, et semblait interdire le désir de l'imitation". Doutre also criticizes the perception that the Canadian author, to be successful, has to write "comme un Dumas, un Eugène Sue, etc." At the same time, Doutre proceeds to evaluate Sue's *Les Mystères de Paris*, "l'ouvrage du célèbre moraliste".

The Dedicatory
Henri-Emile Chevalier's preface to *L'Ile de Sable* (1878) is dedicatory because of its title and content. The preface is titled "Envoi à Monsieur H.-X. Garneau". The content is largely a quotation from Garneau's *Histoire du Canada*. Since the novel is based on the historical description by Garneau which Chevalier quoted in the preface, it implicitly dedicates the novel to Garneau. In the preface to *La fille des indiens rouges* (1888) Chevalier again dedicates his novel to a friend and in it he evokes their youth and enthusiasm for literature. This type of dedication is biographical while the previous one is best classified as a dedicatory preface, because it accounts for the idea of the novel.

The Ethical
Subgroups: 1. Political.
                              a. Patriotic.
                              b. Historical.
                              c. Social conditions.
                         2. Morality.

1. Political.
a. Patriotic.

François-Benjamin Singer's preface to *Souvenirs d'un exilé canadien* (1871) is patriotic in the sense that he discusses the situation of French-Canadian literature in the context of French-Canadian history. Benjamin Sulte's *Au coin du feu: Histoire et fantaisie* (1877) is intriguing already because of its title — in the context of Sulte's importance as a historian. His preface, as mentioned above, is in verse form. The patriotic component of the preface appears in the call for Canadians to know and read their history:

Peut-être dira-t-on que, trompant la rubrique,
J'aborde à tout propos un thème trop ancien:
Qui donc ne voudrait plus se sentir Canadien
Et verrait sans amour une étude historique?

Honoré Beaugrand's preface to *Jeanne la fileuse: Épisode de l'émigration franco-canadienne aux États-Unis* (1878), may be identified as a political-patriotic preface because it takes issue with the situation of emigrant French Canadians in the U.S.A.:

Le livre que je présente aujourd'hui au public, sous le titre de: Jeanne la Fileuse, est moins un roman qu'un pamphlet; moins un travail littéraire qu'une réponse aux calomnies que l'on s'est plu à lancer dans certains cercles politiques, contre les populations franco-canadiennes des États-Unis.

Jules-Paul Tardivel's preface for *Pour la patrie: Roman du XXe siècle* (1895) is thematically patriotic and this is strongly reflected in the author's preface. The post-face of Georges-Isidore Barthe's novel *Drames de la vie réelle: Roman canadien* (1896) contains patriotic rhetoric: "J'ai écrit ces pages, en peu de jours, pour chasser les idées noires, après ma destitution par le gouvernement de Québec". At the same time, the prefacer assures the readers that the novel is morally acceptable: "Le roman à mon sens, doit avoir un but moral et utile. Par mon récit, j'ai voulu surtout, montrer le prêtre canadien tel qu'il a été, tel qu'il est et tel qu'il doit être". Firmin Picard's preface to Rodolphe Girard's novel *Florence: légende historique, patriotique et nationale* (1900) conveys a patriotic purpose for the writing of the text: "C'est donc un bien que l'auteur ait écrit ce livre vibrant de patriotisme, surtout en ces temps de platitude et de courbettes devant le fort: le puissant fût-il l'être individuel ou collectif le plus injuste, le plus cruel que la terre ait porté".

b. Historical.

The context of politics between English and French Canada occurs frequently in French-Canadian prefaces. The political charactersitic is sometimes expressed by or in the context of French-Canadian history, as in the case of the editor's (G.H. Cherrier) preface to Pierre-J.-Olivier Chauveau's novel *Charles Guérin: Roman de moeurs canadiennes* (1853), where the preface is political-historical in its interpretation of the novel's theme: "Les événements peu saisissants que l'écrivain raconte se sont passés à une époque où les passions politiques et les animosités nationales étaient très vives dans notre pays". Similarly, in the 1889 edition of the same novel, the new prefacer, Ernest Gagnon, again writes with a political-historical undertone: "Le problème résultant de la situation de la race conquise (disons cédée pour ne déplaire à personne), en face de la race conquérante, est posé de main de maître dans ce roman dont certaines pages semblent ne dater que d'hier".

A perception of English-Canadian and French-Canadian politics and history is defined in Napoléon Bourassa's preface to *Jacques et Marie: Souvenir d'un peuple dispersé* (1866). Interestingly, his discussion has a conciliatory tone while most other prefacers' perspective is confrontational.

The preface to the second edition of Joseph Marmette's *François de Bienville...* (1883) contains a historical and patriotic perspective. The following paragraph from the long preface is illustrative: "C'est à la suite de ces événements que les colons anglais se décidèrent à envahir le Canada à la fois par terre et par mer, afin d'en chasser les Français et de s'emparer du pays".

The historical role of French Canadians is the subject of Edmond Rousseau's preface to *Le Château de Beaumanoir: Roman canadien* (1886). He speaks about French-Canadian history in the context of contemporary events. There is a quotation from a letter by Mgr. Alexandre Taché, after which Rousseau states:

Ces remarquables paroles de l'une des gloires de l'épiscopat canadien-français résument la pensée qui a présidée à ce livre. En face des insinuations malveillantes et des injures qui ont été dites et écrites depuis quelques mois contre la population canadienne-française, contre nos milices, il n'est pas de meilleure réponse, croyons-nous, de réfutation plus facile et plus complète, que de rappeler les actions héroïques de nos pères, leur courage dans l'adversité, leur vaillance sur le champ de bataille.

Georges Brémond's preface in *Les Jumeaux de Montréal: Épisode de la guerre du Canada* (1889) calls on French-Canadians to love the "mother country", France, using a historical context: "Puisse notre travail servir à l'instruction de nos jeunes lecteurs et raviver leur filiale affection pour la France, pour cette patrie que n'ont jamais cessé d'aimer les victimes de la conquête, aussi bien en Europe qu'en Amérique!"

c. Social conditions.

An interesting perspective is to be found in J.A. David's preface to Charles Marcil's *L'Héritière d'un millionnaire: Roman historique* (1867), because the prefacer apparently refers to a general condition of French-Canadian society. The prefacer assures the reader that he "ne trouvera rien de nature à froisser ses opinions ou ses susceptibilités politiques dans les pages que nous allons livrer à la publicité".

The context of French-Canadian society and some of its aspects often result in political references in the context of the ethical category of prefaces. An example is Joseph Doutre's preface to *Les Fiancés de 1812: Essai de littérature canadienne* (1844): "Par exemple de l'étude du droit public. Je ne connais pas deux jeunes gens à Montréal, ajouta-t-il, qui aient de véritables notions de politique". The context of social conditions is conveyed in the preface to Henri-Emile Chevalier's novel *L'Enfer et le paradis de l'autre monde* (1866). The concern of the prefacer is the economy and its impact on society:

Si quelques-uns des motifs qui l'ont dicté n'existent plus, comme le traité de réciprocité entre le Canada et les Etats-Unis, il n'en est pas moins toujours vrai que la Grande Bretagne décourage systématiquement l'industrie et les arts utiles dans ses colonies; que, chaque année, les Canadiens eux-mêmes fuient une patrie où ils ne trouvent point de travail, malgré les immenses ressources naturelles dont abonde leur pays. Il n'en est pas moins toujours vrai que le Canada ne sera jamais prospère et grand que lorsqu'il se sera annexé à la République des États-Unis.

A specific aspect of social conditions, that of women and literature, appears in Paul-Emile Prévost's preface to the novel *L'Epreuve* (1900): "L'homme serait hardi, qui déclarerait solennellement bien connaître la femme. Ce qu'il en pourrait dire, serait approuvé par les unes, mais fortement démenti par les autres; une seule chose pouvant les mettre toutes d'accord: l'adresse de n'en dire que du bien".

2. Morality.

The religious content of French-Canadian society and questions of morality are often a concern of prefacers. The preface of Philippe-Ignace-François Aubert de Gaspé to his novel *L'Influence d'un livre* (1837) contains ethical components in the context of morality and humanism: "maintenant c'est le coeur humain qu'il faut développer à notre âge industriel". The preface also contains the author's perception of Canadian morality as a source for literature: "Les moeurs pures de nos campagnes sont une vaste mine à exploiter". Napoléon Bourassa's preface to *Jacques et Marie: Souvenir d'un peuple dispersé* (1866) shows concern with morality in a historical and patriotic context. The tone of the preface is that of the author's indignation with the misfortunes of the Acadians. The editor's preface to Charles Marcil's novel *L'Héritière d'un millionnaire: Roman historique* (1867) connects concern with morality with the theme of the novel:

La morale y est aussi rigoureusement respectée, de sorte que ce livre pourra circuler sans danger dans les mains de n'importe quelle classe de lecteurs. ... Maintenant, nous devons dire que nous ne sommes animé, dans la tentative que nous entreprenons aujourd'hui, que par deux motifs parfaitement désintéressés: répandre le goût d'une saine et utile littérature parmis les classes populaires....

François-Benjamin Singer's preface to his novel *Souvenirs d'un exilé canadien* (1871) has a perspective of morality in that his ideological position is based in a general context of humanism of the Rousseau persuasion.

A good example of concern with morality appears in the editors' preface to Alphonse Thomas's novel *Gustave ou un héros canadien: Roman historique et polémique* (1882):

Dans un pays habité par une population mixte en fait de croyances religieuses, il est bon et utile que les catholiques aient sous la main un manuel de controverse qui soit comme un arsenal où ils puissent trouver avec facilité une réponse aux arguties qui leur sont tous les jours répétés par les protestants.

Another example of the preoccupation with morality appears in Alphonse Thomas's preface to his *Albert ou l'orphelin catholique* (1885) and which has a religious tone likely due to the theme of the novel. The perspective of morality and religion appears in Edmond Rousseau's preface to *Les Exploits d'Iberville* (1888), with its scathing condemnation of the contemporary French novel: "Le roman français du jour, c'est-à-dire, même parmi ceux qui sont réputés les moins mauvais, ce qu'il y a de plus dangereux pour le coeur et l'esprit de la jeunesse".

Firmin Picard's preface to Rodolphe Girard's *Florence: Légende historique, patriotique et nationale* (1900) displays concern with French-Canadian values in the context of patriotism and morality: "Plût à Dieu que les Canadiens-français eussent encore le courage, l'énergie montrée par leur pères! ... Son roman est la glorification des plus belles vertus".

The Explanatory
Subgroups: 1. Background (History/Geography).
                2. Intention.
                3. Genesis.

1. Background (History/Geography).
The most frequent explanatory characteristic of French-Canadian prefaces is the background (History and Geography) type. In the case of the French-Canadian prefaces they are largely very similar in their structure and content. They usually contain descriptions of and references to facts of French-Canadian history without ideological discussions. Also, there are very few cases where a reference is made to a published historical source. I will list here a few examples of such explanatory prefaces: Honoré Beaugrand's preface to *Jeanne la fileuse: Épisode de l'émigration franco-canadienne aux États-Unis* (1878), Napoléon Bourassa's to *Jacques et Marie: Souvenir d'un peuple dispersé* (1866), Georges Brémond's to *Les jumeaux de Montréal épisode de la guerre du Canada* (1887), Henri-Emile Chevalier's "Envoi" to *L'Ile de Sable* (1878), Joseph Marmette's to *François de Bienville: Scènes de la vie canadienne au XVIIe siècle* (1883) and to *Les Machabées de la Nouvelle-France: Histoire d'une famille canadienne* (1882) and to *Le Chevalier de Mornac: Chronique de la Nouvelle-France, 1664* (1873), and Edouard Duquet's to *Pierre et Amélie* (1866).

2. Intention.
The explanatory character of the preface may also derive from the author's intentions and his/her reason for the writing of the novel or her/his choice of the novel's theme. For example, Edmond Rousseau's preface to *La Monongahéla* (1890) contains the following passage: "le but que je poursuis dans les pages qui vont suivre est toujours le même: vulgariser, populariser l'Histoire du Canada et la présenter sous la forme la plus agréable possible".

3. Genesis.
There are few examples among French-Canadian prefaces of the explanatory type of preface that contain descriptions of the genesis of the novel. One example is Jean-Baptiste Proulx's preface to *L'Enfant perdu et retrouvé, ou, Pierre Cholet* (1887) that contains a description about the novel's genesis in the form of testimonies by individuals attesting to the "truth" of the novel's contents.

The Integral
Perhaps the most illustrative example of the integral preface among the French-Canadian prefaces is Philippe Aubert de Gaspé's to *Les Anciens canadiens* (1863): "Ce chapitre peut, sans inconvénient, servir, en partie, de préface".
There is a fairly large number of integral prefaces among the French-Canadian prefaces. The majority of them are from the type in which Chapter I is titled "Prologue". The anonymous *Le Chasseur canadien* (1885), Vinceslas-Eugène Dick's *L'Enfant mystérieux* (1890), Pierre Durandal's *Le Vengeur de Montcalm* (1887), Auguste Fortier's

Les Mystères de Montréal (1894), Hector Berthelot's *Les Mystères de Montréal: Roman de moeurs* (189-), Charles-Arthur Gauvreau's *Captive et bourreau* (189-), Pamphile Lemay's *Le Pèlerin de Sainte-Anne* (1877), *L'Affaire Sougraine* (1884), and *Picounoc le maudit* (1878), Joseph Marmette's *L'Intendant Bigot* (1871), Joseph-Ferdinand Morissette's *Le Fratricide: Roman canadien* (1884) are a number of examples, which illustrate the frequency of this type of preface.

The Preemptive
Subgroups: 1. Readership.
              2. Depreciation.
              3. Inexperience.

1. Readership.
The first subgroup of the preemptive preface is the type which is oriented toward the readership and/or is written to forestall criticism of the literary value, style, genre, etc., of the novel. This prefatory characteristic can be found already in Philippe Aubert de Gaspé's preface to *L'Influence d'un livre: Roman historique* (1837): "L'opinion publique décidera si je dois m'en tenir à ce premier essai. En attendant, j'espère qu'en terminant cet ouvrage mon lecteur aura une pensée plus consolante, pour l'auteur, que celle de Voltaire: Tout ce fatras fut du chanvre en son temps". J. Doutre's preface to *Les Fiancées de 1812...* (1844) contains similar characteristics. Later, in Antoine Gérin-Lajoie's preface to *Jean Rivard, le défricheur...* (1874) this attempt to position oneself in a relationship with the readership and to guide it, becomes a rhetoric of "baiting": "Jeunes et belles citadines qui ne reves que modes, bals et conquetes amoureuses; jeunes élégants qui parcourez, joyeux et sans soucis, le cercle des plaisirs mondains, il va sans dire que cette histoire n'est pas pour vous".[12]

The appeal to the public to judge is preemptive in character and this characteristic is fairly frequent. For example, it appears in Eraste d'Orsonnens's preface to his *Une Apparition: épisode de l'émigration irlandaise au Canada* (1860). The author evaluates apologetically his work, which he first published six years earlier in a journal. He assesses his novel as the work of "un écolier". Among the specifics he lists as weaknesses of his *Une Apparition ...* we find "les matériaux n'y sont pas disposés dans le meilleur ordre et ... les personnages y sont trop nombreux". After this the author proceeds to say that

Que les lecteurs qui aiment à critiquer attendent, pour satisfaire leur goût, la publication d'un roman intitulé: Le Parricide Huron, que je livrerai au public dans quelques semaines. Pour cette dernière production, je ne pourrai, comme pour la précédente, fair valoir les circonstances dans lesquelles je l'ai écrite.

---

12 While the prefacer appears to appeal to a specific, educated, and literary readership, the rhetoric of the preface certainly indicates a secondary intention. This is to direct the willing reader (the "citadines" and the "élégants") to position him/herself in the group of the educated readers.

Napoléon Bourassa's preface to *Jacques et Marie: Souvenir d'un peuple dispersé* (1866) makes an implicit appeal to the readership:

Si, dans l'expression des sentiments de quelques-uns de mes personnages, on trouve parfois de la violence, il ne faudra pas oublier dans quels moments ils s'exprimaient: ils étaient dépouillés, chassés, dispersés sur les côtes de la moitié de notre continent; et pourquoi? ... Non, aucune arrière-pensée, aucun but indirect, sournoisement caché, n'a guidé ma plume; je proteste d'avance contre toute imputation de ce genre.

Charles L'Epine's preface to his *Le Secrétaire d'ambassade* (1878) contains a paragraph that is preemptive in the context of both the readership and the text. He uses a pun to get the point across:

Quant au style, nous prenons sur nous d'assurer au public que nous nous sommes rigoureusement piqués de rester en tout et partout fidèle à notre nom; tout en nous efforçant également, sous cet aspect, de donner à notre faible production le plus de relief et de piquant qu'il nous était possible.

L'Epine also continues with preemptive devices to "protect" his work:

Au reste, ne peut-on pas dire d'un livre, ce que le Fabuliste latin a dit d'un homme: ...ille notus quem per te cognoveris? (Phèdre, liv. III, Fab.IX.) — Je prétends que si. — Or, puisque l'on ne connaît un livre qu'àprès l'avoir étudié par soi-même, à quoi bon alors tant de vaines paroles? Lecteur, qui que tu sois: prends, lis et prononce.

2. Depreciation.

The short novel of Alphonse Cynosuridis, *Mémoires d'un vieux garçon recueillis et commentés* (1865) has in its preface several preemptive characteristics. The author's belittling of the work is one: "tu ne seras pas la première sottise que le public aura dû lire et cette pensée me console". Another characteristic is the opposite, nonchalant attitude, but again in reference to the value of the work. It also addresses the readership and thus the preface contains a readership preemptive aspect:

Si l'on trouve que j'ai fait là une blague très-peu intéressante, pourvu qu'on me lise, le reste m'est parfaitement égal, on n'a pas vingt ans pour se soucier énormément de l'opinion publique. Si on me lit, le peu de bien que cet ouvrage est destiné à faire se fera peut-être et on n'aura plus raison de faire trop de reproches à votre très-humble, l'Auteur.

François-Benjamin Singer's preface to *Souvenirs d'un exilé canadien* (1871) is also depreciative in its tone. He mentions Jean-Jacques Rousseau only to depreciate himself in comparison: "je viens, moi, le plus déshérité de la création et inconnu au monde littéraire". At the same time, while he continues to decry his own literary efforts, he invokes the strength he finds in the creation of a new literature. But the depreciative attitude is thus carried over into French-Canadian literature in its totality:

Le Canadien n'a pour toute ressource que son imagination. Il faut qu'il soutienne son récit par d'éternelles fictions. Telles sont les causes qui empêcheront pour longtemps notre littérature d'avancer aussi rapidement que nous pourrions l'espérer. Mais faudra-t-il jeter, de dépit, notre lyre, et condamner du même coup l'avenir littéraire de notre pays? Nous ne le croyons pas, et malgré les obstacles innombrables qu'il nous faille surmonter, nous devons, en courageux soldats de l'avenir, lutter contre l'aridité de notre histoire, et nous efforcer de faire jaillir des cendres de cacique, de nos grands lacs et de nos forêts vierges, des récits qui puissent, au moins, aplanir ces difficultés à la postérité.

François-Benjamin Singer's preface contains a preemptive undertone because he addresses the reader with a description of the Canadian literary situation in a depreciative context, "Le Canadien n'a pour toute ressource que son imagination". Alphonse Thomas too, in the preface to his *Albert ou l'orphelin catholique* (1885), parries criticism by devaluing his own work and by appealing to the readership:

Encore un mot, cher lecteur; n'ayant aucune prétention littéraire, je sais que ce livre pèche beaucoup par la forme; le lecteur instruit verra qu'il a été écrit par un ouvrier plus habile à manier l'outil que la plume. Quoi qu'il en soit, j'espère que, malgré ses défauts, vous lui trouverez quelque qualité et qu'il vous sera agréable.

Some prefaces contain preemptive characteristics with reference to the novel genre, although this does not occur too often. There are two clear examples: Gérin-Lajoie, in the preface of *Jean Rivard, le défricheur...* (1874) goes as far as denying that his novel is a novel. Edmond Rousseau's preface to *Les Exploits d'Iberville* (1888) contains a similar denial.

3. Inexperience.

The preemptive characteristic eliminating criticism by claiming youth and inexperience is used in Eraste d'Orsonnens's preface to *Une Apparition...* (1860). He excuses the faults of his novel by reference to his youth, thus hoping for a less severe criticism of his work: "*Une Apparition*, comme je l'ai dit, est une composition d'écolier; j'espère que, comme telle, elle sera accueillie avec indulgence". Eduard Duquet's preface to *Pierre et Amélie* (1866) contains a similar excuse: "On me pardonnera, sans doute, cette humeur bizarre, j'aime à rêver, c'est peut-être là le plus grand défaut de ma vingtième année".

The Promotional
Subgroups: 1. Genre.
                2. Other than author prefacer's promotion.
                    a. genre.
                    b. emerging literature.
                    c. biographical.
                3. Thematic.
                4. Morality.

1. Genre.

Although rare, genre-promotional characteristics do occur in French-Canadian prefaces. Philippe Aubert de Gaspé (fils), in his preface to *L'Influence d'un livre: roman historique* (1837), promotes his novel as a "roman de moeurs": "J'offre à mon pays le premier Roman de Moeurs canadien, et en le présentant à mes compatriotes je réclame leur indulgence à ce titre". The perspective of genre is to be found in the author's resolution to write a historical novel in the context of a "Canadian morality" and the fact that he indeed introduced this genre into French-Canadian literature. Later examples of genre-promotional characteristics include Alphonse Thomas's preface to *Gustave, ou, un héros canadien* (1882) and Joseph Marmette's preface to *François de Bienville: Scènes de la vie canadienne au XVII*ᵉ *siècle* (1883); the latter also promotes the genre of his novel, in this case the historical novel.

2. Other than author prefacer's promotion.
a. genre.

Of the genre-promotional prefaces, G.H. Cherrier's preface to Pierre Chauveau's *Charles Guérin...* (1853) shows genre-promotional characteristics. Charles Marcil's novel *L'Héritière d'un millionnaire: Roman historique* (1867) contains a preface by the editor J.A. David. The "avis au lecteur" advertises the genre of the historical novel, praises the style of the work, and promotes its author: "Du reste, nous aimons à constater, sans aucune adulation, que la plume de l'auteur, comme plume littéraire et politique, est déjà favorablement connue dans les lettres canadiennes". The promotion of the novel as a genre appears also in Eusèbe Senécal's preface to Georges Boucher de Boucherville's *Une de perdue, deux de trouvées* (1874):

> Il n'est donc que juste de reconnaître que celui qui a eu le mérite de concevoir une oeuvre littéraire qui a obtenu un accueil aussi légitime que le Roman Canadien *"Une de perdue deux de trouvees,"* a le droit de s'enorgueillir ou du moins de se considérer comme un auteur privilégié parmi tant d'autres écrivains qui n'ont rencontré qu'indifférence et découragement dès leur début dans la carrière des lettres.

b. emerging literature.

The promotion of a novel based on the perception that French-Canadian literature has established itself and that authorship is honourable, appears in the editor's preface to Pierre-Joseph-Olivier Chauveau's *Charles Guérin: Roman de moeurs canadiennes* (1866). In the preface to the same novel in a new edition forty-seven years later (1900), the prefacer (Ernest Gagnon) promotes the novel based on its critical reception and on the observation that the previous editions are hard to find in libraries.

c. biographical.

Benjamin Sulte's already quoted verse-preface promotes *Au Coin du feu, histoire et fantaisie* (1877) by the assurance of the author's literary and personal qualities:

> Je viens te saluer sans fracas, ni réclame,
> Et, mon livre à la main, instamment te prier
> D'être indulgent pour l'humble et candide ouvrier
> Qui l'a fait par plaisir et qui l'offre avec l'âme.

3. Thematic.

The thematic-promotional characteristic occurs in French-Canadian prefaces frequently. It already appears in J. Doutre's preface to *Les Fiancées de 1812...* (1844). Eduard Duquet, in the preface of his *Pierre et Amélie* (1866), implicitly promotes his novel's theme by allusion to the perception that there is a "sentiment de la nature qui manque le plus à nos écrivains". Although his work is not on Canadian nature and the Canadian countryside, he believes writing about human lives to be more important. Thus, he argues, his work deserves to be read. The promotion of the novel's theme occurs also in Napoléon Bourassa's preface to *Jacques et Marie...* (1866), in Joseph Marmette's preface to *Francois de Bienville...* (1870), in F.-B. Singer's preface to *Souvenirs d'un exilé canadien* (1871), in Honoré Beaugrand's preface to *Jeanne la fileuse...* (1878), and again in Edmond Rousseau's preface to *Le Château de Beaumanoir...* (1886). Antoine Gérin-Lajoie addresses the readership in two groups who will, in his view, appreciate and perhaps criticize his novel, *Jean Rivard, le défricheur...* (1874). His promotional perspective is concentrated on the novel's theme: "Le but de l'auteur était de faire connaître la vie et les travaux des défricheurs, et d'encourager notre jeunesse canadienne à se porter vers la carrière agricole".

4. Morality.

Jules Paul Tardivel promotes his novel *Pour la patrie: roman du XXᵉ siècle* (1895) on the basis of his moralistic and religious convictions which provide him with enough confidence to believe that his type of novel is the right one for the reader:

Mais le roman, tout satanique que peut être son origine, n'entre pas dans cette catégorie. La preuve qu'on peut s'en servir pour le bien, c'est qu'on s'en est servi *ad majorem Dei gloriam*. Je ne parle pas du roman simplement honnête qui procure une heure d'agréable récréation sans déposer dans l'âme des semences funestes; mais du roman qui fortifie la volonté, qui élève et assainit le coeur, qui fait aimer davantage la vertu et haïr le vice, qui inspire de nobles sentiments, qui est en un mot, la contre-partie du roman infâme.

The Subversive

Among French-Canadian prefaces there are few examples containing subversive characteristics. Benjamin Sulte, in his verse preface to *Au Coin du feu, histoire et fantaisie* (1877), writes the second stanza with a humorous intention:

> S'il amuse quelqu'un, j'en bénis le bon Dieu.
> Heureux celui dont l'art égaye un front morose.
> Les vers ne m'allant plus, je m'adresse à la prose,
> Car elle est moins farouche, et sait plaire en tout lieu.

Charles L'Epine employs punning in his preface to *Le Secrétaire d'ambassade* (1878): "Quant au style, nous prenons sur nous d'assurer au public que nous nous sommes rigoureusement piqués de rester en tout et partout fidèle à notre nom".

CHAPTER THREE

Systemic Data in the Canadian Novel Prefaces

Preamble

The category of systemic data — category four as described in the *Preamble* of Chapter two — is necessary because the structure of the typological characteristics limits the kinds of information that can be extracted from the prefaces. But more importantly, specific tenets of the *Empirical Theory of Literature*, such that allow for particular attention being paid to systemic characteristics, are here presented. These tenets and their corresponding areas are an integral part of the typology, as shown on the *Data Sheet* in Chapter two. Further, areas of particular and systemic interest discovered in the typology of the prefaces, are here applied in a supplementary testing of the prefaces.

From preliminary indications on the *Data Sheet* and after further reading and interpretation of the prefaces, the systemic data categories of literary theory and genre, references to literary figures and texts, the mention of other arts, and references to or address of the readership will be here presented. The results of this testing are not exhaustive but representative.

The categories of literary theory and genre, although separate categories on the *Data Sheet* for reasons of more precise indication, will be presented together here. This is advantageous because of the similarity of these two categories.

1. The English-Canadian Novel Prefaces

1.1 Literary Theory and Literary Genre

The most frequent genre- and theory-oriented aspect of English-Canadian novel prefaces is the insistence, assurance, the "proof", that the novel is based on "facts" and "truth".[1] This element of prefatorial discourse — in its most frequent and compact formulation, "Truth is stranger than fiction" and "This novel is founded on fact", may be summarized in the following formula. Fact + Fiction = Novel (FFN). From the English-Canadian prefaces studied, 69% contained some form of FFN statement. The following selected examples will illustrate this prefatorial phenomenon.

In most cases, the FFN is explicit yet ambiguous. It is so in the sense that the prefacer appears to have balanced his/her assertions between the importance and relevance of the relationship of "Fact" *and* "Fiction". Annie G. Savigny's preface to *A ROMANCE OF TORONTO. (FOUNDED ON FACT.) A NOVEL* (1888) is illustrative of this ambiguity. In this example, the title already indicates typographically an ambiguity that will be more precisely formulated in the preface. The title *A ROMANCE OF TORONTO* is in capital letters. Underneath, the subtitle *(FOUNDED ON FACT)* is also in capital letters but half the

---

1   Although marginally related to the discussion here, for interesting suggestions as to the nineteenth-century preoccupation with the relationship of truth and fiction see Chapter nine, "Textual Construction: Truth-Producing Fiction" in Marie-Christine Leps's recent book, *Apprehending the Criminal: The Producing of Deviance in Nineteenth-Century Discourse* (167-220).

size of the above. *A NOVEL* is again in capital letters but its size is between the *A ROMANCE OF TORONTO* and *(FOUNDED ON FACT)*. The typographical differentiation is analogous to the prefatorial explanation: "In the following pages are two plots, one of which was told me by an actor therein; the other I have myself watched from its first page to its last, being living facts in living lives of fair Toronto's children".

In other words, the prefacer wants to assure the reader, on the one hand, that the novel is based on facts. On the other hand, the assurance is constructed semantically within the parameters of literature: the story was "told" and "watched", and then written. Thus, the weight of "Facts" and "Fiction" is evenly distributed in the FFN. In a somewhat longer format, R.M. Ballantyne's preface,[2] which he placed, unchanged, in several subsequent American, British, and Canadian editions of different novels, contains a similar FFN formulation:

Truth is stranger than fiction, but fiction is a valuable assistant in the development of truth. Both, therefore, shall be used in these volumes. Care will be taken to ensure, as far as is possible, that the facts stated shall be true, and that the impressions given shall be truthful. As all classes, in every age, have proved that tales and stories are the most popular style of literature, each volume of the series (with, perhaps, one or two exceptions) will contain a complete tale, the heroes and actors in which, together with the combination of circumstances in which they move, shall be more or less fictitious.

John Mackie (*The Heart of the Prairie*, 1876) goes even further by attacking authors who, in his opinion, "still think that no matter how absurd and misleading their local colouring may be, the pictorial element is everything". He then proceeds to argue that he can "claim truthfulness of detail for this story".

Historically, the concept of the FFN seems to have been prevalent in English-Canadian novel literature since Julia Beckwith Hart's *St. Ursula's Convent...* (1824) where she wrote in her preface: "Our Readers, in these Provinces at least, may likewise be gratified with the assurance, that mother St. Catherine is not a mere creature of imagination, but had a real existence in Canada, and that even the name of her daughter is preserved". The formula, in the case of Julia Beckwith Hart, is connected to the emerging North American (i.e. Canadian and American) literature: "Can the patriotic Canadian, then, refuse a kind reception to his own kindred?" Obviously, the prefacer is promoting the novel because it is about Canada. The promotional characteristic is equally rooted in the prefacer's attitude with regard to the concept of FFN and the emerging Canadian literature. In another early English-Canadian preface, in Charles E. Beardsley's written for *The Victims of Tyranny: A Tale* (1847), the preface begins thus: "The following work, though assuming the character of a fiction, is founded on fact". Throughout the two pages of preface, the author returns to the theme of FFN. For example, he writes that

Incidents acted apart, have, indeed, been brought in juxtaposition. The high colors of reality, nevertheless, have been partially hidden, rather than fully exposed, lest the descriptions should

---

2   E.g., *Fast in the Ice, or, Adventures in the Polar Regions* (1880?).

appear unnatural, and even absurd, to the reader unacquainted with the petty and criminal resorts of a Colonial Government — Colonial officials, and their satellites.

The FFN is merged here implicitly with questions of narrative, style, the explanatory characteristic with reference to history, and, in an exception among the English-Canadian prefaces, with an explicit criticism of Canadian officialdom and bureaucracy.

The FFN formula, as mentioned above, was a construct balanced between its two components, "Fact" and "Fiction". But the formula had variants. While "Fact" was by far the dominant FFN component in the prefaces, "Truth", an analogue of "Fact", was also frequent. Enoch Wood, in his preface to John Carroll's novel (*The School of the Prophets...*, 1876), discusses FFN, contrasting the novel to a similar publication fifty years before. In his discussion, he contends that while the title of the previous work included the words "No Fiction" although the work was wholly fictitious, the present novel is based on facts of history. He then admits to fiction stating that "The opinions and inferences of the writer are fairly open to criticism". He then returns to FFN: "but in the racy narratives which are presented to the reader there is nothing 'More strange than true'". What he is saying is that no matter what the imagination of the writer allowed him to put into his novel, fiction is based on reality rather than imagination. Another good example of this variation of the FFN formula is found in Wallace Lloyd's preface to *Houses of Glass...* (1899): "Believing, that truth after all, is stranger than fiction, I have not gone afield for highly coloured heroes and villains, but have taken characters from real life — men and women, with all their faults and imperfections".

Other examples show that prefacers of both canonical and non-canonical novels, in general, adhered to the FFN concept. A canonical example is the preface to the anonymously published (the novel was published by "A.S.H.", Abraham Holmes) *Belinda or the Rivals* (1843). The author asserts in several ways that "nothing but truth has been intentionally given a place". Another early example of the FFN is to be found in the preface of J.H. Alway's ("H.H.B.") *The Last of the Eries: A Tale of Canada* (1849). The author merges such as the narrative, the explanatory characteristic with reference to history, and, in an exception among English-Canadian prefaces, an explicit criticism of Canadian officialdom and government:

In delineating the Indian character, the writer has endeavored to give the reader some information regarding the principle tribes of western Canada, and those people generally known as the Five or Six Nations; and, although, it was not his intention to attempt anything like a biographical history of the Eries, yet he has availed himself of a knowledge of their early history to make them the prominent characters of this tale — and he has always kept in view that great desideratum in the compilation of books, namely, the obligation under which an Author rests to his readers, that in furnishing them with amusement for an idle hour, he should not only avoid presenting to them language, which it might be beneficial to forget, and ideas or characters which it would be pernicious to emulate, but that on the contrary, he should endeavor to entwine the fictitious and real portions of his subject in such a manner, that many, who have only commenced its perusal for the purpose of acquiring some useful information, or banishing a tedious hour, may have a pleasing recollection of its most striking passages.

This preface is the more interesting because it introduces the idea of entertainment with the concept of the FFN. Examples of this connection are rare.

W.R. Ancketill's preface to *The Adventure of Mick Callighin* (1875) is, in a way, an exception because it presents a subverted FFN by poking fun at the formula "Truth is stranger than fiction".

Ralph Connor's novel, *Black Rock: A Tale of the Selkirks* (1900) has a preface written by George Adam Smith: "He writes with the freshness and accuracy of an eye-witness, with the style (as I think his readers will allow) of a real artist". R.M. Ballantyne defines the novel, or the way a novel should be written in the context of FFN, in the preface to *The Young Fur-Traders...* (1881):

In writing this book my desire has been to draw an exact copy of the picture which is indelibly stamped on my own memory. I have carefully avoided exaggeration in everything of importance. All the chief, and most of the minor incidents are facts. In regard to unimportant matters I have taken the liberty of a novelist, — not to colour too highly, or to invent improbabilities, but, — to transpose time, place, and circumstance at pleasure; while, at the same time, I have endeavoured to convey to the reader's mind a truthful impression of the general effect, — to use a painter's language — of the life and country of the Fur Trader.

Ballantyne was consistent in his perception of what a novel should be, because he paraphrased the above in the preface of another novel, *The Fugitives...* (1887): "It is almost allowable, I think, to say that this is a true story, for fiction has only been introduced for the purpose of piecing together and making a symmetrical whole of a number of most interesting facts". And again, in his preface to *The Buffalo Runners ...* (189-): "Nearly all the incidents in this tale are either facts, or founded on fact".

Although in the case of historical novels the prefacers' proposition that the novel is based on facts is more obvious, the FFN formula as such is often an important element in the prefatorial discourse. At the same time, as we shall see, the proof of "fact" is not backed by references to historical secondary literature or archival sources, unlike the custom established by Walter Scott and followed by virtually all European authors of the time (for example, in Manzoni's *I promessi sposi* or in Eötvös's *Magyarország 1514-ben*, to use two examples of historical novels from two from each other relatively distant literatures). This may be explained by the lack of such sources in contemporary Canada. David Hickey's *William and Mary: A Tale of the Siege of Louisburg* (1884), Edmund Forest's *Vellenaux: A Novel* (1874), or Blanche Lucile Macdonnell's *Diane of Ville Marie: A Romance of French Canada* (1898) are good examples of the authors' insistence on "Facts" but without citation of sources.

In sum, the FFN is an important and frequent element in English-Canadian prefaces. Its importance as a prescribing formula showing continuous concern with a "national" (English)-Canadian literature and often with adding to the formula another frequent characteristic of the Canadian prefaces in general, namely the concern with morality (see the ethical category in Chapter two), is perhaps best represented in the preface of Joseph H. Hilts's novel *Among the Forest Trees...* (1888):

1st. The facts and incidents must be substantially true. 2nd. All the drapery and coloring must be in strict harmony with pure morality, and with the demands of a sound religious sentiment. 3rd. And the whole must be illustrative of pioneer life, in its conditions and surroundings, and calculated to show something of the toils, privations, hardships, difficulties and sorrows of the early settlers.

As mentioned above, a very high percentage of English-Canadian prefaces contain the FFN formula in one form or another. Still, there are some examples to the contrary. In Richard Ryland's preface to *The Coiners of Pompeii: A Romance* (1845), an early example, the author says that

A "Novel or a Romance," we will all at once admit, is written not so much for instruction, or for the giving of a moral lesson to the reader, as for the amusement of his or her mind in their leisure moments, and when they have nothing else to engage their attention: hence we conclude, that as every one, when in search of amusement, generally seeks for that which affords him the greatest pleasure — the best of the two, whether a novel or a romance, is the one that would be required. The novel merely tells of events which have happened or do happen around us every day: but the romance tells of matters and things far more exciting; it speaks of the marvellous — of blood and murder — of things which do not happen before us *every day*, and consequently of those things which being strange and new to us, would be likely to give us the most pleasure in those leisure moments, of which we have just now spoken. But, you will say, a romance may be written in a much worse style than a novel: well, perhaps it may; and so we have to ask pardon for thus presuming to pass our comments on a work which we are concerned in.

Thus emerges the author's support for the genre of the romance, expanded by a discussion of the genre. In a later example, Louie Barron (*Zerola of Nazareth*, 1895) refutes completely the FFN concept and pleads for fiction as a genre of entertainment:

In offering this oriental story in book form to the reading public I do so in the hope that it may entertain and help to make leisure hours pass pleasantly. ... To entertain is the mission of fiction. In the present decade of realism and naturalism, of the nasty sort, there is undoubtedly a place in the hearts of thousands of people for wholesome romance which will arouse and hold the attention by means of methods that are admirable.

Similarly, Janet Conger (*A Daughter of St. Peter's*, 1889) begins her preface by saying that "The characters in this book — the author's first attempt at novel-writing — are, with a single exception, 'of imagination all compact'". And, in an overlap of implied FFN negation and in support for the notion of literature as amusement, Flora MacDonald, in the preface to her *Mary Melville...* (1900) claims to have written the novel for "literary entertainment".

Theoretical discourse about the genre of the novel was present in the English-Canadian prefaces, although not as frequently as the FFN concept. In most cases the theoretical discourse about genre was implied rather than explicitly stated. For example, in the above quotation from Richard Ryland's preface to *The Coiners of Pompeii...* (1845), the prefacer clearly delineates the genres novel and romance. In the same vein and importantly, in the context of literary history, fifty years later, in the above quoted preface by Barron (*Zerola of Nazareth*, 1895) it is important that he uses the term "romance", and not the term "novel", when he argues that the mission of fiction is to entertain. He is saying that the FFN formula is for novels which belong to the types of realistic and naturalistic literature, and therefore are not fit for enjoyment. A similar argument for the popular novel is presented by Joseph Edmund Collins (*The Four Canadian Highwaymen...*, 1886), who pleads for this form of reading and calls his genre "blood and thunder". The reason for his choice of genre is that he believes that he will be able to sell the novel and thus: "I will not, even for my best friend, write anything but what the people will buy from me". This is a clear case where in the theoretical discourse about genre it becomes apparent how an economic concern influences literature.

In the preface to *Tim Dolan, the Irish Immigrant...* (Author of "Mick Tracy", 1869) the prefacer obviously avoids calling his text by any genre-defining term. His reasons for doing this are open to speculation, but most likely he avoids calling the novel a novel because of the period's general aversion to this genre:

The tale here presented is one composed of actual incidents, many of them, even the majority of which, have come under his own observation. They are interwoven in the form of a narrative, because that form appears to be most agreable to a very large number of the reading public.

An exceptional perception of the genre of the novel is contained in Ebenezer Clemo's preface to his *Canadian Homes...* (1858). It is exceptional, because except for references that a novel has been previously published in a magazine, or that it is a second edition, the discourse about genre with reference to the voluminous magazine and journal industry has not often occurred in the prefaces:

To bring before the reader in a more popular and readable form than can usually be done through the medium of a newspaper, some of the leading features of this subject, and also to point out that which the author conceives to be true remedy for the evil, are the objects of the present work.

The preface in J.B. Kennedy's *Afloat for Eternity...* (1893) begins with the polemical question "Why write another book? — when the Earth already groans beneath the ponderous productions of pen?" The answer is partially given by the justification that this "Book is certainly original and unique in conception and style", written in a second preface by the editors.

The argument that the history of Canada ought to be popularized by the historical novel is explicitly presented in David Hickey's preface to *William and Mary...* (1884): "It was long a matter of surprise to me, why the story of the remarkable siege of 1745 had never been presented to the public in popular form. The present work is an attempt to do this". Hickey then discusses the "religious novel" (for this author obviously a distinct genre) and, anticipating a critical attitude toward that genre, attempts to justify it by referring to the fact that he himself is a preacher, a Methodist minister. The claim that the historicity of a novel rests on accidentally found "documents" (diaries, letters, etc.) occurs in W.D. Lighthall's (*alias* Wilfrid Châteauclair) preface to *The False Chevalier...* (1898): "This story is founded on a packet of worm-eaten letters and documents found in an old FrenchCanadian house on the banks of the St. Lawrence". The prefacer then continues to balance between "Facts" (the letters) and "Fiction": "A packet of documents of course is not a novel, and the reader may be able to guess what is mine and what is likely to have been the scanty limit of the original hint". Thus, he creates the impression that the reader is presented with a "historical" novel, i.e., that it is based on "facts". Interestingly, W.D. Lighthall's preface to his earlier novel, *The Young Seigneur...* (1888) contains a denial that his novel is a novel: "Lastly, the book is not a novel. It consequently escapes the awful charge of being 'a novel with a purpose'". Apparently, Lighthall felt it necessary to use such rhetoric to escape the uncomfortable feeling that if "The chief aim of this book is the perhaps too bold one — to map out a future for the Canadian nation", he may be accused of political partisanship. He attempts to avoid such an accusation by insisting that "The book is not a political work".

J. Macdonald Oxley, who is better known for his adventure stories for adolescents, "creates" a new genre of the novel in the preface to *The Romance of Commerce* (1896):

There has been a romance of commerce no less than a romance of war. Men have shown an equal enterprise and daring in the pursuit of wealth as in extending the bounds of empire, and gold has run rivalry with glory in adding brilliant pages to the world's history.

An example of the defense of naturalism as a technique for a specific genre can be found in the preface of Edmund E. Sheppard (*Dolly, the Young Widder...*, 1886), who defends naturalism as a component of his own work. At the same time, he promotes naturalism as a morally acceptable form of writing: "If you want to find pleasure in the naturalism of it, read it slowly and find where it tells the inner truth".

The preface is generally not often discussed in the prefaces. There are some examples, however, which will give us an indication of the prefacer's/ novelist's views. Barnas Freeman Ashley humorously titled his preface "0" to *Tan Pile Jim...* (1894) and wrote that "The above cipher is placed there because a preface generally counts for nothing in the reading of a book" and then proceeded to write another half page addressing the readership and promoting his novel. R.M. Ballantyne wrote twice in his prefaces about the preface. To his novel *The World of Ice* ... (1894) he wrote: "Dear Reader, most people prefer a short to a long preface. Permit me, therefore, to cut this one short, by simply expressing an earnest hope that my book may afford you much profit and amusement". The second "prefatorial" preface is the already quoted humorous preface to *Charlie to the Rescue...* (1890): "Having got nothing prefatorial to say, I avail myself of this blank page to say so".

In the preface to her first novel, *Honor Edgeworth* ... (1882), Kate Bottomley ("Vera") argues that the writing of prefaces is unnecessary because of the large number of books published, except to make "sure that he [*sic*] will be rightly interpreted by his readers". Her second novel, *The Doctor's Daughter* (1885) also discusses the preface in a similar way. She quotes Dickens, who said that "though seldom read, prefaces are continually written". She agrees with him on that point and attempts to explain why this might be so. The explanation of why prefaces are written, she relates to the situation in society in which one wants or has to introduce a less than impressive relative. In essence, the preface is, then, a necessary evil, useful to introduce a first attempt, or, by implication, a not-so-good attempt on the literary scene. In the next three pages the author uses the preface as a vehicle for a variety of purposes, ranging from a depreciatory comparison of her own work with the novels of Dickens to the promotion of her novel.

John R. Gair, a less recognized author than Bottomley, but who is mentioned in Klinck (I 317), begins his preface for *Fun on the Road* (1886) with a reference to Pope: "I am inclined to think the words of Pope, in his preface, are true, that both the writers of books and the readers of them are generally not a little unreasonable in their expectations". What is of note here is that the author legitimizes his own preface by the reference to a canonical author and his preface.

Edward Lane (*The Fugitives...*, 1830), whose Canadian status is somewhat dubious (Klinck I 145-46), demonstrates in his preface the typological and terminological uncertainty of the preface:

On discoursing with an acquaintance, (for friends are scarce) he told me that my little book needed a Preface, Introduction, or Dedication, I almost forget which. — Now, gentle Reader, your humble servant is not at all prepared for the performance of any thing of the sort.

Although he claims ignorance in the writing of a preface, the author discusses at some length (2.5 pages) the merits of both his novel and the preface: "Really, when I look back, I find that I shall actually succeed, either in writing a preface, or an apology for one". Although the author is, in the end, favourable to the preface, there is an underlying tone that degrades it. A half a century later, a more ambiguous perception of the preface is found in Bruce Weston Munro's preface (*A Blundering Boy...*, 1886); Munro uses the preface to discuss the preface first in a positive tone but at the end dismisses it by telling his readers that prefaces are usually not read. More importantly, his discussion includes references to the genre characteristics of the preface:

Notwithstanding that our preface is so grandiloquent, the story opens, the reader will observe, very modestly. But if he should persevere a little way, he will find that the writer soon strikes out boldly. Of course this preface was written after the story; but, let the reader be entreated, if he will excuse the Hibernicism, to read it first. If he does not, we are only too confident he will never read it. This is not prophecy, but intuition.

The general attitude toward the preface, as the above examples over sixty years demonstrate, was more negative than positive. Perhaps the best example of a negative perception of the preface, both in its systemic structure and because of its early date, is Richardson's preface to *Wau-Nan-Gee* (1852). Richardson explains that the only reason he wrote the preface is because his publisher requested it and goes on to assert that the preface is unnecessary because the novel is based on "historical fact". By this he must have meant that a preface is justified only if there is a need to explain something to the readers about the novel. But there are examples of prefaces in which the prefacer's intention is to promote the preface. Rosanna Leprohon wrote in the preface to *Antoinette de Mirecourt...* (1864): "The simple Tale unfolded in the following pages, was not originally intended to be issued with any prefatory remarks. Advised, however, that it is usual to do so, the author, having no wish to deviate from the established custom".

A confirmation of the systemic character of the preface occurs in John Richardson's preface to *Wacousta...* (1851):

As the reader may be curious to know on what basis, and in what manner this story ... was suggested to me, and on what particular portions of History the story is founded, I am not aware that this introductory Chapter, which I have promised my Publishers, can be better devoted than to the explanation.

The systemic components of producer, product, receiver, and post-production processing, are all mentioned in this paragraph, justifying the use of the preface for the novel.

1.2 Literary Figures and Texts

The preface of Julia Beckwith Hart's *Tonnewonte...* (1825) contains a list of canonical authors, consisting of Addison, Corneille, Hume, Milton, Racine, Robertson, Shakespeare, and Tasso. These authors are cited as proof of the European "genius" as opposed to North American culture that has not produced anything like them yet, although Franklin and Washington are cited as proof of the emerging North American "genius". A later example of the listing of canonical authors is the preface of Joseph Hatton's novel *By Order of the Czar* (1890). The prefacer presents the genesis of the novel and provides a long list of known and less known historical and literary works. Among the canonical authors are Gogol, Dostoevsky, Lermontov, and Tolstoy. Today less known authors he mentioned are Karl Emil Franzos, Tomàs de Iriarte, Eugenie Lawrence, Germain de Lagny, Leopold Kompert, Edmund Noble, and Sergej Stepniak. He also listed the authors of a number of articles in magazines, such as *Harper's Magazine*, and in encyclopedias. Kate Bottomley, as already mentioned, referred to Dickens as a prefacer and self-depreciatively compared herself to his literary merits. John R. Gair mentioned Pope and his preface. And, to provide a late example, Flora MacDonald, in the preface of her *Mary Melville...* (1900) refers to a long list of historical, religious, scientific, philosophical, and literary figures: Confucius, Buddha, Socrates, Dante, Shakespeare, Burns, Columbus, Copernicus, Galileo, Kepler, Galvani, Franklin, Stephenson, and Morse.

The comparison with canonical authors in the prefaces written by editors, publishers, or learned men is fairly frequent. John Campbell (*Two Knapsacks...*, 1892) is said in the publisher's preface to have known the works of Wordsworth. Joseph Edmund Collins (*The Four Canadian Highwaymen...*, 1886) compares his own work to the work of the then very popular Charles Reade.

From English literature the following authors are mentioned, either by a simple reference and quotation, or by critical comparison: Bacon (Smith, 1889), Carlyle (Huntington, 1884), Carroll and Coleridge (Rogers, 1900), Cooper (Richardson 1839), Crabbe (Johnson, 1876), Defoe (Traill, 1852), Dickens (Bottomley, 1885; Mercier, 1896), Dryden (Richardson, 1852), and Rider Haggard (Rogers, 1900). Implicit references to the Bible are frequent in the prefaces. Explicit mention appears in J.B. Kennedy's preface (*Afloat for Eternity...*, 1893): "We acknowledge our great indebtedness to the author of the Bible — an author and a book, without which this one could never have been written".

References to authors and works other than English are rare in English-Canadian prefaces. The above cited Hatton preface (c1890) contains references to a number of Russian, German, and French authors but in that case it is the theme and setting of the novel (Russia and the persecution of Jews there) that determines the references to these authors and their works. More exceptional is the usage of the German term "Munchausenisms" [*sic*] in its usual German (and English) context, i.e. tall tales, in the editor's preface to Richard Lanigan's novel (1888). Other references include the Aneid (Smith, 1889) from classical literature, Paul Lacroix (Lighthall, 1898), and Verne (Rogers, 1900) from French literature, and "les Bibaud, les Garneau" (Leprohon, 1861) from French-Canadian literature.

Prefaces to historical novels rarely contain references to secondary literature. However, the following examples may give an indication of the areas of historical and travel writing the prefacers were familiar with: Major Boulton and Lord Garnet Wolseley (Mercier, 1896; Sparrow, 1896); R. Wright, a biographer of General Wolfe (Briton, 1885); d'Abrantes, Bartema, de Bourienne, Burckhardt, Burton, Finati, and Irving (Wilson, 1897); and de Meneval, Metternich, Mulbach, and de Saint-Amand (Sparrow, 1896).

In a few cases historical figures are mentioned: Cleveland and William Tweed (Broome, 1890); Washington, Lansdowne, and Queen Victoria (Leonard, 1888) are good examples.

1.3 Mention of the Other Arts

This category did not yield any meaningful data. R.M. Ballantyne (*The Young Fur Traders...*, 1856) refers to "a painter's language" when he is discussing the "truthful impression of the general effect" and Isaac Broome (*The Brother...*, 1890) mentions in his preface that he was a sculptor as well as a writer.

1.4 References to or Address of Readership

This category, in a limited way, offers some insights into the prefacers'/ authors' perception of the nineteenth-century English-Canadian readership. The readership addressed in the prefaces can be divided into distinct groups: Youth, Women, "Canadians", etc.

Young men are the targeted readers in Robert Wilson's preface (*Never Give Up...*, 1877). Specifically, youth is targeted in a number of prefaces: Mann, 1878; in the prefaces of Ashley, 1896, 1894; Murray, 1871; Oxley, 1892; Traill, 1852. Specific nationalities are also targeted and it is of importance that there was a high frequency of addresses to Canadians in general: Garison, 1890; Mann, 1878; Munro, 1886; Savigny, 1895; Shinnick, 1891; and Skelton, 1876. English (Abbott, 1846 and Ballantyne, between 1894 and 1905), Irish (Clayton, 1884), and American (Beckwith, 1825 and Johnson, 1876) readership were the other occurrences of national targeting. Children (Lanigan, 1888; "L.G.", 1870; Rogers, 1900), women (Clemo, 1858; "L.G.", 1870), immigrants (Darling, 1849), critics (Carroll, 1876 and Barron, 1895), and religious groups (Carroll, 1876) are other, but less frequent readership targets. Specific organizations or social groups are, in a few isolated cases, also targeted: "Readers of a lesser income" (Lauder,

1894; Ballantyne, 1887), alcoholics (Wilson, 1894), "the unhappily married" (Lloyd, 1899), "Readers of popular literature" (Collins, 1886), and a specific club in London (Barr, 1892), may serve as selected examples.

An exceptional case is Susanna Moodie's preface to *Mark Hurdlestone, the Gold Worshipper* (1853), because the prefacer discusses Canadian readership. Moodie contends that there is a larger readership in Canada than before and that books are readily available. The author discusses much of English Canada's contemporary magazine history and the literary activity connected with it. She also makes several comments about the situation of literary production in both the U.S. and English Canada. A somewhat similar voice is to be found in George Bourne's preface to *Lorette...* (1834). An earlier work than Moodie's and its Canadian status questionable, its preface is nevertheless interesting because the author declares that no one would dare to publish the novel in Canada.

1.5 Theme and/or Setting of the Novel

To determine the theme of a novel is at best a daring undertaking. Thus, where the setting of the novel or some major aspect of the novel clearly indicates a country or nation, or the nationality of the major character of the novel, the novel has been classified accordingly.

The English-Canadian novels with prefaces are most often Canadian in theme and/or setting. From the total of 239 novels with prefaces it is possible to determine in 73 cases that the theme and/or setting is Canadian. In contrast, there are 7 novels with clearly American themes and/or setting: four Ballantyne novels (1872, 1881, 1890, 1894), and Broome, 1890; Chaplin, 1876;, and Galt, 1830. There are also two novels with Scottish (Galt, 1831 and Ashley, 1896) and one with Irish (author of *Mick Tracy*, 1869) themes/setting. In a few cases there is a mixture of American/Canadian (Shrimpton, 1867), and British/Canadian (Parker, 1896) themes and/or setting. Several of Haliburton's novels can be classified as mixed themes and setting: Canadian/British (1843) and Canadian/American (1838). There are few cases of British themes and/or setting (Forrest, 1869; Gordon, 1892; and Huntington, 1884). "Exotic" themes and setting include the Orient (Barron, 1895), Madagascar (Ballantyne, 1887), and East India (Emberson, 1897). For the theme of prohibition, Potter (1884) is a good example. There are also ten examples of Continental European themes and/or setting. Austria: Grant Allen, 1900; France: Lighthall, 1898; Spirito Gentil (George Hanna), 1889. Italy: Conger, 1889; Lauder, 1894. The Netherlands: Weaver, 1893. Russia: Hatton, 1890; Smith, 1891. Switzerland: Ballantyne, 1880.

2. The French-Canadian Novel Prefaces

2.1 Literary Theory and Literary Genre

Aubert de Gaspé received unfavourable reactions to the opinion about literature — a theoretical and genre discussion — he expressed in his preface to *L'Influence d'un livre...* (1837) (*Dictionnaire des oeuvres littéraires du Québec* 389). He assessed the nineteenth-century novel as a genre with its focus on "la nature humaine" as opposed to "les belles phrases fleuries ou [les] incidents multipliés". His own novel he designated as a "Roman de Moeurs canadien ... et historique". Aubert de Gaspé's theoretical position in reference to nineteenth-century Canadian prose, or what he proposed the latter should be like, was written in the context of an emerging literature. He argued for the unity of the novel in the eighteenth century — for which he was criticized. Similarly, although thirty years later, the unity of the novel was the concern of Napoléon Bourassa. He claimed to be able to maintain the unity of the novel by drawing on autobiographical data, by analogies to the literature of Antiquity, and implicitly, by the historical, political, and social background of his novel (Acadians).

The genre of the novel is approached in a comparative sense by Doutre in his preface to *Les Fiancés de 1812...* (1844). He deplores the Canadian attitude that allows for a negative perception of native (i.e. French-Canadian) literature when compared to the literature of France, e.g. Dumas père et Dumas fils and Eugène Sue. He counters this attitude by addressing the readership somewhat ironically that "Les Fiancés ne sont pas écrits pour ces messieurs". Doutre's daring alternative, in the context of the time, of literary independence from the "mother country" is credited as a first in French-Canadian literature (*Dictionnaire des oeuvres littéraires du Québec* I 260). Doutre embraces literature as a product of imagination, although he recognizes the prevalent anti-novel sentiment. With a long quotation, whose author he identifies only as "Un autre personnage dont la célébrité est certainement mieux établie que la leur nous a fait", he illustrates the contemporary moral objection to the novel. The author of the quotation opposes the novel also declaring it useless as compared to works of economics, politics, administration, etc.

The anti-novel sentiment is still prevalent thirty years later in Antoine Gérin-Lajoie's preface to *Jean Rivard...* (1874). The preface is genre theoretical in the sense that he too refuses to call a novel "novel": "Mais, que voulez-vous? Ce n'est pas un roman que j'écris", but by implication defines the supposed characteristics of the novel genre:

Si quelqu'un est à la recherche d'aventures merveilleuses, duels, meurtres, suicides, ou d'intriguies d'amour tant soit peu compliquées, je lui conseille amicalement de s'adresser ailleurs. On ne trouvera dans ce récit que l'histoire simple et vraie d'un jeune homme sans fortune, né dans une condition modeste....

The author perceived the novel genre to be what we would call today a gothic novel or romance. The undertone of the definition and his description of what he wrote is negative. The other aspect of the preface is that there is an FFN orientation in the definition of the author's novel. The FFN concept and its prefatorial expressions are much less frequent in French-Canadian prefaces than in English-Canadian prefaces. In addition to the above mentioned example, it appears in Aubert de Gaspé's preface (1837) and in Marmette's (1870, 1883). Jean-Baptiste Proulx (1887) also denies that his work is a novel with an FFN statement:

De ce qui précède, il ressort, je crois, jusqu'à l'évidence, que cette histoire n'est ni une fiction, ni un conte, ni une légende, ni même ce qu'on est convenu d'appeler un roman historique, mais bel et bien, dans toute la force du terme, le récit exact d'événements réels, tels qu'ils se sont passés, sans fard ni couleurs.

Although the author refuses the designation novel or any other genre term for prose literature, his definition — without a name — becomes, at least partially, an FFN confirmation. This is reinforced by the quotations from interviews with "witnesses".

Honoré Beaugrand explained in his preface to *Jeanne la fileuse...* (1878) why he found it necessary to combine the novelistic with the political. This novel of "un romancier d'occasion" (*Dictionnaire des oeuvres littéraires du Québec* I 409) is a before-the-fact example of the twentieth-century phenomenon of "littérature engagée". The author/prefacer is conscious of his choice: "*Jeanne la Fileuse*, est moins un roman qu'un pamphlet; moins un travail littéraire qu'une réponse aux calomnies que l'on s'est plu à lancer dans certains cercles politiques contre les populations franco-canadiennes des États-Unis".

Laure Conan's (Felicité Angers) novel *Angéline de Montbrun* (1884) is important because it contains a twenty-page preface by Casgrain which he wrote for the Royal Society. The preface is a critical assessment of the novel. Abbé Casgrain introduces his topic by quoting Eugénie de Guérin and confirming the latter's view that novels, with the exception of Walter Scott's and those that have a clear moral and religious content, are immoral and corrupting. His criticism of the novel addresses several questions: Casgrain praises the author as the first Canadian (French Canadian) woman author and adds that despite her gender her writing is "masculine". Of interest among his objections are his lament that there are not enough Canadian scenes in the novel and that the author used too many quotations. Casgrain defended the "proper" novel as a genre exemplified by Cardinal Wiseman's *Fabiola* and then cited a number of historical figures who could be used for a novel's subject such as Alexandrine de Ferronnays, Mlle de Verchères, Mme de la Tour, the Chevalier de Lévis, de Saint-Foye, Mme Swetchine, and Lacordaire.

Rodolphe Girard's novel *Florence...* (1900) has a preface written by Firmin Picard. The prefacer is, similarly to the Abbé Casgrain, enthusiastic about the Canadianness of the novel and its religious orientation. It is for these reasons that he assesses the novel in such positive terms: "Son roman est la glorification des plus belles vertus: ce n'est pas un roman à la mode, commençant par des roucoulements quelconques pour se terminer par le mariage. Son roman est original, bien conçu, bien écrit: il a mis son coeur partout". Charles Marcil's novel *L'Héritière d'un millionaire...* (1867) contains two prefaces, one by the author and one by the publisher. The author defines his novel by reference to poetry:

N'écrivant pas un poême, nous n'avons pas cru devoir nous soumettre passivement à une discipline littéraire rigoureuse. Nous avons laissé courir notre plume librement, plus anxieux de plaire par les details que par les combinaisons de l'ensemble. On sera assez bienveillant pour nous tolérer cet acte d'émancipation.

In other words, he defines the novel in relation to the demands of form in poetry and considers the deviation from such demands a positive development in literature. Some of this acceptance of the novel as a result of imagination — rather than intention — appears in the preface by the publisher. He writes: "La partie historique n'est, cependant, que l'accessoire d'une intrigue principale qui se pursuit d'une manière soutenue du commencement à la fin de l'ouvrage".

The publisher, too, accepts the novel as mainly fiction, although the question of FFN ("partie historique") is raised. The publisher assures the readership that the novel is based on acceptable moral standards, thus extending the definition of the novel into that omnipresent dimension. Three decades later, which shows the persistence of moral issues in French Canada, Paul-Emile Prévost defines the novel as a genre concerned with morals. In his preface to *L'Epreuve* (1900) he mentions Balzac, Dumas père et Dumas fils, and Hugo as examples of authors who wrote their works with that conviction. He then expands the responsibility of the novelist to include the description of women. His perception of women is a highly idealized one and their role is, as his description implies, defined. He cites a number of authors whose works, in his view, treat women in the appropriate manner, for example, by drawing attention to their psychology as distinct from that of men. The novel of Jacques Henri Bernardin de Saint-Pierre, *Paul et Virginie* (1787) — in the contemporary context a frequently cited bestseller — and Longus, Goethe, Shakespeare, and *El Cid* are used as examples which, in his opinion, confirm his view.

Jules-Paul Tardivel (1895) discusses the novel in strongly negative terms in the context of morals and religion. He quotes a clerical source in which the French novel is described as an "invention diabolique" and Jules Vallès as evidence and discusses the *Comédie humaine* of Balzac in such terms that his notion that "Le roman est donc, de nos jours, une puissance formidable entre les mains du malfaiteur littéraire" seems justified. In his opinion, since the novel is a fact of literature and society, the writer must write novels "ad majorem Dei gloriam". Thus, Tardivel pleads for the spread of the religious-moralistic novel, which has the ultimate purpose of reinforcing a religious society. Similarly, the editorial preface to Alphonse Thomas's novel *Gustave ou un héros canadien* (1882), although it does not define a genre, implicitly argues for the value of the novel as "une lecture utile au point de vue de l'intérêt et de la religion".

An exceptional way of discussing the theory of the novel appears in the postface of Georges-Isidore Barthe, in his novel *Drames de la vie réelle: Roman canadien* (1896). He quotes several paragraphs of A.B. Routhier's writings on the novel. It appears that Barthe intended to show his compliance by referring to an authority.

The objective of the popularization of Canada's history with historical novels is expressed in the preface of Joseph Marmette to *François de Bienville...* (1870). Marmette begins by telling about his youth when he was reading Walter Scott's novels, thus confirming the commonly occurring phenomenon of Scott's influence. The reason for his own writing of historical novels is explained by his desire to popularize French-Canadian history. Almost two decades later, Edmond Rousseau (*Les Exploits d'Iberville*, 1888), although he too embraces the writing of historical novels, is aware of the negative perception of the novel as a genre. His preface contains a long discussion with a fictitious party, who decries the "abuse of that genre". Rousseau argues for the existence of the novel with the examples of such French authors as Louis Veuillot, George Sand, de Montépin, and Ohnet. He also mentions favourably Canadian authors like Kirby and Marmette. Drawing on examples of authors such as Jean-Jacques Rousseau, and contrasting them with the "monstrueux" Zola and Richepin, he provides an interesting mixture of authors who supposedly argued against the "immoral" novel. Similarly, the popularization of Canadian history is the aim discussed in the long preface of Ernest Myrand in *Une Fête de Noël sous Jacques Cartier* (1890). His argument is that just as Jules Verne popularized science, he will popularize history.

2.2 Literary Figures and Texts

The majority of literary figures mentioned in the French-Canadian prefaces are French and generally the best known literary achievements of the mentioned authors are referred to. In most cases the references are to works of canonical authors: Balzac (Tardivel, 1895; Prévost, 1900), Chenier (Myrand, 1888), Dumas père and Dumas fils (Duquet, 1866; Prévost, 1900), Flammarion (Myrand, 1888), Sand and Soulié (Duquet, 1866), Verne and de Vigny (Myrand, 1888), Voltaire (Aubert de Gaspé, 1837), Zola (Rousseau, 1888), La Fontaine and Molière (L'Epine, 1878), Hugo (Prévost, 1900), Montaigne (Marmette, 1870), Racine (Myrand, 1888), Rousseau (Singer, 1871), Geneviève de Brabant (Proulx, 1887). There are few references to continental European authors: Dante (Conan, 1887; Marmette, 1873), Goethe (Prévost, 1900), or to British authors: Scott (Marmette, 1870), Shakespeare (Aubert de Gaspé, 1837), and one American author Cooper (Marmette, 1870, Brémond, 1889). In criticism Brunetière (Girard, 1900), Fénelon (Gérin-Lajoie, 1874), and La Harpe (Aubert de Gaspé, 1837) are referred to. From specifically French-Canadian literary criticism A.B. Routhier appeared in one preface (Barthe, 1896). From the classics Horace (Bourassa, 1866), Longus (Prévost, 1900), and Virgil (Bourassa, 1866) are mentioned. Historical figures other than English-Canadian and French-Canadian, respectively North American figures, occur seldom in the prefaces, but Lajos Kossuth and Garcia Moreno, both revolutionaries well known at the time in North America, are mentioned (Tardivel, 1895).

2.3 Mention of the Other Arts

The French-Canadian prefaces did not contain any data in this category.

2.4 References to or Address of Readership

This category yielded few data. The type of readership that was referred to in a significant way, both in occurrence and with intensity, was the French-Canadian population in general: Beaugrand, 1878; Bourassa, 1866; Chevalier, 1888; L'Epine, 1878; Girard, 1900; Marcil, 1867; Marmette, 1870; and Myrand, 1890. A Franco-American readership was addressed by Beaugrand, 1878 and Marcil, 1867; and specifically the French readership was addressed by Beaugrand, 1878 and L'Epine, 1878. Youth was addressed by Brémond, 1887 and by Marmette, 1873.

2.5 The Theme and/or Setting of the Novel

The theme and/or setting of French-Canadian novels with prefaces are almost in total French-Canadian with few exceptions such as Beaugrand (1878) and Marcil (1867), who use a mixture of Franco-American and French-Canadian themes/setting.

CHAPTER FOUR

Analysis of the Systemic Dimensions of the Preface Typologies and of the
Systemic Data of the Prefaces

Preamble

In relation to the corpus of the prefaces the lack of studies about nineteenth-century Canadian literature is a serious handicap for the present work. This lack of secondary literature is particularly apparent in the case of nineteenth-century English-Canadian literature. The situation is somewhat better in French-Canadian literature of the period, but there too, there are important areas where basic work is needed.

In this Chapter the systemic dimensions of the preface typologies and the systemic data of the prefaces, introduced in Chapters two and three, will be analyzed and discussed. This will be done based on the four *ETL* categories, namely, A. the *Production*, B. the *Reception*, C. the *Processing*, and D. the *Post-Production Processing* categories.

These four categories contain, in the *ETL* framework, several sub-categories. Within each *ETL* category only those subcategories will be used as bases for the analyses which are pertinent to data obtained from the prefaces. In some instances a subcategory may be implied rather than explicitly stated.

A. *The Production*

The *ETL* category of production includes as subcategories the producer of the literary text (author/prefacer in this study) and the text in its several aspects.

1. The Producer (The author/prefacer)

The CIHM data includes the birth and death dates of authors of 69% of prefaces for the English-Canadian and of 84% for the French-Canadian novels. Unfortunately, the CIHM shows much less consistency in indicating birth and death dates of English-Canadian authors than of French-Canadian authors; this is perhaps a result of the different amounts of research and levels of scholarship.

With the publication dates of the novels with prefaces it is possible to calculate the age of the prefacers at the time of the publication. Figure 1 shows the number of prefacers in relation to their age. Figure 2 shows the proportion of English-Canadian and French-Canadian prefacers to each other.

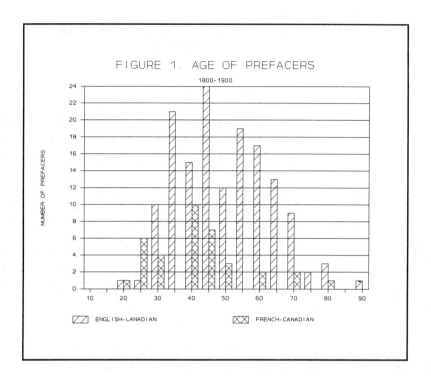

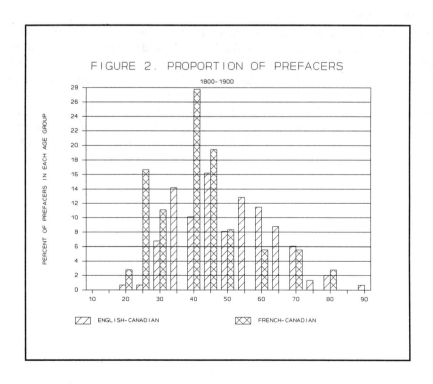

The proportional figures indicate clearly that the French-Canadian prefacers were largely younger than the English-Canadian prefacers. This observation is also borne out by calculation of an average. The mean age of the English-Canadian prefacers is 47.8 $\pm$ 1.1 (mean $\pm$ standard error, n=148) while that of the French-Canadian prefacers is 39.7 $\pm$ 2.3 (mean $\pm$ standard error, n=36). The obvious question here is, why are the French-Canadian prefacers on the average younger? The question, beyond the satisfaction of the statistician's curiosity, is pertinent in several respects. For one, it is not insignificant in the context of literary production, reasons for the writing of a preface, and generally, the "form" of the authorial environment. John Hare, in his article "Introduction à la sociologie de la littérature canadienne-française du XIXe siècle" states that while until 1860 the average age of French-Canadian *authors* was 40, and he designates this average age as very young; it changed after this time, and the average age rose (92). This is not indicated by the average age of the *prefacers* in this study. The reason might be that authors of novels felt the need to write a preface when they were young and were publishing first works. The mean average age of prefacers is the same average Hare gives as the average age of younger authors before the second half of the century. Although it must be kept in mind that before 1860 the authors Hare is speaking about were not novelists but poets, and poets tend to be younger in general, the inconsistency of the younger age of prefacers with that of authors becoming older after 1860 must be an indication of the prefacers' eagerness to speak to the readership or the feeling that some statement ought to be made.

As to the older age of English-Canadian prefacers, this observation confirms the opinion of Mary Lucinda MacDonald in her Ph.D. dissertation *Literature and Society in the Canadas 1830-1850*, that English-Canadian authors tended to be older when they began to publish in Canada than French-Canadian authors (1984, 156; also 1992). It is difficult to confirm the older age of English-Canadian prefacers because MacDonald spoke about an earlier period of only twenty years and about immigrant English authors. Nevertheless, some analogy between the two observations is justified. Unfortunately, MacDonald does not indicate any reason for the older average age of the English-Canadian authors. Without any factual or other source, the answer must be hypothetical. In this case, English Canadians, Protestant and imbued with the proverbial puritan work ethic, perhaps published later in age because writing was not their "real" profession. What MacDonald established between 1830 and 1850, that

Although none of the writers was wealthy, with a few exceptions they would all have considered themselves ladies and gentlemen. Despite the fact that their writing could not have had first claim on their time and energy, they nonetheless took it very seriously.... (1984, 156)

holds for most of the nineteenth century. Patrick A. Dunae, in his book *Gentlemen Emigrants*, postulates that the qualitative and quantitative base of the nineteenth-century English-Canadian educated and/or propertied class and, consequently, the reading public, consisted of the British upper-middle class, of "gentlemen", a concept meaning educated men and women from the ranks of the military, church clergy, the colonial administration, and the "supernumerary gentlemen", i.e., second and third sons of the gentry. These persons were occupied first with their careers, and if they were inclined towards literature, it was a secondary occupation both in reading and writing. Thus, if the authors were writers only after they established themselves professionally and financially, their publications with prefaces also appeared later.

The prefacers' biographical data drawn from the typologies yielded only a limited number of systemic data. In the English-Canadian typological category of the apologetic preface, the autobiographical characteristic is relatively well exemplified. The prefacer's self-referential perception of his own novel is not only a rhetorical device as in the case, for example, of Julia Beckwith Hart, but also a genuine expression of psychologically determinable authorial perceptions. The autobiographical connection between the value of the novel, the prefacer, and the author (who is identical with the prefacer) is a manifestation of the prefacer/author's insecurity as an author and, in some cases also as an individual. The latter case is symptomatic of several women authors, as the examples show. The examples also show that this type of self-referential biographical and apologetic behaviour occurred throughout the nineteenth century.

The ratio of women prefacers is small.[3] Of the 239 English-Canadian prefaces 52 were written by women, or 22% of the total. In the case of French-Canadian prefacers the ratio is even more negligible. Of the 52 French-Canadian prefacers only two were women.

It is an important literary historical observation that in the nineteenth century women wrote a significant body of novels and also published successfully.[4] Carol Gerson's suggestion in her previously cited paper that in English-Canada women novelists constitute a substantial portion of nineteenth-century novel literature confirms this generally accepted view. Interestingly, this is not the case with prefaced novels. Thus, it may be deduced that the prominence of novels written by women did not result in a more assertive attitude on their part, which would have found expression in the prefaces.

Another important systemic dimension of the production category is information about the prefacers'/authors' profession. It has been established that the nineteenth-century English-Canadian and French-Canadian novelist was not a professional writer. With regard to French-Canadian novelists, John Hare's article again contains valuable background information. Of the 58 French-Canadian authors he studied, 18 were lawyers, 10 journalists, 6 priests, 4 government employees, 3 physicians, one an artist, and 16 unknown (Hare 84).[5] This distribution of professions is more than likely paradigmatic for the French-Canadian prefacers of this study. A re-examination of the prefacers' professions in the *Dictionnaire des oeuvres littéraires du Québec* confirms this proposition. In sum, the social position (family background, profession, social status based on family background and profession) of the nineteenth-century French-Canadian and English-Canadian novelist and prefacer places both him and his writing into the privileged class(es).

---

3   Since the overwhelming majority of prefacers is identical with the authors of the novels, the calculation of women prefacers from the total number of prefacers is a statistically acceptable way to determine the ratio.

4   Cf. Lowell 130. In French literature, for example, as in most literatures this is only recently recognized (cf. Waelti-Walters). In English-Canadian scholarship, several important articles appeared in McMullen (1990).

5   Statistically, the 16 authors whose profession is unknown is too high a number to obtain an accurate ratio.

In the case of the English-Canadian prefacers, the period studied here may be divided into pre-Confederation and post-Confederation segments. This periodization is not made only for the sake of historical convenience but because particularly English-Canadian intellectual history shows a dividing line around the time of Confederation. T.D. MacLulich states in his book *Between Europe and America: The Canadian Tradition in Fiction* that "Most of our pre-Confederation novelists, I am arguing, based their cultural frame of reference on an idealized picture of traditional British society. For them, the pyramid of authority and prestige was clearly defined" (32).

The analysis in the present work supports in a round about way MacLulich's assumption that the English-Canadian authors' frame of reference was an "idealized picture of traditional British society", because their family was privileged. The combination of MacLulich's observation and the preface data of this study resulted in the following: while the situation in pre-Confederation English-Canadian novel literature may have had the structure that MacLulich describes, preface data do not explicitly confirm it. Rather, the confirmation of MacLulich's observation lies in the fact that the concern with "ordinary people" appears mainly in post-Confederation prefaces. Therefore, it is the lack of concern in the pre-1867 period that confirms MacLulich's observation. After Confederation, particularly from 1880 onward, MacLulich's observation that post-Confederation novelists were more concerned with the emerging Canadian middle bourgeoisie and that "the majority of our fiction writers were creating stories and novels that dealt directly with the ordinary people" (36) is clearly borne out in the prefaces. Several groups and subgroups of the ethical prefaces illustrate this. While the prefacers and authors of the post-Confederation period were still "gentlemen" and "gentlewomen", their focus expressed in the prefaces and consequently in their novels (or the other way around), changed. Part of the reason for this change is surely what Ramsay Cook convincingly explained as "social criticism in late Victorian English Canada" in his *The Regenerators: Social Criticism in Late Victorian English Canada*. The change, according to Cook, was rooted in the battle over Darwin's theory of evolution by natural selection and its contemporary opponents. The public discussions and arguments about evolution versus the Biblical revelation of devine creation resulted in questions about social responsibility. These, according to Cook, accelerated a democratization of English-Canadian society: "ordinary people" became an important factor of social change. One result of this study will add another, additional, explanation for the interest in "ordinary people". This is the authors'/prefacers' awareness of a changing, i.e., an expanding readership, which, in turn, is a result of the improving literacy rate.

The French-Canadian prefaces, particularly after 1867 (Confederation had a different meaning in French-Canadian society), do not manifest the shift of focus observed in English Canada. Their concerns, in general, were more directed to nature, family, and religion, all three rooted in patriotism.[6] The prefacers' concern with French-Canadian issues in the above configuration is apparent in several typological categories. These

---

6   This aspect of French-Canadian literature has been established in Québécois-Canadian scholarship (cf. Lauzière [1957, 239], [1958, 234]; Hayne [1944, 12 and *passim*], Savard [1967], and Viatte [1980, 46, 52-53, 84]).

instances, however, are more implicit than explicit, as is apparent in the explanatory and ethical categories and subcategories. An explicit, although unusual, dimension is the concern with the situation of the French-speaking population of the U.S., particularly when the prefacers discuss the emigration of French Canadians to the United States. The French-Canadian prefacers do not show antagonism towards Americans when they discuss French-Canadian emigration. In the novels, this attitude also prevails: "The novelists regard the United States as fairly remote from French Canada and seem to feel that Americans should be left alone in the best interests of French-Canadian society" (Hayne 1944, 56).

As the examples show, more specific, if unique, concerns are those with regard to the social condition of French-Canadian youth and women. This has been borne out in the total of French-Canadian novels (Hayne 1944, 96, 101, 103). Their concern is rooted in the recognition that "the fate of their society rested in the hands of 'Les jeunes gens'", within a religious context (Hayne 1944, 103). In addition, the ideology based on morality and patriotism prevalent in French-Canadian society also reinforced a focus on youth and the "sustainers of the family", women/mothers. All this constitutes a blending of the social and the literary: "Le mouvement littéraire québécois est naturellement orienté vers la religion.... Le littéraire et le sociale ne font qu'un; ils invoquent les mêmes principes de justice, de progrès et de liberté" (Lamontagne 108-10. Cf. also Le Moine).

Data included in the previous Chapter, under the heading of literary figures and texts, may be significant in the context of literary influences. However, according to Lauzière's pioneering study of French-Canadian novel prefaces "Primevères du roman canadien français", this was not the case. In his article, Lauzière expresses the view that the prefatorial mention of literary figures proves nothing and he states even more severely: "Aussi, les préfaces de nos premiers ouvrages romanesques n'offrent guère d'intérêt au point de vue de l'évolution de l'esprit littéraire du temps" (1958, 246-47). This is an overall negation of the prefaces' rhetorical direction as far as the position of the prefacer and his relationship with his literary environment is concerned. As will be shown here, Lauzière's verdict is too one-sided, perhaps because he was looking for possible influences of one specific literary period, that of Romanticism. Contrary to Lauzière's observation, it appears that the prefacer's position-taking may be deduced from his use of literary figures and texts, even if only in a limited sense. This mechanism confirms the prefacer's relationship with a certain literary environment, which he chooses to announce for various reasons. It could be a simple listing of authors who, in the view of the prefacer, in some way deal with the topic the prefacer/author also treats in his novel. In the English-Canadian context, such is the case of the English-Canadian prefacer/author Joseph Hatton, who mentions a wide range of canonical authors. The important systemic dimension of Hatton's mention of an international range of canonical authors is that it suggests that Hatton probably read the works of these authors or at least had heard of them and found their mention in the preface as "signals" useful and appropriate. This does not suggest a literary influence, but it gives a clue to the range of literary culture and perception of the literary canon. This is important, because it must be assumed that Hatton did not know the several languages (Russian, Ukrainian, Spanish, German, French) necessary to read the original texts, but had become acquainted with them in translation. Since we still know very little of the literary environment in nineteenth-century Canada, data inform us that European authors were brought to Canada and, consequently, were read in translation. (Of course, depending on the stage of his life when the author immigrated to Canada, he could have read the foreign authors prior to his immigration.) Data presented in the previous Chapter indicate that the prefacers were familiar with contemporary literature or at least with the names of many contemporary authors. Many of these contemporary authors, perhaps the majority, have since become canonical authors. In general, the literary figures mentioned were novelists. Most likely due to the precarious state of novels and novel reading in nineteenth-century Canada, no contemporary bestsellers or their authors are referred to in the prefaces, with the exception of Reade. In French-Canadian society the reading of both "serious" and bestselling novels by French authors seems to have been more common before 1830 than after (Dostaler *passim*). In the period between 1830 and 1860, that is, before the publication of a larger number of French-Canadian novels, French bestsellers (i.e. high numbers of cheap printings sold) started to gain popularity and the reading of more serious French authors such as Balzac decreased. By 1860 and after, the reading of popular novels provoked the wrath of educators, intellectuals, and the church (Dostaler *passim*). This atmosphere was a result of the increasing power of Roman Catholicism (cf., for example, Rioux). Together, the strong influence of the church, the situation of the novel *per se*, and the influence of the "realist aesthetic" (Lowell 74) resulted in the writing of *credos* in prefaces, described by Yves Dostaler in his *Les infortunes du roman dans le Québec du XIXe siècle* thus:

Le goût de ce réalisme les mena vers des formes plus ambitieuses et plus audacieuses: on se mit à décrire des moeurs et à peindre des caractères. Ce fut le réalisme social puis moral qui s'imposa malgré la critique traditionnelle que les romanciers s'efforcèrent d'amadouer, par des préfaces ou des traités d'une ingeniosité fort habile. (139)

The mention of historians, and of memoir and travel authors as sources in the prefaces may offer some leads. Besides confirming the concern for "truth" and "facts", the indication of historical sources may explain the prefacer's/author's historical and ideological predisposition. For example, Mercier (1896) used uncritically Charles Arkoll Boulton's memoirs of the Riel Rebellion and Lord Wolseley's articles on the "Red River Expedition". Considering the part Major Boulton played in the Riel Rebellion, and considering Lord Wolseley's position as a representative of the British government, the historical and ideological direction of the author is predetermined, although some sympathy is expressed to the "half-breeds" in the novel (cf. on Boulton *The Canadian Encyclopedia* 3 1871). The use of travel descriptions from Irving, Burton, Burckhardt, etc. by Wilson (1897) is not so much an element of historical and ideological groundwork as a source for the description of the story's geographical scenes. At the same time, the use of works by Burckhardt, for instance, must mean a certain level of ideological disposition. The case of Sparrow's *The Lady of Chateau Blanc: An Historical Romance* (1896) and its acknowledged historical sources is perhaps indicative of a given conservative English-Canadian historical ideology. Such sources as the totally anti-liberal

Bourienne, or Metternich and Laure Junot d'Abrantès, cannot but indicate the prefacer's conservative ideology.

2. The Product (The Preface)

In this category one of the more important questions is the following. What is the statistical relationship between the prefaces and the novels? Questions about the preface, its specificity as a genre, its frequency, and other aspects can be put into perspective once this statistical relationship is clarified. Again, the CIHM corpus, by its impressive coverage of nineteenth-century monograph publications and the possibility of a numerical count offers a manageable, therefore unique literary historical situation: it is possible to work with a (an almost) clearly defined and delineated corpus of literary texts. As explained in Chapter one, electronic extraction from the CIHM allows for the selection of titles of fiction. Keeping in mind the possibility of 10% to 15% of missing titles in the CIHM, in the case of English-Canadian literature (C813) the extraction of fiction yielded 1,080 titles. Of these 1,080 fiction titles, 556[7] titles were visually (on the microfiche) established as novels. Of the 556 novels 239 contain a preface.[8] This results in 43% of the English-Canadian novels containing a preface. In the case of French-Canadian literature (C843), the fiction extraction yielded 146 titles. Of the 146 titles, 102 were established as novels.[9] Of these 52 contained a preface.[10] The proportion here is 51% of the novels containing a preface. Thus, French-Canadian novels had a slightly higher percentage of prefaces. In more general terms, in both cases roughly half of all novels had a preface. The distribution of prefaces in the novels bears out the notion that in the nineteenth-century Canadian novel literatures the preface has been a frequent type of text. The frequency of the preface is of course one factor that allows for a categorical classification of the nineteenth-century English-Canadian and French-Canadian novel preface as a genre. An anecdotal, perhaps spurious, "proof" of the importance of the preface in nineteenth-century Canada is indicated by a publication in Halifax in 1876: *The Preface: A Poem of the Period* (Shiels). The author of the volume named his volume of verse "preface", wrote a "note" explaining the title, and called his long poem "introduction".

In Genette's genre classification of the preface, the dedication and the motto may be considered as related forms of texts. In this study, these types of texts have not been included because the preface has been defined in a narrower sense. However, a simple numerical count and its results again strengthen the argument for the frequent occurrence

---

7 This number does not include re-editions such as those of Haliburton's and Richardson's novels. Prefaces of re-editions do not contain significantly different data. Usually, in addition to the original preface of the work, a biographical preface on the author is added.

8 This number does not include re-editions of novels with prefaces and it does not include cases where the novel contains more than one preface. Consequently, the number of prefaces is actually higher. However, the structure of the typology prohibits the duplication of prefaces and thus the lower, typologically speaking, and more exact number was chosen.

9 Cf. Hare who lists 52 French-Canadian novels, excluding re-editions between 1831 and 1900.

10 These numbers were arrived at with the same exclusion of re-editions and multiple prefaces, as in the case of the English-Canadian figures.

of the preface as a defined type of text. Among the English-Canadian novels, of the 556 novels, 239 of which have prefaces, an additional 132 contain dedications and/or mottoes. Also, the 239 prefaced novels contain in many cases not only the preface but also a dedication and/or motto. Of the 102 French-Canadian novels, 52 of which have prefaces, another 15 contain a short dedication and/or motto. Similarly, several of the 52 prefaced novels also contain dedications and/or mottoes.

To facilitate the interpretation of the systemic dimensions of the preface as a text type and the type's characteristics, the following series of graphs will be useful.

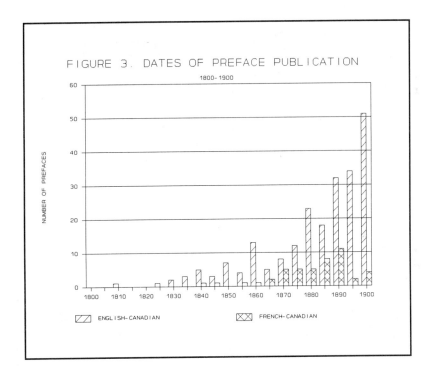

FIGURE 3. DATES OF PREFACE PUBLICATION
1800-1900

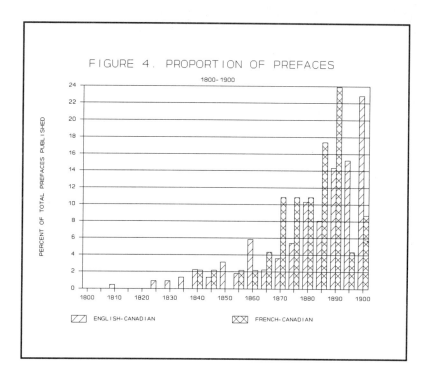

FIGURE 4. PROPORTION OF PREFACES
1800-1900

ENGLISH-CANADIAN   FRENCH-CANADIAN

Figure 3 compares the numbers of English-Canadian and French-Canadian prefaces published between 1800 and 1900. The trend of the occurrence of prefaces can be more easily determined by the conversion of the numbers on Figure 3 into proportions. Figure 4 shows English-Canadian and French-Canadian prefaces published in their proportional relationship. The proportion of prefaces published is divided into ten-year intervals. Between 1840 and 1860 the proportions are similar, with the exception of the period between 1855 to 1860, where the English-Canadian prefaces show an increase. Between 1860 and 1880 the situation is similar, again with one exception, between 1870 and 1875 where the French-Canadian prefaces show a sudden surge. Again between 1890 and 1895 there is a disproportional increase of French-Canadian prefaces. Between 1895 and 1900 there is a decrease in French-Canadian prefaces and an increase in English-Canadian prefaces. To attempt to find an explanation of these variations, the following analysis may be helpful. Figures 5A to 5F show the occurrence of preface characteristics in English-Canadian and French-Canadian prefaces at twenty- and ten-year intervals.

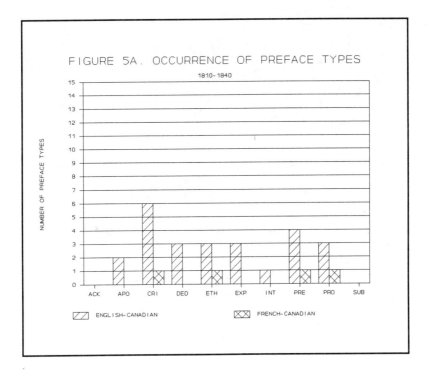

FIGURE 5A. OCCURRENCE OF PREFACE TYPES

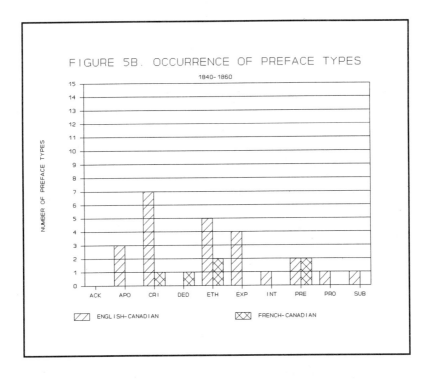

FIGURE 5B. OCCURRENCE OF PREFACE TYPES

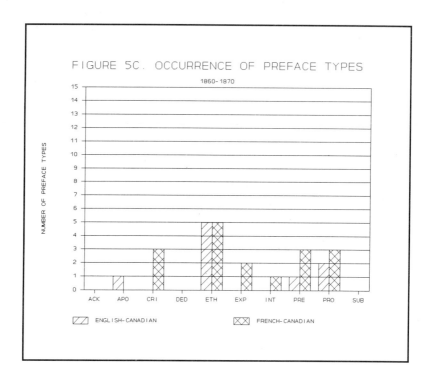

FIGURE 5C. OCCURRENCE OF PREFACE TYPES

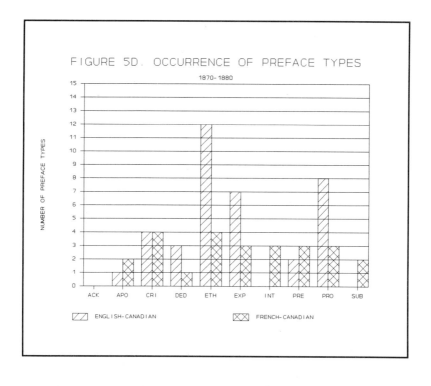

FIGURE 5D. OCCURRENCE OF PREFACE TYPES

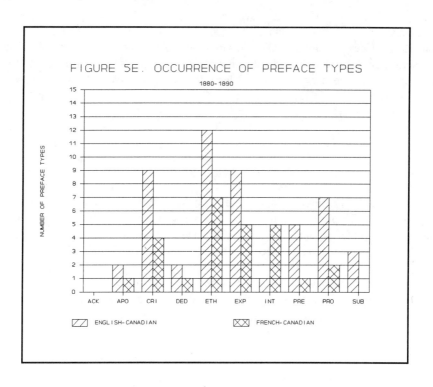

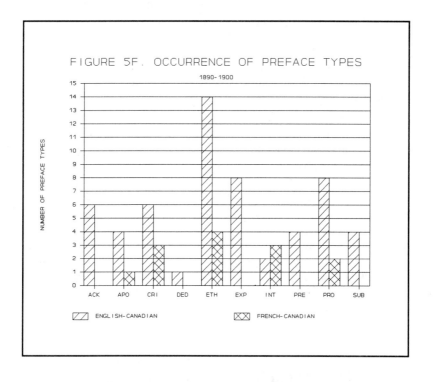

The preceding tables of figures show that during the 1855 to 1860 period, when there was an upsurge in English-Canadian prefaces, critical and ethical prefaces dominated among the prefaces (Figure 5B). This observation can be seen in the following context: if the period 1855 to 1867 is defined as the period of "Pre-Confederation" and 1855 to 1880 generally as the period of "Confederation", as in Klinck's *History of Canadian Literature*, Klinck's description of the period 1855 to 1867 underlines what has been found in the prefaces:

The English literature of the Canadas had played its part in the building of the country's culture. A regional character had been formed and a national character was emerging out of trial and error, tradition and independence, observation and insight, during years of preparation. (Klinck I 176)

In other words, in English-Canada the period of 1855 to 1880 was one of literary emergence, and the prefaces confirm this by a strong voice of the Canadian author/ prefacer. The prefaces, both in occurrence and in the dominant types within the occurrence, show that the emergence of English-Canadian literature took place during a period of higher critical awareness and a more pronounced ethical concern.[11] The literary emergence of English Canada occurred along with what MacLulich defined as "political maturation" (45). In comparison, the same can be said about French Canada. As shown, the French-Canadian prefaces show an increase between 1870 and 1875. In this period the French-Canadian prefaces are predominantly critical and ethical (Figure 5D). Again MacLulich: "Both French-Canadians and English-Canadians realized that the most distinctive feature of their history was the British Conquest of New France, followed by the accommodation that allowed both linguistic groups to live in comparative harmony" (45-46). This "political maturation" seems to manifest itself in literature, i.e., in the prefaces of both novel literatures. But the "political maturation" of English Canada differed from that of French Canada. David M. Hayne, for example, considered the nineteenth-century French-Canadian novel "militant", "marshalling its forces for the preservation and perpetuation of clearly defined national ideals" (1944, 1) and thus, according to Hayne, "In French Canada, literature has always been at the service of the national ideals to an even greater extent than in the European countries" (1945, 149).

Québécois-Canadian scholarship has generally maintained that from the second half of the nineteenth century into the twentieth century "quand la production connaît une expansion considérable, le glissement intime s'affiche jusque dans les titres où se trahit le discours amoureux en parfaite concurrence avec le discours patriotique toujours privilégié et par les meilleurs écrivains et par la réception" (cf. Allard 9-18, 16 and Lemire [1970]). If patriotism and morality were the building blocks of French-Canadian nationalism as revealed by the dominance of the French-Canadian historical novel, and this meant "political maturation", the situation was different in English Canada. The English-Canadian novel, historical and other, did not display an ideology of patriotism or nationalism, although "Britishness" was an important attitude, as Dick Harrison observes in reference to Anne Mercier's *The Red House by the Rockies* (1896): "The

---

11 "Critical" and "ethical" are used here in the sense of the definitions established in Chapter two of this work.

source of the characters' honour, courage, and stamina is their Britishness, and an old concern for birth and breeding accompanies that pride of nationality" (59). But this "Britishness" did not carry a pronounced nationalism. John Pengwerne Matthews observed in his comparison of Australian and English-Canadian literature that "this Canadian literary nationalism, as much as its Australian equivalent, was intimately involved with many complex political, social, and moral issues. In Australia these issues encouraged literary nationalism. In Canada they did not" (Matthews 103). At the same time, as Harrison and Dunae observe, it must be recognized that "Britishness" had a powerful cultural and social hold on English Canada. In French-Canadian novel fiction "political maturation" meant nationalism emanating from an ideological and social homogeneity. It is important, however, that in French Canada nationalism manifested itself in literature in a specific French-Canadian configuration. Already in the nineteenth century the Swiss literary scholar Virgil Rossel wrote about French-Canadian poetry and prose that "elle a bien sa physionomie particulière, son caractère propre, cette littérature du Canada; elle ne ressemble ni à celle de la France, ni à celle de la Suisse ou de la Belgique" (94).

In English-Canadian literature "political maturation" was based on different elements than in French Canada. It meant a more pluralistic dialogue of ideological, social, economic, and other, issues emanating from a more pluralistic society, but which closely associated itself with the mother country, Britain. On the other hand, pluralism in "political maturation" could also mean an orientation towards the concept of political biculturalism: "Contrarily, English-Canadian nationalists ascribed literature mainly the function to assist the creation of an all-Canadian identity" (Goetsch 79). This bicultural pluralism is manifest in the historical phenomenon that McInnis described as "The Conservative Ascendancy", and whose initiator and keeper was the Conservative party:

The dominant force in national politics in the quarter century following confederation was the Conservative party of Sir John Alexander Macdonald. ... The foundations of the party still rested on those two anomalous elements, the big business interests in English-speaking Canada and the French Catholic hierarchy in Quebec. (McInnis 410)

On the other hand, the importance of patriotism in French Canada and in English Canada, although in different configurations, manifested itself in the prefaces as obviously as in the novels themselves and the above discussed configurations of the historical situation, termed "political maturation", explain the dominance of the ethical characteristics of both English-Canadian and French-Canadian prefaces. In sum, this dominance was the result of different social and ideological structures in English and French Canada.

Another important aspect of the English-Canadian and French-Canadian historical novel is the often asserted view that they show a strong influence of Walter Scott. Although the influence of Scott and his novels has been demonstrated by some studies, for example in Dandurand's work on the French-Canadian novel or in Eva-Marie Kröller's Ph.D. dissertation *The Function of Place in the Canadian Literatures*, the prefaces do not show the authors' awareness or acknowledgement of this influence (cf. Kröller 46-64; Dandurand 69; Hayne 1945, 68-69; and Matthews 115). Notable exceptions are John Richardson's preface to *Wacousta* (1832) and Joseph Marmette's to his *François de Bienville...* (1870).

The sharp drop in French-Canadian prefaces between 1895 and 1900 is perhaps explicable according Madeleine Ducrocq-Poirier's analysis of the period 1860 to 1900:

Le roman n'est pas né malgré ses auteurs mais bien grâce à eux. Gêné par le discrédit jeté sur lui au nom de la morale, des bonnes moeurs, et de la "saine littérature", il a hésité à s'engager dans une voie originale. Au seuil de 1900, il ne savait quoi choisir, de l'histoire ou de la réalité villageoise, tout en sachant que l'objet à atteindre était l'homme, abstraction faite du moi de l'auteur. (149)

It has been found that the situation of French-Canadian fiction was significantly influenced by mediocre French-Canadian literary criticism (Dostaler 136). The critics' general and often poignant negation of the novel itself and the reading of French novels created an insecure atmosphere for both novel reading and novel writing in French Canada at least until 1890 (Dostaler 96, 136). On the other hand, the prefaced French-Canadian novels confirm Dostaler's finding that after 1890 and until 1900 the French-Canadian novel became stronger both as a genre written and read.

The surge of French-Canadian prefaces in the period 1890 to 1895 (Figure 4), when related to the occurrence of preface characteristics (Figure 5F), shows that in that period the dominant French-Canadian preface characteristics were critical, ethical, and integral, with a number of other preface characteristics not occurring at all. J.-S. Tassie, in an article entitled "La Societé à travers le roman canadien-français" divided the history of the French-Canadian novel into three periods. The colonial period until the Conquest, the period of stabilization until about 1885, and the period of modern transformation (153-64). If the second period is described by Tassie as "le calme d'une société rurale essentiellement statique" (155) and the third period as a "transformation sociale par l'industralisation" (155), it is possible that the initial impetus of this transformation was the cause of the more assertive, i.e., prefatorial, behaviour of French-Canadian authors. In the context of French-Canadian intellectual history, a similar if not analogous, tripartite development is described by Michel Brunet, in his *Écrits du Canada Français* (1975), where he argues that the three dominant ideologies of French-Canadian writing have been "l'agriculturalisme, l'anti-étatisme et le messianisme" (cf. also Boynard-Frot and Servais-Maquoi). These dominant ideologies also explain some of the French-Canadian authorial strategies evident in the prefaces. A look at who the prefacers in that period were, may also confirm this hypothesis. Dick, Myrand, Rousseau, and Tardivel, the prefacers of the period, were authors who are today, if not fully canonized, at least authors who appear in most French-Canadian literary histories. The results of this analysis are congruent to the findings of Falardeau in his study of the French-Canadian novel of the last decade of the century. For example, the transformation of French-Canadian society, in relation to the novel *Pour la patrie* (1895) of Tardivel is described thus by Falardeau in his *Notre societé et son roman*: "Au fur et à mesure que la société canadienne-française se diversifie et se pluralise et que le climat humain des villes devient anonyme et anomique, la littérature a commencé à exprimer le relâchement du réseau des contraintes qui retenaient les individus" (54).

In sum, the demonstrated increases and drops in French-Canadian prefaces may indicate a more nuanced situation, as suggested by the larger climate of society and literature discussed above. Of course, they may also be a result of the specific prefacers' attitude towards the preface itself. But again, is this attitude not, in more ways than one, the response to the social and literary environment?

The last period in which the prefaces show a proportional discrepancy, is between 1895 and 1900, when the numbers of English-Canadian prefaces rise and those of the French-Canadian drop. As said above, the period 1890 to 1895 shows a short-lived confidence, because it was the beginning of a new era in French-Canadian society and letters. The drop in French-Canadian prefaces between 1895-1900 cannot be explained at this point, especially because of the vitality of writing between 1890 and 1895. Perhaps in the last few years before the turn of the century the domination of the church had become stronger. The increase in English-Canadian prefaces just before the turn of the century is of course significant. This increase is a result of what most Canadian literary historians understand as the first "major watershed for Canadian authorship" because fiction is written for an expanding readership (Jones and Jones 42). At the same time, prefatorial assertion may have been a result of the social and literary ferment that characterized English Canada in the period between 1880 and 1900.

The most prominent typological characteristic, the ethical, indicates the prefacers' concern with morality and religion. While in the case of the French-Canadian prefaces this concern is somewhat more focussed than in the case of the English-Canadian prefaces, the latter show a wider range of ethical concern. Within the ethical prefaces the subgroup of social consciousness/patriotism indicates that both the English-Canadian and French-Canadian prefaces contain proportionally more concern with the Canadian situation than with the configuration of British/English-Canadian or French/French-Canadian. This is also implied in the discourse manifested by other characteristics, such as the subgroup of emerging literature. The awareness by the prefacers of French-Canadian issues is not surprising in the French-Canadian prefaces but is in the English-Canadian prefaces because of the generally accepted view that English Canada was strongly attached to the "mother" country, England.

The frequent concern with ethical matters in the English-Canadian prefaces raises another important question. Ramsay Cook, in his book *The Regenerators*, argues that in English-Canada "The challenge to traditional Protestant teachings in the nineteenth century was both intellectual and social" (229). This challenge to the status quo does not appear clearly in the English-Canadian prefaces, although it is implied in issues of social criticism. This view is implicit in Robin Mathews's paper "The Social Question in English Canadian Literature, 1880-1940: Document, Dialectic, and Dream", in which the author positions ethical concern ("ethical" in the definition of the present study) in the nineteenth century with reference to poetry, but not to novel literature (33-41). However, Ramsay Cook interprets this period in a wider context as dominated by questions of social criticism, and if Cook's interpretation of the period is taken in this wider context, rather than in its specificity, i.e., the challenge to the Protestant ethic, the prefaces show this dominance (174-95). And indeed, the most prevalent English-Canadian preface characteristic in this period is the ethical one (Figure 5F).

As mentioned, in the French-Canadian prefaces the concern with ethical issues is more homogeneous. Michel Lord, in his book *En quête du roman gothique québécois 1837-1860* argues that "L'usure (que l'on peut voir aussi comme une forme d'adaptation) du genre gothique vers 1860 est un signe révélateur du glissement de notre littérature vers un conformisme passéiste et catholicisant" (137). The French-Canadian prefaces confirm the religious cohesion and rigidity of most of nineteenth-century French-Canadian society. This rigidity continued to create an unfriendly atmosphere for novels. In general terms and with reference to the novelist and the novel as reading material, Dostaler found that "Le terme roman fut, au XIXe siècle canadien-français, un de [ces] mots chargés de valeur diffamante: il devint synonyme de légèreté, de perversion" (140). Although it is true that the moral and social consciousness of the French-Canadian novelist/prefacer, under the influence of the church, resulted in the moral/realist attitude manifest in the thematics and types of the novel, at the same time and in the final analysis, "Une telle pression sociale a certainement contribué à paralyser l'effort romanesque" (Dostaler 141). Yet the novel was important in French Canada. While the novel and novel reading *in general* were unfavourably regarded, novels written in a context of patriotism and morality were legitimized. Virgil Rossel observed that "L'Histoire, le roman historique, le roman de moeurs même, tels sont les genres littéraires qu'on cultive de préférence et avec le plus succès au Canada" (343). And, in an article that takes an institutional/systemic approach to this question, Jacques Allard confirms that

Je pars d'un de ces romans dont la forme est scolaire sinon enfantine. Il s'agit de *Pour la patrie* de Jules-Paul Tardivel, la caricature incarnée du discours clérical, qui décide tout à coup de s'emparer de la forme romanesque pour retourner contre Satan et le mal moderne ses armes mêmes. Ne serait-ce pas là un signe que le discours social puisse subir un effet pervers venant du littéraire? (12)

The numbers of preface characteristics also show that in the period between 1810 and 1860 the critical dimension of both English-Canadian and French-Canadian prefaces was prevalent, with the remaining characteristics evenly distributed. It is interesting that in the period 1860 to 1870 (Figure 5C) the critical aspect disappears from English-Canadian prefaces. This can perhaps be explained by the observation that in those years political awareness, due to the events surrounding Confederation, discouraged authors from expressing prefatorial views on literature. In general, this period, with regards to prefatorial characteristics, shows a diminished level of occurrence, which may be due to a lack of general prefatorial assertion. The strong showing of promotional characteristics in the period 1880 to 1900 (Figures 5E and 5F) may be an indication of the above mentioned "watershed" for Canadian literary publications and the authors' sudden awareness of a larger readership.

The difference in the explanatory characteristics between English-Canadian and French-Canadian prefaces is not significant. But perhaps the different occurrence of subgroups should be noted. The French-Canadian explanatory characteristics tended to consist of background explanations while the English-Canadian prefaces had a wider range, e.g. autobiographical and intention-explanatory characteristics.

Promotional characteristics in the typology show that both English-Canadian and French-Canadian authors were very seriously concerned with the state of their respective Canadian literatures. At the same time, the promotional characteristic often merged with the ethical, because in the case of thematic-promotional characteristics both expressed a religious-moral preoccupation. The English-Canadian prefaces showed some extraordinary deviation from the usual didactic and moral purpose: the promotion of novels written to entertain *only*. The exceptional effort of some English-Canadian prefacers to promote novels for entertainment may also have been the result of an awareness that the English-Canadian readership might be large enough to be able to absorb this type of novel. In other words, the author/prefacer was confident that there would be enough readers who admitted to reading without considering the morality of the story as the priority. This characteristic did not occur in the French-Canadian prefaces.

The overall typology of critical characteristics shows a wider range in the case of the English-Canadian prefaces as compared with the French-Canadian. However, the French-Canadian prefaces tended to be more elaborate and interested in literary theory and criticism. This can be seen in the previous Chapter where the data on literary theory and literary genre are presented.

The analysis of the length of prefaces offers some interesting results. Meaningful statistical comparison between English-Canadian and French-Canadian preface lengths could only be made after 1860, because before that time there were too few French-Canadian prefaces. The average length of the English-Canadian prefaces between 1800 and 1860 was 3.7 ± 0.8 (mean $\pm$ standard error, n=39) pages. After 1860 twenty-year periods were analysed. Between 1860 and 1880 lengths were 1.4 ± 0.2 (mean $\pm$ standard error, n=50) pages and 3.9 ± 1 (mean $\pm$ standard error, n=17) for English-Canadian and French-Canadian prefaces, respectively. This average shows a decrease in the length of English-Canadian perfaces to less than half from the 3.7 in the previous period. Between the English-Canadian and the French-Canadian prefaces the comparison shows that the French-Canadian prefaces were significantly longer. This discrepancy is even more pronounced in the next twenty-year period: 2.2 ± 0.3 (mean $\pm$ standard error, n=169) pages for the English-Canadian prefaces and 6.8 ± 1.42 (mean $\pm$ standard error, n=30) pages for the French-Canadian prefaces.

The first question here is why were the English-Canadian prefaces shorter? The answer may be found partially in a linguistic argument. If it is true that the English language is less verbose in comparison to French, that is, one tends to say in fewer and shorter words what one wants to say in English, the English-Canadian prefacers did just that. However, such an argument is obviously exaggerated. Another, perhaps more socio-literary, reason may be that the French-Canadian prefacers felt a greater need to communicate directly with their readers because they felt that the aim of patriotism and morality can thus be better and more clearly served. Since French-Canadian society and the French-Canadian readership were more homogeneous than the English-Canadian, the explanation of this authorial strategy is perhaps an acceptable hypothesis. The length of a preface may also have been dictated by the publisher. It may be that from the time of Julia Beckwith Hart, who said that it was her publisher who requested a preface, until later in the century English-Canadian (American, British) publishers wanted to save on space while the French-Canadian publishers did not. However, at this point there is no evidence to support this hypothesis.

An interesting dimension of the prefaces is the FFN phenomenon, introduced as data in the previous Chapter. This dimension is a link between the preface and the novel and as such, it usually contains theoretical discussions. For this reason it is difficult to classify it clearly in only one *ETL* category. The most appropriate *ETL* category for this dimension is the one which includes the text, i.e., the preface. The FFN of the prefaces is chiefly an *ETL* production component because it shows the literary and genre-theoretical views of the nineteenth-century English-Canadian novelists in the preface.

The high occurrence and importance of the FFN in English-Canadian prefaces does not, of course, preclude that the novels themselves were indeed "literary documentaries" or that their authors intended them to be such.[12] The phenomenon is analogous to what has been found in the novels of late nineteenth-century English literature. Terry Lowell, in his *Consuming Fiction* explains that "the restoration of the novel's literary credentials was marked by a decided shift back towards the dominance of a realist aesthetic" (74). If it is true that the English-Canadian novel was influenced in the nineteenth century by English literary developments, and this is an accepted view, then Lowell's observation confirms the genological interdependence between England and English-Canada. The primary aspect of the FFN orientation in the prefaces is that the English-Canadian novel, if its author aspired to reach a larger, general readership, had to write the novel with the "realist aesthetic" in mind.

Although the FFN phenomenon was not pronounced in the French-Canadian prefaces, the concern with the configuration of "facts and fiction" was present. With reference to the French-Canadian historical novel, David Hayne observes that "The whole problem of the relationship of history and fiction in historical novels puzzled the authors of nineteenth-century French Canada much more that it does their successors" (1945, 159). As mentioned previously, authors of historical novels did not follow, for obvious reasons, the pattern established by Walter Scott in providing historical sources in the preface, they still expressed their concern with it in the preface.

Literary theoretical discourse was fragmented as well as wide ranging in the English-Canadian prefaces. Terms such as "novel" and "romance" were not consistently used or defined. In the French-Canadian prefaces the theoretical discourse was usually combined with ethical (moral-religious) considerations. In general, the main thrust of French-Canadian prefaces seems to have been moral-religious *and* patriotic, hence, for example, the frequent justification for the historical novel in the prefaces.

It can be safely said that the nineteenth-century prefaces of English-Canadian and French-Canadian novels are homogeneous in many areas. At the same time, there are aspects of the English-Canadian prefaces that show "deviations" from this homogeneity. The prefaces' homogeneity consists of aspects such as the length and the general literary attitude of the time. Of course, this is a very general observation. As shown in the

---

12 The English-Canadian predominance of the FFN configuration could also be understood as a more stringent commitment to what Lennard J. Davis described in the history of the early English novel the "unity of news, novels, ideology, history, fact, and fiction" (223).

typology and as discussed in this Chapter, there are interesting and surprising exceptions. Importantly, neither the English-Canadian nor the French-Canadian prefaces show, either in their theoretical discourse or in their ethical (social, political, moral, etc.), characteristics of a defined progression or development. At the same time, the above Figures indicate a limited number of "trends", as I have attempted to show by the analysis of the graphs based on preface data.

3. The Theme and/or Setting of the Novels

As the data presented in Chapter three show, the theme and/or setting of both English-Canadian and French-Canadian novels was in the majority Canadian. This is a curious, if not surprising, aspect of the Canadian novel. If any analogy may be drawn, it would be facetious to propose that English, French, or German novelists of the nineteenth century wrote, thematically speaking, novels with mainly English, French, or German themes, respectively. It is true, however, that authors such as Dickens, Trollope, Reade, Balzac, Hugo, Freytag, Fontane, or Spielhagen wrote novels in which the characters and the setting were those of the author's nationality. But who would venture to classify these authors based on the themes or setting of their novels? Perhaps the "New World" was more important to the Canadian author than other settings, or, it was believed that book sales might be higher if the novel had a Canadian theme or setting. In contrast to canonical European authors, the thematics of Canadian novels becomes a factor because of the complex concept of the emerging literature. Obviously, this extends to questions of the mechanism of canonization and the designation of "Canadian".[13] Nevertheless, the themes and setting of Canadian novels are a valuable systemic indicator. In particular, the French-Canadian novels have often been analysed in their relationship to French-Canadian society. English-Canadian novels have not been as rigorously discussed. This is, of course, again a result of the canonization mechanisms of English-Canadian literature. It is obvious that the "survival" and "nature" themes were explored already in the nineteenth century.

In the *ETL* system of literature the data sheet category of the other arts belongs to the category of "Themen, Stoffe, Motive" (cf. Schmidt 1982, 104). The results from both English-Canadian and French-Canadian prefaces show that most likely there was little interaction between different forms of the arts. The situation of painting, sculpture, the performing arts in the nineteenth-century Canadas is generally marked by an "emerging Canadian" spirit, similar — although to a lesser extent — to what happened in literature. This is particularly true after 1840 (*The Canadian Encyclopedia* 3 1603-05). However, the objective output, at least according to the present perception of the period, was neither very dynamic, nor extensive (*The Canadian Encyclopedia* 3 1604, 1964, 2137, 2144). The low profile of the other arts in the Canadas may have been partially responsible for the lack of references to them in the prefaces.

---

13 For an interesting treatment of canon-building in the Canadian literatures see Lecker (1991), containing a number of articles dealing with this question from various points of view and of various levels of insights.

4. Prefatorial Discourse

The typology of the prefaces is of course an overall, however implicit, assessment of prefatorial discourse. The addressing of issues, the direct or indirect addressing of the readership or a specific readership group are intrinsically forms of discourse. Thus, the typological evaluation of the prefaces is implicitly a form of discourse analysis. Similarly, the length of the prefaces discussed above belongs also, in part, to that subcategory.

It is obvious from the data in the list of novels with prefaces that the majority of both English-Canadian and French-Canadian prefaces was titled "preface" and "préface", respectively. This follows the observation of Genette, pointed out in Chapter one, that the term "preface" is the most frequently used title for such text types. Another noteworthy term'nological and discursive feature in the English-Canadian prefaces is the frequent use of the word "perusal". The prefacers used the word "to peruse" or "perusal" when they were discussing the novel and they used these more frequently than the terms "to read" and "reading". The usage of this term is somewhat of a puzzle. The *OED* contains several meanings and definitions (1961, 7 738). These definitions suggest that "to peruse" means a more thorough reading. The examples in the dictionary of its use in the nineteenth century include several literary ones. For example, "1887 T. Hardy *Woodlanders* iv. 26 Our new neighbour is a strange deep perusing gentleman" (*OED* 1961, 7 738). In this quotation too, the term has the connotation of intensity. On the other hand, this is not my interpretation of its use in the prefaces, where the flavour of the term is more that of reading for relaxation — although this is not equivalent with reading for entertainment.

With regard to prefatorial narrative techniques, the majority of prefacers used the authorial "I" and the discourse was thus conducted in the form of *Ich-Erzählung*. A second frequent form of discourse was the third person narrative. This form of discourse usually identified the third person narrator as the "Author" of the preface at the end of the preface. Both discourse forms, *Ich-Erzählung* and the "Author"-signed third person narration, are a sign that the prefacer and the author of the novel are identical.

The fact that the majority of the prefaces were written mainly in the above two forms of narrative, is another indication in favour of the argument that the nineteenth-century English-Canadian and French-Canadian preface is a genre — if the argument that a certain level of uniformity is necessary for the characteristics of a genre is acceptable. The two dominant forms of narration indicate an attitude on the part of the prefacers best described as "direct". At the same time, this directness may also be perceived as a less sophisticated narrative technique and evidence of a less sophisticated relationship between prefacer and readership. The prefatorial narrative is of course connected to the narrative of the novel, since, as I pointed out previously, the majority of the prefacers are identical with the authors of the novels. Thus, findings about the narrative in the novel can serve as an indication of or analogy to the findings about the preface in this study. In the French-Canadian novel David M. Hayne observed that "Nine out of every ten of our stories are told from the point of view of an omniscient author, who recounts everything that happens everywhere" (1945, 114). Conceptually — although the first-person narrative is often limited both geographically and chronologically while the omniscient author's is not — the narrative technique of the omniscient author can be similar to the technique of the *Ich-Erzählung*, and thus Hayne's observation connects the shape and form of discourse in the French-Canadian novel and its preface:

The autobiographical narrative, moreover, is to all intents and purposes non-existent in French-Canadian historical novels; the device of telling a story from the point of view of a secondary actor, or from several simultaneous points of view, is also almost unknown. Here as elsewhere, we find that the novelist's art is still at a rudimentary stage: perhaps our contemporaries will capitalize on techniqies overlooked by their predecessors. (1945, 116)

Hayne's analysis of narration in the French-Canadian novel and the analysis of narration in the prefaces of the present study show that nineteenth-century French-Canadian narration was based on "directness", an attitude that was rooted in the context of patriotism and morality, leaving ambiguity and a changing of narrative voices, the essentially fictional, to be developed by later generations.[14] Generally, in the English-Canadian prefaces "directness" is also the prevalent narrative technique. However, the reason here may be somewhat different from that in the French-Canadian prefaces. It may be due to a larger thematic element of the nineteenth-century English-Canadian novel, namely, that of "local colour". Novels of local colour obviously aimed at a specific readership and the authors/prefacers may have felt that the preface ought to express the thematic proximity between the novel and its potential readership.[15]

The narratological "directness" of both the English-Canadian and French-Canadian prefaces predetermined the structure of the preface typology. Genette's proposed types of prefaces presupposed a large number of narrative forms in the preface, which Heyden showed in his work on the nineteenth-century French novel preface. As explained above, this was not the case in the English-Canadian or the French-Canadian prefaces. This is why Genette's types of prefaces were useful only from a limited perspective in the construction of English-Canadian and French-Canadian preface characteristics.

A last, but not least, important aspect of the prefaces is the prefacer's intentional manipulation of the reader. This study of the English-Canadian and of the French-Canadian prefaces did not result in finding such a discourse nuance. Unlike Wordsworth's manipulation of his readers in his preface to the *Lyrical Ballads*, discussed in Nabholtz's book *"My Reader My Fellow-Labourer..."*, or as in James's prefaces, this does not seem to be the case in the English-Canadian or the French-Canadian prefaces. Whether this is a sign of less sophistication or less self-confidence or of a more direct relationship between the prefacer and the readership as discussed above, cannot be established with certainty at this point. The assumption that because of the prefacer's clearly delineated aims, his "directness", the manipulation of the readership either did not occur to the prefacers/authors, or they decided against such strategies precisely for ethical reasons which, after all, is manifest in both English- and French-Canadian prefaces may be viable.

---

14 Although, as Rosmarin Heidenreich convincingly demonstrated, exceptions to this general observation occurred (cf. Heidenreich's analysis of Conan's *Angéline de Montbrun*).

15 On the local colour in nineteenth-century English-Canadian fiction cf. Bissell 24-40, 77-92.

B. *The Reception*

The reception of the preface has one feature that belongs to the *ETL* category of post-production processing. This aspect, essentially the ways that scholars use information found in prefaces, will be discussed in that category. Here, the reception of the preface by the readership is of importance. There are limited possibilities to analyse this relationship. The most immediate possibility is to see how the readership is mirrored in the preface. It must be noted, however, that the data of this relationship are limited and limited to data in English-Canadian prefaces.

Generally speaking, the prefacer perceived the preface negatively. This observation holds, if the few instances where there is a discernible reaction of the prefacer to the preface are acceptable as representative data. Most examples in Chapter three are, even if in nuances, more deprecative than appreciative. Overall, the prefacers' view seems to be that prefaces are not read by the readers. It may be of interest that in the two representative instances where the prefacer discusses the preface in a positive light, the prefacers have become canonical authors (Leprohon and Richardson).

The most obvious aspect of the reception category is the prefacer's address to the readership. The typology of the English-Canadian prefaces resulted in several subcategories that contain readership data. These subcategories show that the prefacers were aware of their readership, even if in a limited sense. On the other hand, the available data do not suggest that the prefacers/authors targeted certain readership groups as Heyden found in the prefaces to nineteenth-century French novels. Other preface studies, for example Ehrenzeller's or Riefstahl's, also demonstrate that prefacers consciously targeted certain readership groups. The answer why this was not so in nineteenth-century English or French Canada is to be found in the general composition of the readership in nineteenth-century Canada. Unfortunately, there has apparently been no study made on this topic. Thus, the answer, again, is hypothetical, based on information inferred from analogous data.

There is a general understanding in works on nineteenth-century Canadian literatures that the readership was limited to the privileged and that these privileged were not a numerous class. Although at this time there is virtually no empirical foundation for this accepted view, some data have been collected. Harvey J. Graff's Ph.D. thesis "Literacy and Social Structure in the Nineteenth-Century City" contains data which, although limited to a few cities in Ontario, offer the possibility of postulating a hypothesis about the nineteenth-century English-Canadian urban readership. Graff's findings were that in Ontario in 1861 93% of all males and 92.5 of all females were literate (cf. also Graff 1979). But, as Graff concedes, these percentages do not "always signify an ability to understand what was read" (1975, 413). He is obviously speaking about the difference between literacy and functional illiteracy. His most revealing statement about the nineteenth-century urban Ontario literacy rate is this: "All indicators, thus, suggest that the reading ability commonly attained was an imperfect one" (1975, 441). If this information is combined with what we may assume about the reading of novels in nineteenth-century English Canada, namely, that novel reading was frowned upon and that only certain novels, the morally acceptable ones, were generally read, the readership indeed becomes almost homogeneous and relatively small. Graff sees the cause of functional illiteracy in the poor state of institutional education. In his discussion of the secondary school system of nineteenth-century Ontario, he also mentions reading habits and concludes that

Reading fiction represented a negative, unwise use of literacy, wasteful to the individual and dangerous to society. "Novel reading," the *Christian Guardian* [Jan. 28, 1852] exclaimed, "is pernicious to man as an intellectual and a religious being. Novels make few appeals to reason. This neglect soon engenders an aversion to profound thought, which results in inability." Good men, moreover, were not often authors of novels; good men and women should not therefore be their readers. (1975, 446-47)

Examples found in prefaces confirm this attitude. Prefacers attempted to persuade against this generally accepted negative attitude towards the novel of the time. But their persuasion rested on their awareness of the importance of morally acceptable writing. This explains why the ethical aspect of the prefaces was so strong. The prefacers indeed needed to attempt to advocate the ethical, moral, and religious acceptability of their work — in response to what they thought their readership was like. Addressing of youth and women, as the examples show in the case of the English-Canadian prefaces, was particularly important. Graff writes that "The threat [of novel reading] was perhaps greatest to young unmarried women and to children, whose moral innocence it was most important to protect" (1975, 447). The resistance to novels, as Graff's study shows, was an almost total social fact. He documents his finding that "Schoolmen, not surprisingly, added their voices to the cries against novel reading" (447). Interestingly, the resistance to novel reading was not an attitude of only the leading strata of society (clergymen, educators, politicians, the upper classes). Graff found that the working class too, decried novel reading:

Importantly, however, the working class press censured the school system itself for the prevalence of this state of affairs. The public system, they reported, made attendance and reading instruction compulsory, and "then gives them dime novels for perusal, having previously given them a taste for such reading." (447)

Although it must be assumed that this negative attitude towards novel reading was all-pervasive, in my view its effect must have been more differentiated. Graff's study contains this seemingly contradictory observation:

The rise and easy availability of cheap, popular literature, aimed at the pleasure and amusement of the lower as well as the middle class, provided material which many would quite naturally find suited to their tastes. Easy to buy, sold on street corners and hawked on the pavements, within the financial grasp of all but the very poorest, this was material simply read, easily understood, appealing, pleasing, and exciting.... (447)

In this context, we must assume that although novel reading was decried, this was done with reference to a certain type of novel. Due to the fact that we do not have readership data as to what kinds those "cheap, popular" novels were, this part of the question too, must be hypothetical. The question and answer become even more complicated, because the "good" and "bad" novels, with regard to the novels examined in this study, are difficult to relate to each other. As we shall see in the appropriate *ETL* category, the canonization mechanisms of nineteenth-century English-Canadian literature were ethically and aesthetically oriented.

The literacy rate in French Canada was lower than in English Canada. David M. Hayne declared categorically that in nineteenth-century French Canada "Only a fraction of this tiny population could read and write" (1945, 67) and Allan Greer's study, "L'Alphabétisation et son histoire au Québec: état de la question", contains valuable information on the nineteenth-century Lower Canadian readership in statistical and descriptive forms. Greer's data are somewhat broader than those of Graff because they include rural and urban literacy ratios. A complicating aspect of Greer's data is that he used census numbers for his literacy calculations, thus limiting his data points. Greer, similarly to Graff, found that literacy did not necessarily mean a full ability to read *and* comprehend (27-45).[16] In 1861, when the Lower Canadian population was approximately 1.2 million (*The Canadian Encyclopedia* 3 1796), 61.8% of the rural, and 81.8 % of the urban population was moderately literate ("lire au moins") (Greer 44). By 1891 this did not change significantly, although the population did not increase by much either (*The Canadian Encyclopedia* 3 1796). The ratio was 67.3% for the rural, and 82.2% for the urban population (Greer 44). The limited readership of French-Canadian fiction is confirmed also by Maurice Lemire, in his article "Les Relations entre écrivains et éditeurs au Québec au XIXᵉ siècle". He states that fiction authors "donnent leurs livres aux institutions", i.e., to "bibliothèques de collèges, d'écoles et de paroisses" (1983, 217). This observation allows for the inference that the at this time higher output of published fiction did not mean a significantly higher level of readership, because it is more than likely that these libraries and parishes had a low rate of borrowing. In fact, the type of institutions receiving the donations did not indicate readership at all, because they were not public libraries. Based on these observations, the situation of novel reading was analogous with the situation in Ontario. However, one interesting aspect of Greer's data begs attention. He found that Lower Canadian female readers were more literate by 20% than male readers (38-44). This is dramatically different from the almost equal ratio found by Graff. At the same time, Greer questions the exact meaning of literacy. Thus, it appears that the majority of this group was functionally illiterate and therefore not capable of serious novel reading.

Had there been a significant ratio of urban Lower Canadian female novel readership, surely some preface data would have indicated this. However, the readership data of the French-Canadian prefaces are generally scarce and no targeting of any readership group occurred. On the contrary, as the data show, presented in the previous Chapter, the prefatorial readership address is general. Thus, we must accept that the readership is

---

16 This differentiation is important. In second language acquisition research distinction is made between the BICS (Basic Interpersonal Communication Skills) and CALP (Cognitive Academic Language Proficiency) levels. For novel reading a lower level of CALP would be necessary. It appears that Graff's or Greer's literacy figures would include no more than 40% of a lower level CALP.

perceived by the prefacers as a homogeneous, Roman Catholic, French-Canadian, and conquered population.

Another important question with regard to the readership is that of the type of novels read in the nineteenth-century Canadas and, consequently, the relationship between this choice and the preface. Mary Vipond contended in her study "Best Sellers in English Canada, 1899-1918: An Overview" that

By and large, Canadian middle-class reading tastes seem to have been more conservative than American ones; Canadians were slower to pick up a new author, but slower to abandon an old favourite too. ... The popular fiction of both countries depicted for the most part the lives of members of the middle class or aspirers to it. Religious, idealistic, filled with good intentions and thus able ultimately to triumph over both dilemma and adversity, the characters were guides and models for readers searching for hope and happiness in their own lives. (109-10)

This "conservative" attitude of the English-Canadian readership is reflected in the prefaces. As explained above, the readership was most likely a middle-class readership throughout the nineteenth century.[17]

In summary, nineteenth-century English-Canadian novel readership of the kinds of novels under study here, i.e., the novels with prefaces listed in the *Appendix* and in the majority "popular fiction" i.e., non-canonical, must be assumed to have been fairly small and homogeneous in English Canada. Although for slightly different reasons, the readership in French Canada appears to be similarly constituted. A further differentiation can be made that in English Canada the readership of these novels must have been somewhere between the "masses" of the "cheap, popular" novels and those, who were against the reading of novels because of their bad reputation. Both the French-Canadian and the English-Canadian novel readership and the prefacers/authors demonstrably knew of the negative attitude towards the novel and hence the prefacer wanted to assure the reader that his/her novel was not a "bad" or "immoral" one. It must be also considered that the popularity of "cheap" novel reading Graff discussed is in reference to an urban readership. This is important, when considering that the majority of the population in the Canadas was rural. The situation was similar in French Canada where the negative attitude towards novel reading existed and had been propagated by the Roman Catholic church. Taken together, the above observations indicate that the relationship between the prefacers/authors and the readership contained elements of strain in both English and French Canada in the sense that the readership consumed one type of reading material and the prefacers/authors were attempting to attract them to read another. At the same time, the authors/prefacers needed readership and needed to sell their product. It is perhaps for this reason that readership groups were only rarely targeted by the prefacers of nineteenth-century Canadian novelists. They recognized the necessity to speak to a "non descript" readership. The small readership and the hostile environment for the novel on the part of the educated, the churches, schools, etc., did not allow for the singling out

---

17 Although the "proletarian" novel existed in English Canada, neither the genre nor the readership could have been significant (cf. Watt 41-59).

of specific groups which were large enough to buy the novel specifically offered to them. This was, for obvious reasons, a situation dissimilar to that of England, France, or the United States.

C. *Processing*

In the case of nineteenth-century English-Canadian and French-Canadian novels it is important to note that a very large percentage of the novels first appeared in a serialized format. Exact statistical data are not available and it would go beyond the scope of this study to establish how many novels had been first published in a magazine or newspaper. However, the CIHM is presently working on the accumulation of the total magazine, newspaper, pamphlet, etc. publication of the nineteenth-century Canadian English and French publication industry. With reference to the prefaces, some examples in the typologies (i.e., acknowledgement) show that prefacers sometimes thanked the magazine or newspaper for the permission to re-publish the novel, now in book form.

The statistical figures for the place of publication of the English-Canadian novels confirms the generally accepted view that in the nineteenth century English Canada had strong ties with the "mother" country, England. At the same time, Canadian locations dominate in the publication figures. The following figures are a selection of the most frequent places of publication: Toronto (74), London, England (69), Montreal (33), New York (24), Boston (8), Chicago (5), Detroit (3), Philadelphia (1), Ottawa (4), Saint John (4). In comparison to French-Canadian locations, there was a smaller number of small cities as places of publication, such as Hamilton, London (Ontario), Fredericton, Guelph, Halifax, Charlottetown, and Windsor (Nova Scotia). Obviously, these figures have limited value because they would have to be related to the places of publication of all novels.

The analysis of the English-Canadian publishers offers some interesting observations. According to George L. Parker, in his *The Beginnings of the Book Trade in Canada*, the Toronto publisher Hunter and Rose had the longest list of Canadian fiction (179). This is not borne out by the publishers' numbers of this study. Hunter and Rose published novels *without* prefaces. In fact, they published only four novels with prefaces. Why this was so may be explained precisely by the larger publishing capacity of this publisher. Perhaps smaller publishers thought it more necessary to include a preface. Other publishers, some of which are not mentioned in Parker's book, were as follows: Toronto: Briggs (24), Musson (7), Poole (2), Williamson, Clougher, Cooper (1 each); Montréal: Lovell (15), Drysdale (3), Coates (2), Gazette, Grafton (1 each).

The figures for the publication places of French-Canadian novels with prefaces indicate a minimal attachment to the "mother" country, France. Montréal was 26 times the place of publication, Québec City 16 times, while Paris only 4 times. The publisher with the highest number (4) of novels is Senécal, followed by Desbarats (2) and Beauchemin (2), all in Montréal, and Brousseau (3) in Québec City. The following publishers appear with one book each: Chenevert, Patrie, Pigeon, Chevrier, Leprohon, Rolland, Darveau, David, Cérat, Cadieux, and Germany. This distribution indicates a higher level of individuality on the part of the authors/prefacers in the selection of their publishers in comparison to the number of publishers of English-Canadian novels with prefaces. It does not seem probable that the proportionally high number of publishers of French-Canadian novels with prefaces is a result of specific publishing trade idiosyncrasies. Rather, the shape and form, the presentation of the novels is also a subcategory of processing. It is of note that while of the total of English-Canadian novels with prefaces, 14 contain illustrations, none of the French-Canadian texts does. The illustrations may be an indication of the fact that many English-Canadian novels had an adventure or nature theme, while the French-Canadian novels more often had a historical theme. In essence, the novels with illustrations had a different, perhaps less "intellectual", readership, because they had an adventure theme. For this reason, the author and/or the publisher may have decided to include the illustrations.

Among the publishers perhaps the Lovells of Montreal and the U.S. are the most interesting. The bad treatment of Kirby by John Lovell is well known in English-Canadian literature (cf. Parker 161-65, 190-93). What is interesting is that the dedications and acknowledgements of novels, from the number of novels with prefaces, to the Lovells, is very high. In most of these dedications and acknowledgements the prefacer refers to the efforts of Lovell, either the individual or the firm, to promote and aid *Canadian* literary production. This may be, of course, a result of the authors' more or less obligatory gratitude because they were published, but not necessarily so. According to Parker,

It is safe to say that many of these books [fiction by Canadian authors] issued by local booksellers and printers were paid for by the authors themselves. Such books do not seem to have been issued or marketed abroad, even though some of them had modestly good sales in this country. (183)

If this were indeed the case, perhaps the prefacers/authors did not *need* to acknowledge Lovell's support of Canadian literature. Also, the absence of similar acknowledgements and dedications to other publishers indicates more than just rhetoric. Based on these prefatorial data, it is possible to say that the Kirby affair was an exception and that the Lovells were indeed very important and instrumental in the development of nineteenth-century English-Canadian literature.

D. *Post-Production Processing*

The systemic significance of the distribution between canonical and non-canonical novels with prefaces is negligible. Canonization in English-Canadian fiction is at best debatable and although it is possible to provide an account of canonical *versus* non-canonical novels with prefaces from the lists in the *Appendix*, the count would not be meaningful. The reason for this is the following. Klinck's *Literary History of Canada* is the most comprehensive (detailed/factual and analytical) work on English-Canadian literature. If canonization means, among other things, a mention in a literary history such as Klinck's, many authors on the CIHM list are non-canonical. However, Klinck often mentions authors and works in a non-canonical perspective. In the case of French-Canadian prefaces the problem of the canon is less complicated because the novels with prefaces are, in the majority, from the canonical literature. These observations, sweeping as they may be, are an appropriate introduction to one of the more important issues of the nineteenth-century Canadian literatures, namely, "what was, if there was, the literature of nineteenth-century Canada?" But first, what is canonization? On its most self-explanatory level, canonization means a *cumulative process*, among other factors such as the appearance of literary production in literary post-production processing. In other words, authors and texts, minimally, must appear in the secondary literature, including literary histories; thus, the more exhaustive the literary history, the more extensive the canonical literature. In the history of the nineteenth-century Canadian literatures this preliminary element of canonization did not occur. The reason for this lies in the strongly aesthetically oriented literary environment of nineteenth-century Canada, particularly that of English Canada. At the outset, the literary establishment of English Canada, more specifically, the bureaucratic machinery such as the National Library for instance, did not keep any lists of books published in Canada (Parker 178). Until the recent compilation of the CIHM, the most complete bibliography of Canadian works was the *Check List of Canadian Literature and Background Materials 1628-1950* by R.E. Watters, first published in 1959. In English-Canadian literature this list was the only reference work in which nineteenth-century authors appeared. Of course, it was but a list. Thus, while this list was a first step toward canonization in the above sense, it was a limited one. Canonization obviously means, as a next step, the analysis and evaluation of literary texts. This happens, in a cumulative manner, by the writing of literary histories. To date, as mentioned, the only English-Canadian literary history that has shown an attempt to be factual and analytical at the same time, is Carl F. Klinck's *Literary History of Canada: Canadian Literature in English* of 1965 (2nd edition 1976, 3rd edition 1989). At the same time, one must take into account that the canonization of nineteenth-century English-Canadian novelists did, on the other hand, occur in works written by Logan and French, Rhodenizer, Pacey, Lecker, or Moss. These literary histories contain analyses of selected novelists, who were "chosen" based on aesthetic and belletristic criteria.[18] The underlying reason for the lack of adequate literary histories, analytical works, and generally, the largely unrecognized state of nineteenth-century English-Canadian literature is well summarized in the *Canadian Encyclopedia*:

Samuel Taylor Coleridge, a principal source of modern literary theory in English, made little direct impression in 19th-century Canada, largely because literary life in Canada shared the anti-theoretical biases of Victorian England. ... Great or successful literature was the occasion for ostensive definition (comparison with similar points of excellence drawn from Homer, Dante, Shakespeare or Milton) or the invocation of a moral standard; it was not the occasion for reflection on particular literary arts, or for isolation and analysis of a text's distinctive features. (2 1227)

Obviously, such a clearly aesthetic and "high-brow" environment did not permit the notation and study, and therefore canonization, of English-Canadian authors. (I should like to mention here that in the English-Canadian prefaces, references were made to the

---

18 Cf. e.g., J.D. Logan and Donald D. French, *Highways of Canadian Literature* (1924); Desmond Pacey, *Creative Writing in Canada* (1952); Vernon Blair Rhodenizer, *Canadian Literature in English* (1965); John Moss, ed., *The Canadian Novel: Beginnings* (1980); and Robert Lecker, Jack David, Ellen Quigley, eds. *Canadian Writers and Their Works* (1983).

same authors. Thus, the article in the *Canadian Encyclopedia* is confirmed by data in the prefaces).

It is acknowledged among comparatists of the English-Canadian and French-Canadian literatures that English-Canadian literary scholarship is in need of much work in many areas, particularly in those of the nineteenth century. The next two quotations will illustrate the necessity of a Canadian literary history of the nineteenth century (or of the twentieth century, for that matter) that is detailed and analytical, and at the same time is systemic, thus taking account of the totality of the literary period. George Parker writes in his *The Beginnings of the Book Trade in Canada*, when discussing nineteenth-century English-Canadian fiction: "Many, perhaps all, of these books [i.e., nineteenth-century novels] are relevant to our understanding of late nineteenth-century colonial society as it struggled towards a new identity and self-assurance" (183). In an earlier publication, Elizabeth Waterston stated that

reading these old books as social historians or as literary critics, however, we suddenly realize with a blush of self-awareness that we turn the pages with quickened interest not because they prove something about evolution or illustrate national motifs. We read these best sellers of the past basically because they give us the same pleasures they gave their thousands of readers when they first came out.... (445-46)

The situation is somewhat different with French-Canadian novels of the nineteenth century. Thanks to the work of several groups of scholars which resulted in the *Dictionnaire des oeuvres littéraires du Québec*, one may assume that attention was paid to the whole of nineteenth-century French-Canadian literature. In short, the *ETL* definition that canonization occurs, in part "nach dem Ziel, bestimmte ästhetische Normen durchzusetzen (sei es stabilisierend, sei es gegen konkurrierende Normen)" (Schmidt 1982, 116), is exemplified in French-Canadian post-production processing.

As the example of Cook's *The Regenerators* shows, information contained in English-Canadian prefaces was used. These instances are an indication, however limited, of the level of post-production processing of the prefaces. Importantly, the French-Canadian prefaces underwent a different history, mainly due to the canonization mechanisms explained above. It is significant, indeed, that the French-Canadian prefaces were recognized earlier than the English-Canadian prefaces as valuable texts. For example, the nineteenth-century scholar Du Bled used the contents of a preface by Taché to underscore his analysis of French-Canadian literature (880). In the twentieth century, when Canadian scholars began to study nineteenth-century French-Canadian literature, the preface again caught their attention. The following quotation from David Hayne's M.A. thesis (1944) will illustrate this early attention paid to prefaces in Canadian scholarship:

In general, French-Canadian novels of the last century are eminently moral works, yet criticism of the novel on moral grounds continued until the end of the century. The prefaces of several of our novels reveal the authors' concern lest their works be classed with the "mauvais romans" everywhere in disrepute. (82)

This interest in the prefaces remained with French-Canadian scholars and as recently as 1983 Javier Garcia-Mendez published an article "Les Romanciers du XIXe siècle face à leurs romans: notes pour la reconstitution d'une argumentation" in which he ascribes "topos" to the prefaces, and discusses the FFN phenomenon (331-45). Thus he preceded, at least conceptually, this study's French-Canadian typology and one systemic aspect.

Concerning the problem of canonization it can be said that the authors on the French-Canadian list are almost in their totality canonical authors — because of the exhaustive inclusion of authors in the compilation. From the authors on the English-Canadian list, depending on the secondary source used, at the most 45% are canonical.

As a last aspect of the *ETL* categories, the subject of the literary institution must be discussed. In *The Canadian Encyclopedia* it is noted that:

The history of English-Canadian literary criticism has also involved a struggle to promote Canadian literature by providing it with a literary institution: publishers, readers, reviewers, booksellers, literary associations, journals, reference works, textbooks and university courses. Even before Confederation, Edward Hartley Dewar concerned himself with the economic difficulties of Canadian authors and publishers. (2 1228)

Although theoretically there is a distinction between the "literary institution" and the "literary system", as discussed in Chapter one, this short reference to the literary institution shows an awareness of the concept. Unfortunately, there are very few data with regards to the prefaces and their relationship with elements of the literary institution or system. George Parker, in his previously mentioned book, *The Beginnings of the Book Trade in Canada*, discusses in one section the relationship between Canadian authors and their publishers. With regard to John Lovell, there seems to have been a strong awareness among English-Canadian novelists that this publisher effectively supported Canadian fiction publishing, and that this is observable in the preface data. Parker's study indicates that for copyright, economic, and market reasons the situation of publishing in the 1870s was gloomy in English Canada (233). He observes that Canadian imprints as a rule did not sell outside Canada. Thus, many authors had to find publishers abroad. This does not seem to be the case with prefaced novels, although there is at least one example of prefatorial advertisement for the "Canadian" product, which indicates the necessity to attract readers. John Lovell inserted a publisher's advertisement into Ebenezer Clemo's novel *Canadian Homes, or, the Mystery solved...* (1858).[19] As shown above, the majority of these novels were published in Canada. In turn, this may be an indication that prefaces were thought to be more necessary in Canadian imprints than in British or American imprints. Parker's impression, based on primary sources such as Sara Jeanette Duncan, is that the feeling of English-Canadian authors was that it was necessary to write for American readership and that the reason for the lack of Canadian publishers of fiction was that "there was still considerable antagonism in the country towards popular fiction as time-wasting and immoral" (234). This observation, taken together with the fact that the majority of prefaced novels were Canadian imprints, allows

---

19 A discussion of this issue is included in Edwards 147-54.

a hypothesis that English-Canadian authors found it necessary to write prefaces because of the place of imprint (Canada, i.e., "colony") and because of the precarious, although accepted, position of the genre *per se* — whether the book was then sold in Canada or abroad. As mentioned before, the choice of publishers by the French-Canadian prefacers/authors is greater than that of the English-Canadian. The data show that the French-Canadian novel with preface was published in Lower Canada, mainly in Montréal, by a relatively large number of publishers. These publishers, for whatever reason, do not seem to have issued a number of novels, but only one each. Maurice Lemire, in his article "Les Relations entre écrivains et éditeurs au Québec au XIXᵉ siècle" presents, based on a few examples, the observation that the Lower Canadian publishing industry was very limited with regard to fiction (Lemire speaks mainly of poetry publications [1983, 207-24]). The case of Fréchette is telling: he succeeded in getting some financial reward for his work, but only when a translated copy of his *La Noël au Canada* was simultaneously published in the U.S., Canada, and Britain. And even then he sold very little in English Canada and England (Lemire 1983, 221). Ultimately, "Par une ironie du sort assez cruelle, Fréchette se rend compte que son meilleur marché reste le Québec" (Lemire 1983, 221). Generally, the situation of the French-Canadian author was similar to that of the English-Canadian: most had to pay for the publication of their work or they had to rely on subscription sales. Obviously, this situation was not conducive to an economically rewarding relationship between authors and publishers in either English or French Canada.

Although translation is not an explicit category in *ETL*, it can be deduced from cursory references that it belongs to the category of post-production processing (Schmidt 1980, 278, 286-87). The Canadian scholar Barbara Godard wrote in one of her prefaces that "One could write a history of translation, a history of the relationships between author and translator, indeed between author and reader, by writing a history of the preface as genre" (3). This does not seem to be true, however, in the case of the Canadian literatures. Reflecting the state of translation in the nineteenth-century Canadian literatures, prefaces to translated texts are rare.[20] From the CIHM list of novels with prefaces, five prefaces to translations from English to French, three from French to English, and one from English to German can be identified.[21] In the case of English to French, the number will have to be reduced to three *bona fide* prefaces, because in one case (Clemo's *Canadian Homes...*, 1858) the preface is the literal translation of the original English preface. The same applies to the number of French to English translations in the case of Proulx's preface to *Pierre Cholet...* (1888).

---

20 On the precarious state of nineteenth-century translations see, for example, Hayne 1983, 35-46. Also, Kathy Mezei's *Bibliography of Criticism on English and French Literary Translations in Canada / Bibliographie de la critique des traductions littéraires anglaises et françaises au Canada* contains important sources.

21 English to French: Clemo, *Le Foyer canadien...*, tr. H. Émile Chevalier (1859), De Mille, *Le Baron americain...*, tr. Louis Ulbach (1877), Kirby, *Le Chien d'or: Légende canadienne*, tr. Pamphile LeMay (1884), Leprohon, *Le Manoir de Villerai...*, tr. E.L. de Bellefeuille (1861), *Antoinette de Mirecourt...*, tr. Joseph-Auguste Genand (1881). French to English: d'Ennery, *A Martyr...*, tr. Aristide Filiatreault (1886), Proulx, *Pierre Cholet...*, tr. M.J. Murphy (1888), Aubert de Gaspé, *The Canadians of Old...*, tr. Charles G.D. Roberts (1890). English to German: Saunders, *Der schöne Sepp...*, tr. A. Henrich (1896).

In comparison with the "normal" corpus the prefaces to translated novels do not reveal typological novelties. There are, however, some systemic indicators worthy of note. The earliest translation preface is among those to English texts rendered into French, de Bellefeuille's translation of Leprohon's *Le Manoir de Villerai...* (1861). David Hayne, in his article mentioned above, wrote that "When the full story is told, it will undoubtedly constitute a revealing chapter in the history of literary translation as religious politics" (Hayne 1983, 40). Unfortunately, the preface does not contain an indication of "religious politics" or other systemic data of significance. However, the translated novel indicates already on the title page a systemic environment, because the translator is introduced by "Traduit de l'Anglais avec la bienveillante permission de l'auteur". This statement is there for the legitimization of the novel and not for reasons of publication regulations.[22] The preface is titled "Note du traducteur", thus clearly distinguishing author from translator. De Bellefeuille wrote a preemptive preface but without any reference to possible faults, stylistic or otherwise, that the original might have had in his view. The original is highly praised on moral, patriotic, and narratological grounds; hence the preface's critical nature. The translator asserts that the reader of this historical novel will be satisfied: "Celui qui lira avec attention le *Manoir de Villerai*, aura une connaissance assez étendue de l'histoire de cette époque". With reference to the preface as a genre, de Bellefeuille added an interesting critical note, albeit of a rhetorical type: "Je devais ces remarques à l'auteur, au public et au livre. Sans vouloir faire une préface, dont un roman n'a pas besoin, le lecteur me permettra de lui dire quelques mots sur le *Manoir de Villerai*, avant de commencer à le parcourir". The "Note des editeurs" in the translation of Leprohon's *Antoinette de Mirecourt...* to the 1881 edition, a translation made by Joseph-Auguste Genand in 1865 (Hayne 1983, 40), is largely a necrology on Rosanna-Eleanor Leprohon née Mullins, with some critical excerpts from journals. The preface again asserts that her novels are morally acceptable literary works.[23] A more interesting preface is the one provided for the translation of James De Mille's *Le Baron américain* (1877), translated and prefaced by Louis Ulbach and published by Ulbach as his own work in Paris.[24] The "Avis au lecteur" contains a correction of the decision to publish under the translator's name, and Ulbach strongly promotes the "romancier americain" James De Mille to the French readership. Ulbach also mentions the need to "franciser" the original text. Thus he alludes to problems of translation, however briefly. The most important translation preface is in Kirby's *Le Chien d'or...*, titled "Pourqoui Le Chien d'Or traduit en Français" and signed "Les Éditeurs". The translation contains a second preface by Pamphile LeMay, titled "La Légende du Chien d'Or". This preface is a historical explanation of the novel's theme. The preface titled "Pourquoi..." has been ascribed to Pamphile LeMay in Québécois-Canadian scholarship,[25] although it was more likely written by F.-X.-A. Trudel, editor of *L'Étendard*. The preface is mainly

---

22 Literary texts or authors were not, at the time, legally protected with regards to translation.

23 It may be of note that in this preface the author is described as having been born in 1832. In the CIHM she is listed as born in 1829.

24 This translation is not listed in the *Dictionnaire des oeuvres littéraires du Québec*.

25 Cf. Guildo Rousseau's *Préfaces des romans québécois du XIXe siècle* (75).

explanatory and ethical. As the title of the preface suggests, its author explains why this novel is worthy of a French-Canadian readership. The religious-historical polarity of English and French Canada is alluded to, in this case in a positive context:

Nous avons voulu faire apprécier par nos littérateurs l'admirable parti qu'un homme, qui pourtant n'a ni notre foi, ni nos sentiments nationaux, et dont la langue maternelle est la langue anglaise, a su tirer d'une courte période de notre histoire.

LeMay proceeds to praise French-Canada's religiosity by a comparison with French literature and society. He mentions the French "immoral" novel, while at the same time he praises the contemporary religious and moral section of French society, which, in his view, is the basis of French cultural superiority: "La France catholique est encore, Dieu merci, au premier rang des nations civilisées, par la science, l'inspiration et le génie littéraire de ses auteurs catholiques". He mentions several examples of these "auteurs catholiques": Féval, Lamothe, Buet, de Navery, de Chandeneux, Fleuriot. His argumentation for the morally and religiously acceptable novel includes a correct assessment of the situation of the English-Canadian novel:

Les ouvrages de certains romanciers anglais, dûs même à des auteurs protestants, sont sous ce rapport beaucoup meilleurs que nombre de romans français que l'on s'accoutume à considerer comme n'étant pas mauvais. Parce que sans cesse la foi chrétienne y est affirmée et les personnages y adorent et servent Dieu. L'enseignement chrétien s'en dégage et exerce son influence sur le lecteur.

Thus, the "moral" novel becomes a Canadian trademark, perhaps even a genre. Although the prefaces appreciates the morally acceptable status quo of the French-Canadian and English-Canadian novel, the polarity of religion, which implicitly results in French-Canadian and English-Canadian historical adversity, forces him to acknowledge the difference in religion, i.e., Catholic versus Protestant: "Nous n'oserions pas recommender ce livre comme une oeuvre de doctrine parfaitement irréprochable. On ne doit pas oublier que c'est un protestant qui écrit".

In the case of French to English translations, Proulx's *L'Enfant perdu et retrouvé ou Pierre Cholet* (1887) published as *Pierre Cholet, or, the Recovered Kidnapped Child* in 1888 is similar to the novel of Ebenezer Clemo. The translation of the novel included the literal translation of the original French preface. Its characteristics have been discussed in Chapter two and its statistical and systemic elements have been incorporated into the discussion presented in Chapters three and four. This is also true of Clemo's translated preface.

Philippe Aubert de Gaspé's *The Canadians of Old* (1890) contains the well known "Introduction" by Charles G.D. Roberts. It is a critical preface, including a historical perspective with reference to the English-Canadian and French-Canadian question of history, and biographical notes on the author. Another noteworthy preface is Aristide Filiatreault's to the French author's Adolphe d'Ennery's novel *A Martyr; or, a Victim of the Divorce Law: A Novel* (1886). Although this novel is not French Canadian, the preface was written by an important French-Canadian critic and author (*Dictionnaire*

669-71) and it contains references to French-Canadian literary life. The preface is significant in that it defends the French novel in general, although, at the same time, it rejects the "pornographic" and "immoral" writings of Zola and other such authors. Filiatreault analyses the novel he translated as a novel with "stirring scenes of the greatest effect", in which "from the first page to the last the reader is kept in a state of thrilling excitement". Beyond this promotional element, he inserted preemptive and apologetic elements into the preface claiming that this was his first translation and that its publication was the result of the insistence of "some literary friends, who, I am afraid, were partial to its merits".

An exceptional case is Saunder's *Der schöne Sepp...* (1896), a translation of *Beautiful Joe...* (1895). The promptness with which the translation appeared is by itself significant. More importantly, the fact that it was translated into German and published in Philadelphia is an indication of a sizable German-American readership. On the CIHM copy, there is a hand-written note, most likely by Marshall Saunders herself:

This book is presented to McMaster University by Marshall Saunders. 1932. Sec. pa.tem of the American Baptist Pub. Sty. The German book was first brought out in Hamburg Germany by the Baptist Pub. house. Then the Baptists moved to Cassel. Col. Banes had this edition for the U.S.A. and Canada.

The German edition differs from the English one in the structure of the prefaces. The English edition contains three: one by the author, one by Ishbel Aberdeen, and one by Hezekiah Butterworth, an official with the Boston Humane Society. The English edition was obviously intended for a Canadian readership and this is underscored by the preface from the Countess Aberdeen. The printed prefaces in the German edition do not suggest publication for a Canadian readership, the American being obviously due to the fact that it was published in Philadelphia. The preface by the Countess Aberdeen has been dropped. Although the "Einleitung" by Hezekiah Butterworth in the German edition is almost a verbatim translation of his "Introduction" for the English edition, there are some interesting differences. For example, in the German text there is a section in which this prefacer explains his reasons for awarding the prize to the novel, as the "Mitglied des Prüfungskomitees für die der humanen Gesellschaft gesandten Preisschriften". This section is not in the English version and neither is the prefacer's function in the Humane Society mentioned. Most likely, these changes are the result of decisions with reference to the need to assure the readership that the novel had already obtained a significant level of recognition by winning the Humane Society's prize, thus vouching for a certain quality. The reason for dropping the preface by Ishbel Aberdeen is obvious. Although the hand-written note indicates a Canadian readership, the Philadelphia edition was obviously intended for an American audience. Most likely, the publisher did not think it opportune to include the preface of the wife of a Canadian Governor-General in an edition intended to attract a mainly American readership.

CONCLUSION

J.G. Bourinot, in his *Our Intellectual Strength and Weakness*, said in 1893: "there is one respect in which Canadians have never won any marked success, and that is in the novel or romance" (27). This, of course, may be a valid statement in the context of traditional, aesthetics/"high brow" oriented literary criticism. From a socio-literary point of view, literature ought not be studied by measuring the value of a literary text by standards derived from canonical texts only. Rather, it ought to be studied by paying attention to a "whole", i.e., a system of literature. This does not mean that all literary texts included in systemic literary studies will become canonical texts; the systemic study of literature entails value differentiation, too. But such an approach specifically requires the study of non-canonical literature. Thus, in the *terra incognita* of nineteenth-century comparative Canadian literature a minor type of text, the preface, becomes the object of literary study. The preceding study has attempted the discovery and analysis of the nineteenth-century English-Canadian and French-Canadian novel preface. The study was based on a body of prefaces which, at least in the case of the English-Canadian novels, has not, until now, been compiled or studied. The study of the prefaces was based on the theory and methodology of the systemic and empirical approach to literature, *ETL*.

Recently, several well-known scholars have postulated that there is a need for a preface typology. Within this framework and because a typology intrinsically responds to this theory's demand for empirical data, a typology of English-Canadian and French-Canadian prefaces forms an important part of this work. The typology thus serves two purposes: it serves to establish the preface as a genre and provides data for the systemic analysis of the prefaces.

The English-Canadian and French-Canadian prefaces in this study consist of a delineated corpus of prefaces to novels in the nineteenth-century English-Canadian and French-Canadian literatures. The possibility of electronic data accumulation and the possibility of reading the actual texts on microfiche made the delineation of the corpus possible. If this study is a work on the preface as a genre and an element of the literary system, more importantly it is an attempt to chart more precisely the relatively unknown period of nineteenth-century English-Canadian literature and the still insufficiently recognized comparative dimension of the Canadian literatures.

The results of the empirical data, i.e., accumulation, typology, and analysis of the prefaces are multi-faceted. The structure of the *ETL* categories, of course, determines this. At the same time, the *ETL* categories also determined the analytical aspect of this study. The *ETL* categories and their analytical aspects resulted in some unexpected observations. For example, the lack of address of specific readership groups is evidence that nineteenth-century English-Canadian and French-Canadian novel readership was homogeneous and privileged, i.e., from and for the educated classes only. This confirms the assumptions of such scholars as Yves Dostaler, Harvey J. Graff, Ramsay Cook, and Dennis Duffy. Both English-Canadian and French-Canadian prefaces show that morals and religion were an important socio-literary factor in nineteenth-century Canada, emanating from Protestantism and Catholicism, respectively. The prefaces seem, in general, to reflect major social and literary trends within nineteenth-century Canada. At the same time, they do not contain manifestations of more detailed attitudes or opinions about specific social, intellectual, economic, and/or literary development, or occurrences. Although in their totality the prefaces represent a more or less homogeneous authorial attitude in the two literatures, several examples illustrate exceptions. (E.g. the assertion of some prefacers that their novel is strictly to entertain and not to edify.)

The number of the novel prefaces, in relation to the number of published novels, their form, contents, the typological characteristics, etc., summarily establish that the novel preface in the nineteenth-century Canadian literatures was a genre on its own. Based on the demonstrated typological characteristics — specifically those of emerging literature, the apologetics due to the prefacer/authors' inexperience, etc. — even the argument that the nineteenth-century English-Canadian and French-Canadian preface is a *specific Canadian literary genre* could be put forward. As a genre, by virtue of its properties presented in this study, the prefaces show that they act as an element of the literary system and that, at the same time, systemic mechanisms have been embedded in their text. The comparison of the prefaces revealed that, although for different reasons, this genre is characterized by more similarities than differences within the Canadian literatures. Having said this, the prefaces also reveal specific English-Canadian or French-Canadian properties which, in turn, point to differences in the mechanisms of the Canadian literary system.

WORKS CITED

Angenot, M., J. Bessière, D. Fokkema, and E. Kushner. *Théorie littéraire*. Paris: PUF, 1989.

Asor Rosa, A. "Il letterato e le istituzioni", *Letteratura italiana*. Torino: Einaudi, 1982-.

Adams, T.D. "To Prepare a Preface to Meet the Faces That You Meet: Autobiographical Rhetoric in Hawthorne's Prefaces", *ESQ* 23.2 (1977): 89-98.

Allard, J. "Du Littéraire et du social au Québec: l'influence des livres", G. Kurgan-van Hentenryk, éd. *La Question sociale en Belgique et au Canada: XIXᵉ-XXᵉ siècles*. Bruxelles: U de Bruxelles, 1989. 9-18.

Ansorge, H.-J. *Art und Funktion der Vorrede im Roman von der Mitte des 18. Jahrhunderts bis zum Ende des 19. Jahrhunderts*. Würzburg: Julius-Maximillians-Universität, 1969.

Awuyah, C.K. *The Development of a National Literature in Ghana*. Ph.D. diss. U of Alberta, Comparative Literature, 1991.

Bales, K. "Hawthorne's Prefaces and Romantic Perspectivism", *ESQ* 23.2 (1977): 69-88.

Barsch, A. "Empirische Literaturwissenschaft", V. Meid, ed. *Literatur Lexikon: Begriffe, Realien, Methoden*. München Gütersloh: Bertelsmann Lexikon Verlag, 1992a. Vol. 13. 206-09.

Barsch, A. "Handlungsebenen des Literatursystems", *SPIEL — Siegener Periodicum zur Internationalen Empirischen Literaturwissenschaft* 11.1 (1992b): 1-23.

Bélisle, L.-A. *Dictionnaire général de la langue francaise au Canada*. Québec: Bélisle, 1954.

Bennett, T. *Outside Literature*. London and New York: Routledge, 1990.

Bissell, C.T. "Literary Taste in Central Canada during the Late Nineteenth Century", L. McMullen, ed. *Twentieth Century Essays on Confederation Literature*. Ottawa: Tecumseh, 1976. 24-40.

Blase, M.G. *Institution Building: A Source Book*. Columbia: U of Missouri P, 1986.

Blodgett, E.D. "Canadian Criticism and European Theory", *Zeitschrift der Gesellschaft für Kanada-Studien* 11.2 (1986): 5-16.

Bourdieu, P. "Questions of Method", E. Ibsch, D. Schram, and G. Steen, eds. *Empirical Studies of Literature: Proceedings of the Second IGEL-Conference, Amsterdam 1989*. Amsterdam-Atlanta, GA: Rodopi, 1991. 19-36.

Bourdieu, P., K. van Rees, S.J. Schmidt, and H. Verdaasdonk. "The Structure of the Literary Field and the Homogeneity of Cultural Choices", E. Ibsch, D. Schram, and G. Steen, eds. *Empirical Studies of Literature: Proceedings of the Second IGEL-Conference, Amsterdam 1989*. Amsterdam-Atlanta, GA: Rodopi, 1991. 427-43.

Bourinot, J.G. *Our Intellectual Strength and Weakness: A Short Historical and Critical Review of Literature, Art and Education in Canada*. Montreal: Foster Brown — London: Bernard Quaritch, 1893.

Boynard-Frot, Janine. *Un Matriarcat en procès: analyse systématique de romans canadiens-français, 1860-1960*. Montréal: PU de Montréal, 1982.

Brunet, M. *Écrit du Canada Français III*. Montréal: Hurtubise, 1957.

Brumm, U. "Hawthorne's *The Custom-House* and the Problem of Point of View in Historical Fiction", *Anglia* 93 (1975): 385-415.

Busch, U. "Vorwort und Nachwort", *Neue Sammlung* 1 (1961): 349-56.

The Canadian Encyclopedia 2nd Edition. Edmonton: Hurtig, 1988.

Carlson, T.C. "Fictive Voices in Melville's Reviews, Letters, and Prefaces", *Interpretations* 6 (1974): 39-46.

Caws, P. *Structuralism: The Art of the Intelligible*. Atlantic Highlands, NJ: Humanities Press International, 1988.

Cook, R. *The Regenerators: Social Criticism in Late Victorian English Canada*. Toronto Buffalo London: U of Toronto P, 1985.

Dandurand, A. *Le Roman canadien-français*. Montréal: A. Lévesque, 1937.

Davis, L.J. *Factual Fictions: The Origins of the English Novel*. New York: Columbia UP, 1983.

Daymond, D. and L. Monkman, eds. *Canadian Novelists and the Novel*. Ottawa: Borealis, 1981.

Der Sprach-Brockhaus. Leipzig: Brockhaus, 1935.

Der Sprach-Brockhaus. Wiesbaden: F.A. Brockhaus, 1984.

Derrida, J. *La Dissémination*. Paris: Seuil, 1972.

Dictionary of Canadian Biography (Toronto Buffalo London: U of Toronto P, 1965-. 1982.

Dictionnaire des oeuvres littéraires du Québec des origines à 1900. Montréal: Fides, 1980.

Dimić, M.V. "Polysystem Theory", Irene R. Makaryk, General Editor, *Encyclopedia of Contemporary Literary Theory: Approaches, Scholars, Terms*. Toronto: U of Toronto P, 1993. 151-55.

Dimić, M.V. "Preface", *Canadian Review of Comparative Literature/Revue Canadienne de Littérature Comparée* Special Issue J. Pivato in collaboration with S. Tötösy de Zepetnek and M.V. Dimić, eds. *Literatures of Lesser Diffusion/Les littératures de moindre diffusion* 16.3-4 (1989a): 555-64.

Dimić, M.V. "Canadian Literatures of Lesser Diffusion: Observations from a Systemic Standpoint", *Canadian Review of Comparative Literature / Revue Canadienne de Littérature Comparée*. Special Issue J. Pivato in collaboration with S. Tötösy de Zepetnek and M.V. Dimić, eds. *Literatures of Lesser Diffusion/Les littératures de moindre diffusion* 16.3-4 (1989b): 565-74.

Dimić, M.V. "Friedrich Schlegel's and Goethe's Suggested Models of Universal Poetry and World Literature and Their Relevance for Present Debates about Literature as System", G. Gillespie, ed. *Proceedings of the XIth Congress of the International Comparative Literature Association, Paris 1985*. New York and Bern: Peter Lang, 1991. 39-49.

Dimić, M.V. and M.K. Garstin. "The Polysystem Theory: A Brief Introduction, with Bibliography", E.D. Blodgett and A.G. Purdy, eds. *Problems of Literary Reception/Problèmes de réception littéraire*. Edmonton: Research Institute for Comparative Literature, U of Alberta, 1988. 177-96.

Dostaler, Y. *Les infortunes du roman dans le Québec du XIXe siècle.* Montréal: HMH, 1977.

Du Bled, V. "La Vie politique, sociale et littéraire au Canada, 1840-1884", *La Revue des deux mondes* (15 février 1885): 844-81.

Dubois, J. *L'Institution de la littérature: introduction à une sociologie.* Paris: Nathan, Bruxelles: Labor, 1978.

Dubois, J. "Institution littéraire", J.-P. de Beaumarchais, D. Couty, et A. Rey, éds. *Dictionnaire des littératures de langue français.* Paris: Bordas, 1984. G-O 1087-90.

Duchet, C. "L'Illusion historique — L'enseignement des préfaces (1815-1832)", *Revue d'histoire littéraire de la France* 2-3 (mars-juin 1975): 245-67.

Ducrocq-Poirier, M. *Le Roman canadien de langue française de 1860 à 1958.* Paris: A.G. Nizet, 1978.

Duden. G. Drosdowski, ed. Mannheim Wien Zürich: Bibliographisches Institut, 1980.

Duffy, D. *Sounding the Iceberg: An Essay on Canadian Historical Novels.* Toronto: ECW, 1986.

Dunae, P.A. *Gentlemen Emigrants: From the British Public Schools to the Canadian Frontier.* Vancouver and Toronto: Douglas & McIntyre, 1981.

Durišin, D. *Vergleichende Literaturforschung.* Bratislava: Slovenskej Akademie, 1972.

Duyfhuizen, B. *Narratives of Transmission.* Rutherford Madison Teaneck: Fairleigh Dickinson UP, 1992.

Easthope, A. *Literary into Cultural Studies.* London and New York: Routledge, 1991.

Edwards, M.J. "The Case of *Canadian Homes*", *Canadian Literature* 81 (1979): 147-54.

Ehrenzeller, H. *Studien zur Romanvorrede von Grimmelshausen bis Jean Paul.* Bern: Francke, 1955.

Estivals, R. *Le Livre dans le monde.* Paris: RETZ, 1984.

Estivals, R., éd. *Le livre en France.* Paris: RETZ, 1984.

Even-Zohar, I. *Polysystem Studies* Special Issue *Poetics Today* 11.1 (Spring 1990).

Falardeau, J.-Ch. *Notre Société et son roman.* Montréal: HMH, 1967.

Fokkema, D. and E. Ibsch. *Literatuurwetenschap & Cultuuroverdracht.* Muiderberg: Coutinho, 1992.

Foerster, H. von, E. von Glasersfeld, P.M. Hejl, S.J. Schmidt, P. Watzlawick, *Einführung in den Konstruktivismus.* [München: Oldenbourg, 1985] rpt. München Zürich: Piper, 1992.

Fowler, A. *Kinds of Literature: An Introduction to the Theory of Genres and Modes.* Cambridge, MA: Harvard UP, 1982.

Frow, J. *Marxism and Literary History.* Cambridge: Harvard UP, 1986.

Funk and Wagnalls Standard College Dictionary Canadian Edition. Toronto Montreal Winnipeg Vancouver: Fitzhenry and Whiteside, 1974.

The Gage Canadian Dictionary. Toronto: Gage, 1973.

Garcia-Mendez, J. "Les Romanciers du XIXe siècle face à leurs romans: notes pour la reconstitution d'une argumentation", *Voix et Images* 8.2 (hiver 1983): 331-43.

Genette, G. *Seuils.* Paris: Seuil, 1987.

Gerson, C. "The Presenting Face: Prefaces to English-Language Poetry and Fiction Written by Women in Canada, 1850-1940", E.D. Blodgett and A.G. Purdy in collaboration with S. Tötösy de Zepetnek, eds. *Prefaces and Literary Manifestoes/ Préfaces et manifestes littéraires.* Edmonton: Research Institute for Comparative Literature, U of Alberta, 1989. 56-71.

Gerson, C. *A Purer Taste: The Writing and Reading of Fiction in Nineteenth-Century Canada.* Toronto: U of Toronto P, 1989.

Gilgamesh: Translated from the Sin-leqi-unnini Version. John Gardner, John Maier, Richard A. Henshaw, eds. New York: Alfred A. Knopf, 1984.

Godard, B. "Preface", N. Brossard, *Lovhers.* B. Godard, trans. Montréal: Guernica, 1986.

Goetsch, P. "Kanada", J. Schäfer, ed. *Commonwealth-Literatur.* Düsseldorf: August Babel, 1981. 79-101. 202-03.

Goetz, W.R. "Criticism and Autobiography in James's Prefaces", *American Literature* 51.3 (November 1979): 333-48.

Gorp, H. van, R. Ghesquiere, D. Dalabastita, and J. Flamend. *Lexicon van literaire termen.* 5th ed. Leuven: Wolters, 1991.

Graesser, A.C. *Prose Comprehension Beyond the Word.* New York: Springer, 1981.

Graff, H.J. *Literacy and Social Structure in the Nineteenth-Century City.* Ph.D. Diss. U of Toronto, 1975.

Graff, H.J. *The Literacy Myth: Literacy and Social Structure in the Nineteenth-Century City.* New York San Francisco London: Academic Press, 1979.

Grand Larousse de la langue française. Paris: Larousse, 1975-76.

Greer, A. "L'Alphabétisation et son histoire au Québec: état de la question", Y. Lamonde, éd. *L'Imprimé au Québec: aspects historiques (18ᵉ-20ᵉ siècles).* Québec: Institut québécois de recherche sur la culture, 1983. 25-51.

Grimm, J. and W. Grimm. *Deutsches Wörterbuch.* Leipzig: S. Hirzel, 1862-1951.

Gwyn, S. *The Private Capital: Ambition and Love in the Age of Macdonald and Laurier.* Toronto: McClelland and Stewart, 1984.

Habermas, J. *Strukturwandel der Öffentlichkeit* [1962] 17th ed. Darmstadt: Luchterhand, 1987.

Hare, J. "Introduction à la sociologie de la littérature canadienne-française du XIXᵉ siècle", *L'Enseignement secondaire*, 13 (mars-avril 1963): 68-92.

Harpham, G.G. "Joseph Conrad and the Art of the Preface", Paper presented at the Canadian Learned Societies, Comparative Literature. U of British Columbia, 1983. Unpublished ms. *Canadian Review of Comparative Literature/Revue Canadienne de Littérature Comparée*, U of Alberta.

Harrison, Dick. *Unnamed Country: The Struggle for a Canadian Prairie Fiction.* Edmonton: U of Alberta P, 1977.

Hart, J. *Theater & World: The Problematics of Shakespeare's History.* Boston: Northeastern UP, 1992.

Hart, J. *Northrop Frye: The Theoretical Imagination.* London: Routledge, 1993.

Hatzfeld, A., A. Darmstetter, and A. Thomas. *Dictionnaire général de la langue française du commencement du XVIIᵉ siècle jusqu'a nos jours ....* Paris: Ch. Delagrave, 1895-1900.

Hauptmeier, H., D. Meutsch and R. Viehoff, "Empirical Research on Understanding Literature", *Poetics Today* 10.3 (Fall 1989): 563-604.

Hayne, D.M. *French-Canadian Novelists on the Defensive*. M.A. Thesis, U of Ottawa, 1944.

Hayne, D.M. *The Historical Novel and French Canada*. Ph.D. Diss. U of Ottawa, 1945.

Heidenreich, R. "Narrative Strategies in Laure Conan's *Angéline de Montbrun*", *Canadian Literature* 81 (1979): 7-46.

Helikon Special Issue *La Science empirique de la littérature* 1 (1989).

Heyden, U. *Zielgruppen des Romans: Analysen französischer Romanvorworte des 19. Jahrhunderts*. Heidelberg: Carl Winter, 1986.

Hintzenberg, D., S.J. Schmidt, and R. Zobel. *Zum Literaturbegriff in der Bundesrepublik Deutschland*. Braunschweig-Wiesbaden: Vieweg, 1980.

Holman, C.H. *A Handbook to Literature* 4th Edition. Indianapolis: Bobbs-Merrill, 1980.

Holman, C. Hugh and William Harmon. *A Handbook to Literature* 6th Edition. New York: Macmillan London: Collier Macmillan, 1992.

Ide, N.M. and J. Véronis. "Artificial Intelligence and the Study of Literary Narrative", *Poetics* 19.1-2 (1990): 37-63.

Ingles, E.B. and R.J. Montague. "Canadian Institute for Historical Microreproductions", *Canadian Library Journal* (June 1983).

Jäger, G. *Empfindsamkeit und Roman: Wortgeschichte, Theorie und Kritik im 18. und frühen 19. Jahrhundert*. Stuttgart Berlin Köln Mainz: W. Kohlhammer, 1969.

Jones, K.Y. *A Comparative History of Caribbean Poetry in English, French, and Spanish*. Ph.D. Diss. U of Alberta, Comparative Literature, 1986.

Jones, J. and J. Jones. *Canadian Fiction*. Boston: Twayne, 1981.

Jørgensen, S-A. "Warum und zu welchem Ende schreibt man eine Vorrede? Randbemerkungen zur Leserlenkung, besonders bei Wieland", *Text und Kontext* 4.3 (1976): 3-20.

Kaplan, F. "Fielding's Novel About Novels: The 'Prefaces' and the 'Plot' of *Tom Jones*", *Studies in English Literature 1500-1900* 13.3 (1973): 535-49.

Kayser, W. *Das sprachliche Kunstwerk: Eine Einführung in die Litera-turwissenschaft*. Bern München: Francke, 1964.

Kempcke, G. *Handwörterbuch der deutschen Gegenwartssprache*. Berlin: Akademie, 1984.

Kenyeres, Á., ed. *A kegyes olvasóhoz!: Előszavak és utószavak válogatott gyüjteménye*. Budapest: Gondolat, 1964.

Klinck, C.F., ed. *Literary History of Canada: Canadian Literature in English*. Toronto and Buffalo: U of Toronto P, 1965. Rpt. 1976.

Kohl, B.G. "Petrarch's Prefaces to *De viris illustribus*", *History and Theory: Studies in the Philosophy of History* 13 (1974): 132-44.

Kröller, E.-M. *The Function of Place in the Canadian Literatures*. Ph.D. Diss. U of Alberta, Comparative Literature, 1978.

Labadie, P.B. *Critical Response to the Prefaces of Henry James: A History of the Development of Understanding and Appreciation of James's Theory of Fiction.* Ph.D. Diss. U of Michigan, 1974.

Lambert, J. "L'Éternelle question des frontières: littératures nationales et systèmes littéraires", C. Angelet, L. Melis, F.J. Mertens et F. Musarra, éds. *Langue, Dialecte, Littérature: Études romanes à la mémoire de Hugo Plomteux.* Leuven: Leuven UP, 1983. 362-63.

Lambert, J. *Un Modèle descriptif pour l'étude de la littérature: La littérature comme polysystème.* Leuven: Campus Kortrijk, 1983.

Lamonde, Y., éd. *L'Imprimé au Québec: aspects historiques (18e-20e siècles).* Québec: Institut québécois de recherche sur la culture, 1983.

Lamontagne, L. "Les Courants idéologiques dans la littérature canadienne-française du XIXe siècle", F. Dumont et J.-Ch. Falardeau, éds. *Littérature et société canadiennes-françaises.* Québec: PU de Laval, 1964. 101-21.

Landow, G.P. *Hypertext: The Convergence of Contemporary Critical Theory and Technology.* Baltimore and London: The Johns Hopkins UP, 1992.

Lausberg, H. *Handbuch der literarischen Rhetorik: Eine Grundlegung der Literaturwissenschaft.* München: Max Hueber, 1960. Vols I, II.

Lauzière, A. "Primevères du roman canadien français", *Culture* 18 (1957): 225-44 and 19 (1958): 233-56.

Le Grand Robert de la langue française. Paris: Le Robert, 1985.

Lecker, R. *et al.*, eds. *Canadian Writers and Their Works.* Toronto: ECW, 1983.

Lecker, R., ed. *Canadian Canons: Essays in Literary Value.* Toronto Buffalo London: U of Toronto P, 1991.

Lemire, M. "Les Relations entre écrivains et éditeurs au Québec au XIXe siècle", Y. Lamonde, éd. *L'Imprimé au Québec: aspects historiques (18e-20e siècle).* Québec: Institut québécois de recherche sur la culture, 1983. 207-24.

Lemire, M. *Les Grands thèmes nationalistes du roman historique canadien-français.* Québec: PU de Laval, 1970.

Lemire, M. and M. Lord, éds. *L'Institution littéraire.* Québec: UP de Laval, 1986.

Leps, M-Ch. *Apprehending the Criminal: The Producing of Deviance in Nineteenth-Century Discourse.* Durham and London: Duke UP, 1992.

Le Moine, R. "Le roman au XIXe siècle", René Dionne, ed. *Le Québécois et sa littérature.* Sherbrooke: Naaman, 1984. 76-86.

Levin, H. 1963. *The Gates of Horn: A Study of Five French Realists.* New York: Oxford UP.

Link, J. and U. Link-Heer. *Literatursoziologisches Propädeutikum.* München: Wilhelm Fink, 1980.

Littré, É. *Dictionnaire de la langue française.* Paris: Hachette, 1881.

Logan, J.D. and D.G. French. *Highways of Canadian Literature.* Toronto: McClelland & Stewart, 1924.

Lord, M. *En quête du roman gothique québécois (1837-1860).* Québec: Centre de recherche en littérature québécoise, 1985.

Lowell, T. *Consuming Fiction.* London: Verso, 1987.

Luhmann, N. *Die Wirtschaft der Gesellschaft*. Frankfurt: Suhrkamp, 1988.

Luhmann, N. *Soziale Systeme: Grundriß einer allgemeinen Theorie*. Frankfurt: Suhrkamp, 1984.

Luhmann, N. *Soziologische Aufklärung*. Köln Opladen: Westdeutscher Verlag, 1970-81. 4 vols.

MacDonald, M.L. *Literature and Society in the Canadas 1817-1850*. Louiston, N.Y.: Edwin Mellon P, 1992.

MacDonald, M.L. "Reading Between the Lines: An Analysis of Canadian Literary Prefaces and Prospectuses in the First Half of the Nineteenth Century", E.D. Blodgett and A.G. Purdy in collaboration with S. Tötösy de Zepetnek, eds. *Prefaces and Literary Manifestoes/Préfaces et manifestes littéraires*. Edmonton: Research Institute for Comparative Literature, U of Alberta, 1989. 29-42.

MacDonald, M.L. *Literature and Society in the Canadas 1830-1850*. Ph.D. Diss. Carleton U, 1984.

MacLeod, K. *Henry Handel Richardson: A Critical Study*. Cambridge: Cambridge UP, 1985.

MacLulich, T.D. *Between Europe and America: The Canadian Tradition*. Toronto: ECW, 1988.

Magee, W.H. "Local Colour in Canadian Fiction", L. McMullen, ed. *Twentieth Century Essays on Confederation Literature*. Ottawa: Tecumseh, 1976. 77-92.

Mandler, J.M. *Stories, Scripts, and Scenes: Aspects of Schema Theory*. Hillsdale, NJ: Lawrence Erlbaum Associates Inc., 1984.

Marcotte, G. "L'Institution: institution et courants d'air", *Liberté* (mars-avril 1981): 5-20.

Martial. *The Twelve Books of Epigrams*. J.A. Pott and F.A. Wright, trans. London: George Routledge & Sons, New York: E.P. Dutton, n.d.

Mathews, R. "The Social Question in English Canadian Literature, 1880-1940: Document, Dialectic, and Dream", G. Kurgan-van Hentenryk, éd. *La Question sociale en Belgique et au Canada: XIXᵉ-XXᵉ siècles*. Bruxelles: U de Bruxelles, 1989.

Matthews, J.P. *Tradition in Exile: A Comparative Study of Social Influences on the Development of Australian and Canadian Poetry in the Nineteenth Century*. Toronto: U of Toronto P, 1962.

McGann, J.J. *The Textual Condition*. Princeton: Princeton UP, 1991.

McInnis, E. *Canada: A Political and Social History*. Toronto: Holt, Rinehart and Winston, 1969.

McMullen, L., ed. *Re(dis)covering Our Foremothers: Nineteenth-Century Canadian Women Writers*. Ottawa London Paris: U of Ottawa P, 1989.

Mitterand, H. "Le Discours préfaciel", G. Falconer and H. Mitterand, éds. *La Lecture sociocritique du texte romanesque*. Toronto: Samuel Stevens Hakkert, 1975. 3-13.

Mitterand, H. *Le Discours du roman*. Paris: PU de France, 1980.

Moisan, C. *L'Histoire littéraire*. Paris: PU de France, 1990.

Moisan, C. *Comparaison et raison: essais sur l'histoire et l'institution des littératures canadienne et québécoise*. LaSalle: Hurtubise, 1987a.

Moisan, C. *Qu'est-ce que l'histoire littéraire?* Paris: PU de France, 1987b.

Moss, J. *The Canadian Novel: Beginnings.* Toronto: NC Press, 1980.

Nabholtz, J.R. *"My Reader My Fellow-Labourer": A Study of English Romantic Prose.* Columbia: U of Missouri P, 1986.

Nadeau, V. *Au commencement était le fascicule: Aux sources de l'édition québécoise contemporaine pour la masse.* Québec: Institut québécois de recherche sur la culture, 1984.

Neupokoeva, I. "Dialectics of Historical Development of National and World Literature", *Neohelicon* 1-2 (1973): 116-29.

New, W.H. *A History of Canadian Literature.* Houndmills, Basingstoke, Hampshire: MacMillan Education, 1989.

Nies, F. "Für die stärkere Ausdifferenzierung eines pragmatisch konzipierten Gattungssystems", Ch. Wagenknecht, ed. *Zur Terminologie der Literaturwissenschaft.* Stuttgart: Metzler, 1988. 326-36.

Nies, F. and J. Rehbein. *Genres mineurs: Texte zur Theorie und Geschichte nichtkanonischer Literatur (vom 16. Jahrhundert bis zur Gegenwart.* München: Wilhelm Fink, 1978.

The Oxford English Dictionary. 2nd Edition. Oxford: Clarendon, 1989.

The Oxford English Dictionary. Oxford: Clarendon, 1961.

The Oxford Companion to Canadian Literature. Toronto Oxford New York: Oxford UP, 1983.

Pacey, D. *Creative Writing in Canada: A Short History of English-Canadian Literature.* Toronto: Ryerson, 1952.

Parker, G.L. *The Beginnings of the Book Trade in Canada.* Toronto Buffalo London: U of Toronto P, 1985.

Perosa, S. *American Theories of the Novel: 1793-1903.* New York and London: New York UP, 1983.

Pier, J. "Pragmatisme du paratexte et signification", *Études littéraires* 21.3 (hiver 1988-89): 109-18.

Pivato, J. "Italian-Canadian Writing: A Polysystem", *Canadian Review of Comparative Literature/Revue Canadienne de Littérature Comparée* Special Issue J. Pivato in collaboration with S. Tötösy de Zepetnek and M.V. Dimić, eds. *Literatures of Lesser Diffusion/Les littératures de moindre diffusion* 16.3-4 (1989): 839-51.

Prince, G. *Dictionary of Narratology.* Lincoln and London: U of Nebraska P, 1987.

Purdy, Anthony. *A Certain Difficulty of Being: Essays On the Québec Novel.* Montréal: McGill-Queen's UP, 1990.

The Random House Dictionary. New York: Random House, 1966.

Reallexikon der deutschen Literaturgeschichte. W. Kohlschmidt and W. Mohr, eds. Berlin and New York: de Gruyter, 1977.

Rhodenizer, V.B. *Canadian Literature in English.* Montreal: Quality Press, 1965.

Riefstahl, H. *Dichter und Publikum in der ersten Hälfte des 18. Jahrhunderts, dargestellt an der Geschichte der Vorrede.* Limburg a.d. Lahn: Limburger Vereinsdruckerei, 1934.

Rigolot, F. "Prolégomènes à une étude du statut de l'appareil liminaire des textes littéraires", *L'Esprit créateur* 27.3 (Fall 1987): 7-18.

Rioux, M. "Sur l'évolution des idéologies au Québec", *Revue de l'Institut de Sociologie* (1968): 95-124.

Robert, L. *L'Institution du littéraire au Québec*. Québec: PU de Laval, 1989.

Robert, L. *Prolégomènes à une étude sur les transformations du marché du livre (1900-1940)*. Québec: Institut québécois de recherche sur la culture, 1984.

Rosengren, K.E. *Sociological Aspects of the Literary System*. Stockholm: Natur och Kultur, 1968.

Rosmarin, A. *The Power of Genre*. Minneapolis: U of Minnesota P, 1985.

Rossel, V. *Histoire de la littérature française hors de France*. Lausanne: F. Payot, 1895.

Rousseau, G. *Préfaces des romans québécois du XIXᵉ siècle*. Sherbrooke: Cosmos, 1970.

Sørensen, P.E. *Elementare Literatursoziologie: ein Essay über literatursoziologische Grundprobleme*. E. Meier and J. Glauser, trans. Tübingen: Max Niemeyer, 1976.

Salusinszky, I. "Northrop Frye", I. Salusinszky, *Criticism in Society*. New York and London: Methuen, 1987. 26-42.

Sammons, J.L. *Literary Sociology and Practical Criticism*. Bloomington: Indiana UP, 1977.

Santerres-Sarkany, St. *Théorie de la littérature*. Paris: PU de France, 1990.

Sarkany, St. *Québec Canada France: Le Canada littéraire à la croisée des cultures*. Aix-en-Provence: U de Provence, 1985.

Schmidt, S.J. "Plenumsvortrag: Literaturwissenschaft als interdisziplinäres Vorhaben," Johannes Janota, ed. *Vielfalt der kulturellen Systeme und Stile*. Tübingen: Max Niemeyer, 1993. 3-19.

Schmidt, S.J. "The Logic of Observation: Introduction to Constructivism", *Canadian Review of Comparative Literature/Revue Canadienne de Littérature Comparée* 19.3 (September 1992): 295-311.

Schmidt, S.J. *Grundriß der Empirischen Literaturwissenschaft: mit einem Nachwort zur Taschenbuchausgabe*. Frankfurt: Suhrkamp, 1991.

Schmidt, S.J. "The Empirical Science of Literature ESL: A New Paradigm", *Poetics* 12 (1983). 19-34.

Schmidt, S.J. *Foundations for the Empirical Study of Literature: The Components of a Basic Theory*. R. de Beaugrande, trans. Hamburg: Buske, 1982.

Schmidt, S.J. *Grundriß der empirischen Literatur wissenschaft* Vol. I: *Der gesellschaftliche Handlungsbereich Literatur* Vol. II: *Zur Rekonstruktion literaturwissenschaftlicher Fragestellungen in einer Empirischen Theorie der Literatur*. Braunschweig-Wiesbaden: Vieweg, 1980-82.

Schwanitz, D. *Systemtheorie und Literatur: ein neues Paradigma*. Opladen: Westdeutscher Verlag, 1990.

Schwanitz, D. "Systems Theory and the Environment of Theory", C. Koelb and V. Lokke, eds. *The Current in Criticism: Essays on the Present and Future of Literary Theory*. West Lafayette: Purdue UP, 1987. 265-94.

Selby, J. "Ballantyne and the Fur Traders", *Canadian Literature* 18 (1963): 40-46.

Servais-Maquoi, M. *Le Roman de la terre au Québec*. Québec: PU de Laval, 1974.

Shiels, A. *The Preface: A Poem of the Period*. Halifax: James Bowes, 1876.

Silbermann, A. *Einführung in die Literatursoziologie.* München: R. Oldenbourg, 1981.

Staël-Holstein, G., Mme de. "De la littérature considérée dans ses rapports avec les institutions sociales", *Oeuvres complètes.* Vol. I. Paris, 1861. Rpt. Genève: Slatkine, 1967. 196-334.

Stang, H. *Einleitung — Fußnote — Kommentar: Fingierte Formen wissenschaftlicher Darstellung als Gestaltungselemente moderner Erzählkunst.* Bielefeld: Aisthesis, 1992.

Tassie, J.-S. "La Societé à travers le roman canadien-français", P. Wyczynski, B. Julien, J. Ménard, and R. Robidoux, éds. *Le Roman canadien-français: évolution, témoignages, bibliographie.* Montréal and Paris: Fides, 1964. 153-64.

Tötösy de Zepetnek, S. "Empirical Science of Literature/Constructivist Theory of Literature", Irene R. Makaryk, General Editor, *Encyclopedia of Contemporary Literary Theory: Approaches, Scholars, Terms.* Toronto: U of Toronto P, 1993a. 36-39.

Tötösy de Zepetnek, S. "Selected Aspects of Nineteenth-Century English-Canadian and French-Canadian Novel Prefaces", *TSC — Textual Studies in Canada* (1993b): forthcoming.

Tötösy de Zepetnek, S. "Systemic Approaches to Literature — An Introduction with Selected Bibliographies", *Canadian Review of Comparative Literature / Revue Canadienne de Littérature Comparée* 19.1-2 (March/June 1992a): 21-93.

Tötösy de Zepetnek, S. and Ph. Kreisel. "Urban English-speaking Canadian Literary Readership: Results of a Pilot Study", *Poetics* 21.3 (1992b): 211-38.

Tötösy de Zepetnek, S. "The Empirical Science of Literature and the Nineteenth-century Canadian Novel Preface: The Application of a Literary Theory", *SPIEL - Siegener Periodicum zur Internationalen Empirischen Literaturwissenschaft* 9 (1990a): 343-60.

Tötösy de Zepetnek, S. "The Empirical Science of Literature and the Preface in the Nineteenth-Century Canadian Novel: A Theoretical Framework Applied", *Canadian Review of Comparative Literature / Revue Canadienne de Littérature Comparée* 17.1-2 (1990b): 68-84.

Tötösy de Zepetnek, S. *Prefaces to Nineteenth-century Canadian Novels: Their Function as Genre and Element of the Literary System.* Ph.D. diss. U of Alberta, Comparative Literature, 1989. *Dissertation Abstracts International* 1990 May v50 (11) p3596A-3597A.

Tötösy de Zepetnek, S. "Canonization and Translation in Canada: A Case Study", *TTR — Traduction, Terminologie, Rédaction* 1.1 (1988): 93-102.

Träger, C. "Vorwort-Geschichte als Spiegel bürgerlicher Ideologie- und Methodengeschichte", C. Träger, *Studien zur Realismustheorie und Methodologie der Literaturwissenschaft.* Leipzig: Reclam, 1972. 183-248.

Viatte, A. *Histoire comparée des littératures francophones.* Bruxelles: Nathan, 1980.

Vinge, L. "Ganzheit, System, und Kontinuität — eine Übersicht über einige Theorien zum Zusammenhang der Literatur", A.J. Bisanz and R. Trousson, eds. *Elemente der Literatur: Beiträge zur Stoff-, Motiv-, und Themenforschung. Elisabeth Frenzel zum 65. Geburstag.* Stuttgart: Kröner, 1980. 1-17.

Vipond, M. "Best Sellers in English Canada, 1899-1918: An Overview", *Journal of Canadian Fiction* 24 (1979): 96-119.

Voßkamp, W. "Gattungen als literarisch-soziale Institutionen", W. Hinck, ed. *Textsortenlehre-Gattungsgeschichte*. Heidelberg: Quelle und Meyer, 1977. 27-44.

Waelti-Walters, J. *Feminist Novelists of the Belle Epoque: Love as a Lifestyle*. Bloomington and Indianapolis: Indiana UP, 1990.

Wahrig, G. *Brockhaus Wahrig Deutsches Wörterbuch*. Wiesbaden: F.A. Brockhaus, 1984.

Wartburg, W. von. *Französisches Etymologisches Wörterbuch*. Basel: R.G. Zbinden, 1959.

Waterston, E. "Books and Notions: The Canadian Popular Novel in the Nineteenth Century", *Canadian Review of Comparative Literature / Revue Canadienne de Littérature Comparée*, Special Issue *The Popular Novel in the Nineteenth Century* 9.3 (September 1982): 437-48.

Watt, J.D. "The Growth of Proletarian Literature in Canada, 1872-1920", L. McMullen, ed., *Twentieth Century Essays on Confederation Literature*. Ottawa: Tecumseh, 1976. 41-59.

Watters, R.E. *A Check List of Canadian Literature and Background Materials 1628-1950*. Toronto: U of Toronto P, 1959. Rpt. 1975.

Weber, E. *Die poetologische Selbstreflexion im deutschen Roman des 18. Jahrhunderts: zu Theorie und Praxis von "Roman", "Historie" und pragmatischem Roman*. Stuttgart Berlin Köln Mainz: W. Kohlhammer, 1974.

Weinstein, M. *The Prefaces to the Waverly Novels*. Lincoln: U of Nebraska P, 1978.

Wilpert, G. von. "Empirische Literaturwissenschaft", G. von Wilpert, *Sachwörterbuch der Literatur*. 7th ed. Stuttgart: Kröner, 1989. 233.

APPENDIX

Abbreviations and conventions in the *Appendix*:

1. NO: = Notes (As Recorded by the CIHM).
2.   = The title of preface is indicated between apostrophies. If there is no name after the title, the preface was written by the author of the novel. Otherwise the author of the preface is indicated after the title of the preface.
3. X   = Indication that the preface had no title.
4. p.   = Page or pages.
5. ¶   = Paragraph or paragraphs.
6.   = The lower case spelling in the novel titles originates from the CIHM bibliographical list.

ENGLISH-CANADIAN NOVELS WITH PREFACES

1. Abbott, J. (Joseph), 1790-1862. *Philip Musgrave, or, Memoirs of a Church of England missionary in the North American colonies*. London: J. Murray, 1846. NO: A fictional autobiography of Joseph Abbott--Cf. Dictionary of Canadian Biography, vol. IX, p. 4. '"Then fearless walk we forth ..."' Original issued in series: Murray's home and colonial library; no. 33. CIHM microfiche series; no. 26442. "Introduction" 2.5 p.

2. *The Adopted daughter, or, The trials of Sabra: a tale of real life*. Montreal: J. Lovell, 1863. CIHM microfiche series; no. 10296. "Preface to the Second Edition" 0.5 p.

3. *The Adopted daughter, or, The trials of Sabra: a tale of real life*. Montreal: J. Lovell, 1873. CIHM microfiche series; no. 27752. "Preface to the Fourth Edition" 0.5 p.

4. *Agnes Harcourt, or, "For his sake": a Canadian story illustrative of the power of a child's life*. --. Montreal: Montreal Women's Print. Off., 1879. CIHM microfiche series; no. 04007. "Preface" 2 ¶.

5. Allen, Grant, 1848-1899. *The British barbarians: a hill-top novel*. New York; London: G.P. Putnam's Sons, 1895. CIHM microfiche series; no. 26236. "Introduction" 23 p.

6. Allen, Grant, 1848-1899. *The woman who did*. Boston: Little, Brown; London: J. Lane, 1898, c1895. NO: Original issued in series: The Keynotes series; no. 8. Duplicate of CIHM microfiche no. 27600. CIHM microfiche series; no. 26241. "Preface" 1 ¶. "Note" 1 ¶.

7. Allen, Grant, 1848-1899. *Hilda Wade: a woman with tenacity of purpose*. New York; London: G.P. Putnam's Sons, c1899. CIHM microfiche series; no. 26393. "Note" Publisher 1 p.

8. Allen, Grant, 1848-1899. *Linnet: a romance*. New York: New Amsterdam Book Co., 1900. CIHM microfiche series; no. 26240. "Note" 1 ¶.

9. Alway, J.H. "H.H.B." *The Last of the Eries: A Tale of Canada*. Simcoe, Ontario: Standard, 1849. "Preface" 1 p.

10. Ancketill, W.R. *The adventure of Mick Callighin, M.P.: a story of home rule, and the De Burghos: a romance*. Toronto & Detroit: Belford, 1875. CIHM microfiche series; no. 06446. "Preface" 0.5 p.

11. Ardagh, Alice Maud, 1866-1936. *Tangled ends*. Toronto: W. Briggs; Montreal: C.W. Coates, 1888. NO: Attributed to Alice Maud Ardagh--A checklist of Canadian literature / R.E. Watters. CIHM microfiche series; no. 03969. "To the Readers" 1.5 p.

12. Armour, Agatha, d. 1891. *Lady Rosamund's secret, a romance of Fredericton*. St. John, N.B.: Telegraph Print. and Pub. Office, 1898. CIHM microfiche series; no. 06086. "Introduction 1 ¶.

13. Ashley, B. Freeman (Barnas Freeman), 1833-1915. *Tan pile Jim, or, A Yankee waif among the bluenoses*. Chicago: Laird & Lee, 1894. CIHM microfiche series; no. 05828. "0" 4 ¶.

14. Ashley, B. Freeman (Barnas Freeman), 1833-1915. *Air Castle Don, or, From dreamland to hardpan*. Chicago: Laird & Lee, [1896?] NO: "Some dreams we have are nothing else ..." Original issued in series: Young America series. CIHM microfiche series; no. 27223. "Why Not" 1 ¶.

15. Ashley, B. Freeman (Barnas Freeman), 1833-1915. *Dick and Jack's adventures on Sable Island*. Chicago, Ill.: Laird & Lee, [1896?] CIHM microfiche series; no. 06156. "Instead of a Preface" 4 ¶. "Sable Island - Where and What it is" 1 ¶.

16. Author of "Mick Tracy". *Tim Doolan, the Irish immigrant: being a full and particular account of his reasons for emigrating, his passage across the Atlantic, his arrival in New York, his brief sojourn in the United States, and his further emigration to Canada*. London: S.W. Partridge, [1869?] NO: "Fifth thousand." CIHM microfiche series; no. 13409. "The Author's Bow to His Readers" 4 ¶.

17. Backwoodsman. *Two and twenty years ago: a tale of the Canadian rebellion*. Toronto: McClelland's Book and Job Printing House, 1859. CIHM microfiche series; no. 22755. "Introduction" 0.5 p.

18. Balfour, Grant. *The fairy school of Castle Frank*. Toronto: Poole Print. Co., [1899] CIHM microfiche series; no. 06342. X Publisher 1 ¶.

19. Ballantyne, R. M. (Robert Michael), 1825-1894. *Snowflakes and sunbeams, or, The young fur traders: a tale of the far north.* London; Edinburgh; New York: T. Nelson, 1856 (Edinburgh: T. Nelson) NO: "With illustrations by the author." Title from engraved t.p.: Snowflakes and sunbeams from the far north. CIHM microfiche series; no. 60822. "Preface " 0.5 p.

20. Ballantyne, R. M. (Robert Michael), 1825-1894. *The young fur-traders.* London; Edinburgh: T. Nelson, [1856?] NO: Preface dated: Edinburgh, 1856. CIHM microfiche series; no. 07482. "Preface" 1 ¶.

21. Ballantyne, R. M. (Robert Michael), 1825-1894. *Ungava: a tale of Esquimau land.* London; Edinburgh: T. Nelson and Sons, 1858. CIHM microfiche series; no. 38352. "Preface" 1 p.

22. Ballantyne, R. M. (Robert Michael), 1825-1894. *Snowflakes and sunbeams, or, The young fur traders: a tale of the far north.* Boston: Phillips, Sampson, 1859. NO: "With illustrations by the author." CIHM microfiche series; no. 54089. "Preface" 0.5 p.

23. Ballantyne, R. M. (Robert Michael), 1825-1894. *The dog Crusoe and his master: a story of adventure in the western prairies.* London; Glasgow: Blackie, [1860?] CIHM microfiche series; no. 13518. "Biographical Note" Publisher 3 p.

24. Ballantyne, R.M. (Robert Michael), 1825-1894. *Fighting the whales, or, Doings and dangers on a fishing cruise.* London: J. Nisbet, [186-?]. CIHM microfiche series no. 26467. "Note" 1 p.

25. Ballantyne, R. M. (Robert Michael), 1825-1894. *Away in the wilderness, or, Life among the Red Indians and fur-traders of North America.* London: J. Nisbet, [187-?] NO: Original issued in series: Ballantyne's miscellany. CIHM microfiche series; no. 26465. "Note" 0.5 p.

26. Ballantyne, R. M. (Robert Michael), 1825-1894. *The iron horse.* London: Nisbet, [1871?] CIHM microfiche series; no. 07472. "Preface" 2 ¶.

27. Ballantyne, R. M. (Robert Michael), 1825-1894. *The Norsemen in the west.* London: Nisbet, [1872?] CIHM microfiche series; no. 07475. "Preface" 1.5 p.

28. Ballantyne, R. M. (Robert Michael), 1825-1894. *The lighthouse: the story of a great fight between man and the sea.* London; Melbourne; Toronto: Ward, Lock, [18--?] NO: "Illustrated." CIHM microfiche series; no. 16856. "Preface" 0.5 p.

29. Ballantyne, R. M. (Robert Michael), 1825-1894. *Over the Rocky Mountains, or, Wandering Will in the land of the Red Skin.* London: J. Nisbet, [1879] NO: Original issued in series: R.M. Ballantyne's miscellany of entertaining and instructive tales; 7.

The last two pages contain a list of works in the series. CIHM microfiche series; no. 26866. "Note" 1 ¶.

30. Ballantyne, R. M. (Robert Michael), 1825-1894. *Rivers of ice: a tale illustrative of Alpine adventure and glacier action*. London: J. Nisbet, 1880. CIHM microfiche series; no. 24833. "Preface" 1 ¶.

31. Ballantyne, R. M. (Robert Michael), 1825-1894. *The lonely island, or, The refuge of the mutineers*. [Ottawa ?: s.n., [1880?] (Ottawa: J. Durie)]. CIHM microfiche series; no. 07474. "Preface" 1 ¶.

32. Ballantyne, R. M. (Robert Michael), 1825-1894. *The Red Man's revenge*. London: Nisbet, [1880?] CIHM microfiche series; no. 26867. "Preface" 2 ¶.

33. Ballantyne, R. M. (Robert Michael), 1825-1894. *Fast in the ice, or, Adventures in the Polar regions*. London: J. Nisbet, [1880?] NO: Original issued in series: Ballantyne's miscellany. CIHM microfiche series; no. 27761. "Note" 0.5 p.

34. Ballantyne, R. M. (Robert Michael), 1825-1894. *The giant of the North: pokings round the pole*. Toronto: Musson, [1881?] NO: Preface dated: 1881. CIHM microfiche series; no. 29078. "Preface" 3 ¶.

35. Ballantyne, R. M. (Robert Michael), 1825-1894. *The giant of the North, or, Pokings round the Pole*. London: J. Nisbet, 1882. CIHM microfiche series; no. 26645. X 3 ¶.

36. Ballantyne, R. M. (Robert Michael), 1825-1894. *The pioneers: a tale of the western wilderness: illustrative of the adventures and discoveries of Sir Alexander Mackenzie*. London: J. Nisbet, 1883. NO: Original issued in series: Ballantyne's miscellany. CIHM microfiche series; no. 38351. "Note" 1 p. "Preface" 1.5 p.

37. Ballantyne, R. M. (Robert Michael), 1825-1894. *The fugitives, or, The tyrant queen of Madagascar*. Toronto: A.G. Watson, [1887?] CIHM microfiche series; no. 07470. "Preface" 1.5 p.

38. Ballantyne, R. M. (Robert Michael), 1825-1894. *Life in the red brigade; and, Fort Desolation*. London: J. Nisbet, [1887?] NO: Fort Desolation, or, Solitude in the wilderness. CIHM microfiche series; no. 07473. "Preface" 2 ¶.

39. Ballantyne, R. M. (Robert Michael), 1825-1894. *Charlie to the rescue: a tale of the sea and the Rockies*. New York: T. Nelson, 1890. CIHM microfiche series; no. 07466. "Preface" 1 ¶.

40. Ballantyne, R. M. (Robert Michael), 1825-1894. *The buffalo runners: a tale of the Red River plains*. London: J. Nisbet, [189-?] NO: with illustrations by the author. -- "Fourteenth thousand" CIHM microfiche series; no. 07465. "Preface" 1 ¶.

41. Ballantyne, R. M. (Robert Michael), 1825-1894. *Charlie to the rescue: a tale of the sea and the Rockies*. London: J. Nisbet, [1890?] NO: "With illustrations by the author." CIHM microfiche series; no. 52456. "Preface" 1 ¶.

42. Ballantyne, R. M. (Robert Michael), 1825-1894. *Over the Rocky Mountains, or, Wandering Will in the land of the Red Skin*. Toronto: J. Nisbet, [1890?] CIHM microfiche series; no. 26470. "Note" 0.5 p.

43. Ballantyne, R. M. (Robert Michael), 1825-1894. *The buffalo runners: a tale of the Red River plains*. New York: T. Nelson, [1891?] CIHM microfiche series; no. 32694. "Note" 0.5 p.

44. Ballantyne, R.M. (Robert Michael), 1825-1894. *The walrus hunters: a romance of the realms of ice*. London: J. Nisbet, 1893. CIHM microfiche series no. 07481. "Preface" 1 ¶.

45. Ballantyne, R. M. (Robert Michael), 1825-1894. *The world of ice, or, The whaling cruise of "The Dolphin" and the adventures of her crew in the polar regions*. London; New York: T. Nelson, 1894. CIHM microfiche series; no. 26471. "Preface" 1 ¶.

46. Ballantyne, R. M. (Robert Michael), 1825-1894. *The Norsemen in the West: America before Columbus*. Toronto: Musson Book Co., [189-?] NO: Half title: The Norsemen in the West or America before Columbus. "Twentieth thousand". CIHM microfiche series; no. 36085. "Preface" 2 p.

47. Ballantyne, R. M. (Robert Michael), 1825-1894. *Away in the wilderness, or, Life among the Red Indians and fur-traders of North America*. Toronto: Musson, [between 1894 and 1905] CIHM microfiche series; no. 27760. "Note" 0.5 p.

48. Ballantyne, R. M. (Robert Michael), 1825-1894. *Over the Rocky Mountains, or, Wandering Will in the land of the Red Skin*. London: J. Nisbet, [between 1894 and 1900] NO: Original issued in series: R.M. Ballantyne's miscellany of entertaining and instructive tales; 7. CIHM microfiche series; no. 27165. "Note" 0.5 p.

49. Ballantyne, R. M. (Robert Michael), 1825-1894. *The world of ice, or, The whaling cruise of "The Dolphin" and the adventures of her crew in the polar regions*. London; New York: T. Nelson, 1894. CIHM microfiche series; no. 26471. "Preface" 1 ¶.

50. Barr, Robert, 1850-1912. *In a steamer chair, and other shipboard stories*. London: Chatto & Windus, 1892. NO: Publisher's list--p. [1]-32. CIHM microfiche series; no. 03347. "A Preliminary Word" 1 ¶.

51. Barron, Louie. *Zerola of Nazareth*. Toronto: C.J. Musson, 1895. CIHM microfiche series; no. 25183. "Preface 1.5 p.

52. Beardsley, Charles E. *The Victims of Tyranny: A Tale*. Buffalo: C.E. Young, 1847. "Preface" 2 p.

53. Bech, Birger. *The unknown*. Toronto: Queen City Pub. Co., 1887. CIHM microfiche series; no. 03534. "Preface" 1 p.

54. Beckwith Hart, Julia Catherine, 1796-1867. *St. Ursula's Convent, or, The nun of Canada: containing scenes from real life...* 1824 (Kingston, Upper Canada [Ont.]: H.C. Thomson) NO: "In two volumes. Vol. I." Part of a CIHM set. For individual microfiches in this set, see CIHM microfiche nos. 57557-57559. Attributed to Julia Catherine Beckwith Hart--National Union Catalog, pre-1956 imprints. "The moral world ... in universal good.--Thomson." CIHM microfiche series; no. 57558. "Preface" 2.5 p.

55. Beckwith Hart, Julia Catherine, 1796-1867. *Tonnewonte, or, The adopted son of America: a tale containing scenes from real life*. Watertown, N.Y.: J.Q. Adams, 1825. NO: "Two volumes in one. Vol. I." Part of a CIHM set. For individual microfiches in this set see CIHM microfiche nos. 44189-44191. Attributed to Julia Catherine Beckwith--National Union Catalog pre-1956 imprints. '"Such is the patriot's boast ... "--Goldsmith.' CIHM microfiche series; no. 44190. "Introduction" 5 p.

56. Begg, Alexander, 1839-1897. *"Dot it down": a story of life in the North-West*. Toronto: Hunter, Rose, 1871. NO: Followed by an emigrant's guide to Manitoba. CIHM microfiche series; no. 30055. "Dedication" 1 p.

57. Bottomley, Kate Madeline (Vera). *Honor Edgeworth, or, Ottawa's present tense*. Ottawa: A. Woodburn, 1882. NO: Attributed to Kate Madeline Bottomley--A checklist of Canadian literature /R.E. Watters. CIHM microfiche series; no. 00556. "Preface" 3 p.

58. Bottomley, Kate Madeline (Vera). *The doctor's daughter*. Ottawa: A. S. Woodburn, 1885. NO: Attributed to Kate Madeline Bottomley--A checklist of Canadian literature / R.E. Watters; also attributed to William Wilfrid Walter by University of Fredericton--A checklist of Canadian literature /R.E. Watters. CIHM microfiche series; no. 00557. "Preface" 4 p.

59. Bourne, George. *Lorette: the history of Louise, a daughter of a Canadian nun, exhibiting the interior of female convents*. New York: Charles Small, 1834. CIHM microfiche series; no. 14671. "Introductory Letter" 6 p.

60. Boyle, David, 1842-1911. *The ups and downs of no. 7, Rexville: being a full, true and correct account of what happened in the said school section during a period of twelve months, more or less, and of some things that were enacted beyond its limits, with a few of judicious remarks on religious instruction in public schools, the morality of fresh air, teacher's "recommends" and bogus certificates*. [Toronto?: s.n., 188-] NO: Cover title: The adventures of "no. 7." Attributed to David Boyle -- Checklist of Canadian literature / R.E. Watters. CIHM microfiche series; no. 14019. "Preface" 1 p.

61. Briton, E. Vincent. *Some account of Amyot Brough, captain in His Majesty's 20th Regiment of Foot, who fought (but with no great glory) under H.R.H. the Duke of Cumberland in the Low Countries, and had the honour to be wounded in the left shoulder under the eyes of General Wolfe at the taking of Quebec. Vol. 1.* London: Seeley & Co., 1885. NO: Half-title: Amyot Brough. Vol. 1 of a set of two volumes. For vol. 2 see CIHM microfiche series; no. 05505. CIHM microfiche series; no. 05504. "Preface" 1 p.

62. Briton, E. Vincent. *Some account of Amyot Brough: captain in His Majesty's 20th Regiment of Foot, who fought (but with no great glory) under H.R.H. the Duke of Cumberland in the Low Countries, and had the honour to be wounded in the left shoulder under the eyes of General Wolfe at the taking of Quebec.* London: Seeley, 1886. NO: Includes publisher's list. CIHM microfiche series; no. 29135. "Preface" 1 p. "Preface to the Second Edition" 1.5 p.

63. Briton, E. Vincent. *Some account of Amyot Brough, captain in His Majesty's 20th Regiment of Foot, who fought (but with no great glory) under H.R.H. the Duke of Cumberland in the Low Countries, and had the honour to be wounded in the left shoulder under the eyes of General Wolfe at the taking of Quebec.* London: Seeley & Co., 1886. CIHM microfiche series no. 29135. "Preface" 1 p. "Preface to the Second Edition" 1 p.

64. Brooke, Frances, 1724-1789. *The history of Lady Julia Mandeville.* London: Printed for F.C. and J. Rivington [and 34 others]; Edinburgh: W. Creech; York [England]: Wilson and Son, 1810. NO: Both works are fiction. Edition statement refers only to Mrs. Inchbald's Nature and art. From: The British novelists: with an essay, and prefaces, biographical and critical / by Mrs. Barbauld; v. 27. CIHM microfiche series; no. 37443. "Mrs. Brooke" Publisher 2 p.

65. Broome, Isaac, 1835-1922. *"The brother": splendor and woe.* Paterson, N.J.: J.A. Craig, 1890. CIHM microfiche series; no. 25683. "Preface" 2 p.

66. Butler, W. F. (William Francis), Sir, 1838-1910. *Red Cloud, the solitary Sioux: a story of the great prairie.* London: Sampson Low, Marston, Searle, & Rivington, 1888. NO: Includes publisher's list. CIHM microfiche series; no. 29883. "Foreword" Robert Baden-Powell 4 p.

67. Campbell, John, 1840-1904. *Two knapsacks: a novel of Canadian summer life.* Toronto: Williamson, 1892. NO: Attributed to John Campbell--A checklist of Canadian literature / R. Watters. CIHM microfiche series; no. 00387. "Publisher's Note" Publisher 1 p.

68. Carroll, John, 1809-1884. *The school of the prophets, or, Father McRorey's class, and 'Squire Firstman's kitchen fire: a fiction founded on facts.* Toronto: J.B. Magurn, [1876?] NO: Dated: Toronto, June 10th, 1876. "A book for the Methodists." "Second series." Includes publisher's list. CIHM microfiche series; no. 39561. "Preface" 4 p. "Introduction" Enoch Wood 2.5 p.

69. Carroll, John, 1809-1884. *My boy life: presented in a succession of true stories.* Toronto: William Briggs, 1882. "Introduction" W.H.W. 2 p.

70. Chapin, Gardner B. *Tales of the St. Lawrence.* Montreal: J. Lovell, 1873. CIHM microfiche series; no. 00562. "Introduction" 1.5 p.

71. Chaplin, J. D. (Jane Dunbar), 1819-1884. *Mother West's neighbors.* Boston: American Tract Society, 1876. CIHM microfiche series; no. 27436. "Preface" 4 p.

72. Charlesworth, Maria Louisa. *Oliver of the mill: a tale.* Montreal: Dawson, 1876. CIHM microfiche series; no. 26927. "Preface" 2.5 p.

73. Cheetham, William. *Lights and shadows of clerical life.* Montreal: Lovell, 1879. CIHM microfiche series; no. 00596. "Preface" 2 p.

74. Clark, Graham S.R. Mrs. *Our street.* Boston: D. Lothrop, c1880. CIHM microfiche series; no. 28709. "Dedication" 0.5 p.

75. Clayton, F. H. *Scenes and incidents in Irish life.* Montreal: J. Lovell, 1884. NO: Attributed to F.H. Clayton--A checklist of Canadian literature / R.E. Watters. CIHM microfiche series; no. 00679. "Dedicatory Preface" 1 p. "Preface" 1 p.

76. Clemo, Ebenezer, 1831?-1860. *Canadian homes, or, The mystery solved: a Christmas tale.* Montreal: J. Lovell; Toronto: W.C.F. Caverhill, 1858. CIHM microfiche series; no. 37533. "Preface" 2 p.

77. Collins, J. E. (Joseph Edmund), 1855-1892. *The four Canadian highwaymen, or, The robbers of Markham swamp.* Toronto: Rose, 1886. NO: Includes: Mary Holt's

engagement / by Catherine Owens. CIHM microfiche series; no. 08597. "Preface" 1.5 p.

78. Conger, Janet C. *A daughter of St. Peter's.* [Montreal?: s.n., 1889?] (Montreal: J. Lovell & Son) CIHM microfiche series; no. 00742. "Preface" 1 p.

79. Connor, Ralph, 1860-1937. *Beyond the marshes.* Toronto: Westminster Co., [1898?] CIHM microfiche series; no. 26971. "Foreword" 1.5 p. "Introduction" Ishbel Aberdeen 2 p.

80. Connor, Ralph, 1860-1937. *The sky pilot: a tale of the foothills.* Toronto: Westminster Co., 1899. NO: The author's real name is Charles William Gordon. CIHM microfiche series; no. 30112. X 1.5 p.

81. Connor, Ralph, 1860-1937. *Black rock: a tale of the Selkirks.* Chicago: M.A. Donohue, [1900?] CIHM microfiche series; no. 26972. "Black Rock" George Adam Smith 1 p. "Introduction" 1.5 p.

82. Cureton, Stephen. *Perseverance wins: the career of a travelling correspondent: England, Canada, United States, Hawaiian Islands, New Zealand, Australia, Egypt, Italy.* Toronto: J. Clougher, [1880?] CIHM microfiche series; no. 02242. "To the Reader" 1 p. "Dedication" 2 p.

83. Darling, William Stewart, 1818-1886. *Sketches of Canadian life, lay and ecclesiastical: illustrative of Canada and the Canadian Church.* London: D. Bogue, 1849. NO: Attributed to William Stewart Darling--National Union Catalog pre-1956 imprints. Tables. Includes publisher's list. CIHM microfiche series; no. 55031. "Preface" 2 p.

84. Daunt, Achilles. *The three trappers: a story of adventure in the wilds of Canada.* London: T. Nelson, 1882. CIHM microfiche series; no. 30124. "Preface" 1.5 p.

85. Davison, L. L. (Leslie Loring), 1871-1889. *Stray leaves from "Book of Wonders".* Wolfville, N.S.: Davison, 1890. NO: with a preface by Harl Harlee. -- Attributed to Leslie Loring Davison--Canadian Men and Women of the Time / H.J. Morgan. Afar / L.L. Davison. CIHM microfiche series; no. 06015. "Biography of Leslie Loring Davison" Ben Zeene 5 p.

86. De Mille, James, 1837-1880. *Le baron americain.* Paris: C. Levy, 1877. NO: L'auteur James De Mille mentionné dans L'avis au lecteur. CIHM microfiche series; no 32173. "Avis au Lecteur" Louis Ulbach 1.5 p.

87. Dougall, Lily, 1858-1923. *The zeit-geist .* --. London: Hutchinson, [1895?] NO: A novel. Author identified in advertisement preceding the title page, which lists The

zeit-geist as belonging to the Zeit-Geist library of complete novels in one volume. Original issued in series: Zeit-Geist library. CIHM microfiche series; no. 07102. X 2 p.

88. Duncan, Sara Jeannette. *A daughter of to-day*. London: Chatto & Windus, 1895. CIHM microfiche series; no. 32300. "Opinions of the press on *A Daughter of To-Day*" 1 p.

89. Emberson, F. C. (Frederick C.), d. 1913. *The yarn of the love sick Parsee*. Montreal: W. Drysdale, [1897?] NO: Title at head of table of contents: The yarn of the love-sick Jap. CIHM microfiche series; no. 02913. "An Apology" 1.5 p.

90. Erskine, Douglas. *A bit of Atlantis*. Montreal: A.T. Chapman, 1900. CIHM microfiche series; no. 38356. "Preface" 33 p.

91. Flewellyn, Julia Colliton, b. 1850. *Hill-Crest*. Toronto: Cooper, 1894. CIHM microfiche series; no. 03166. "Preface" 1.5 p.

92. Forrest, E. W. (Edmund William), d. 1880. *Ned Fortescue, or, Roughing it through life: a story founded on fact*. Ottawa; Toronto: Hunter, Rose, 1869. CIHM microfiche series; no. 03153. "Preface" 0.5 p.

93. Forrest, E. W. (Edmund William), d. 1880. *Ned Fortescue, or, Roughing it through life: a story found on fact*. Montreal: Printed for the author by John Lovell, 1871. CIHM microfiche series; no. 13419. "Preface" 1 p.

94. Forrest, E. W. (Edmund William), d. 1880. *Vellenaux: a novel*. Saint John, N.B.: Daily News, 1874. CIHM microfiche series; no. 03154. "Preface" 1 p.

95. Fraser, W. A. (William Alexander), 1859-1933. *Mooswa and others of the boundaries*. Toronto: W. Briggs, 1900. CIHM microfiche series; no. 28734. "Introduction" 2.5 p.

96. Gair, John R. *Fun on the Road*. Toronto: Grip, 1886. CIHM microfiche series no. 03282. "The Author's Preface" 1.5 p.

97. Galt, John, 1779-1839. *Lawrie Todd, or settlers in the woods*. London: H. Colburn and R. Bentley, 1830. CIHM microfiche series; no. 44269. "Preface" 2.5 p.

98. Galt, John, 1779-1839. *Bogle Corbet, or, The emigrants*. London: H. Colburn and R. Bentley, [183-?] NO: "In three volumes. Vol. I." Part of a CIHM set. For individual microfiches in this set, see CIHM microfiche nos. 42427-42430. '"Truth severe by fairy fiction dressed."' CIHM microfiche series; no. 42428. 6 p.

99. Galt, John, 1779-1839. *Annals of the parish; and, The Ayrshire legatees*. New York: MacMillan, 1895. CIHM microfiche series; no. 26261. "Introduction" Alfred Ainger 7 p.

100. Galt, John, 1779-1839. *The entail, or, The lairds of Grippy*. Edinburgh; London: W. Blackwood, 1895. NO: with introduction by S.R. Crockett; illustrations by John Wallace. First ed. published in three volumes, 1823. Original issued in series: Works of John Galt. "Volume I." Part of a CIHM set. For individual microfiches in this set see CIHM microfiche nos. 24600-24602. CIHM microfiche series; no. 24601. "Introduction" S.R. Crockett 7 p.

101. Garison, Isabel. (Mrs. W.R. Smith). *Looking forward*. Montreal: J.T. Robinson, [1890?]. CIHM microfiche series no. 12576. "Dedication" 0.5 p.

102. Glasier, Alfred A. *The Irving Club among the White Hills*. St. John, N.B.: H.J.A. Godard, 1877. CIHM microfiche series; no. 06326. X 1 p.

103. Gordon, W. J. (William John). *Englishman's haven*. New York: D. Appleton, 1892. CIHM microfiche series; no. 03469. "Preface" 1 ¶.

104. Graham, E. Jeffers (Emma Jeffers). *Etchings from a parsonage veranda*. Toronto: W. Briggs, 1895. CIHM microfiche series no. 03891. "Preface" 1 p.

105. Grodenk. *My own story: a Canadian Christmas tale*. Toronto: A.S. Irving, 1869. NO: In double columns. CIHM microfiche series; no. 06368. "To the Reader" 0.5 p.

106. Haliburton, Thomas Chandler, 1796-1865. *The clockmaker, or, The sayings and doings of Samuel Slick of Slickville* ... Concord [N.H.]: W. White; Boston: B.B. Mussey, 1838. NO: '"--Garrit aniles ex re fabellas"--Horace.' Attributed to Thomas Chandler Haliburton--National Union Catalog, pre-1956 imprints. CIHM microfiche series; no. 25838. "Advertisement" Publisher 0.5 p.

107. Haliburton, Thomas Chandler, 1796-1865. *The clockmaker, or, The sayings and doings of Samuel Slick of Slickville* ... Philadelphia: Carey, Lea and Blanchard, 1838. NO: Attributed to Thomas Chandler Haliburton--National Union Catalog, pre-1956 imprints. "Ecce iterum Crispinus." "If here aint the clockmaker again, as I am alive!" "Second series." CIHM microfiche series; no. 10449. "To Colonel C.R. Fox" 1.5 p.

108. Haliburton, Thomas Chandler, 1796-1865. *The letter bag of the Great Western, or, Life in a steamer*. Paris: A. and W. Galignani, 1840. NO: "Dulce est desipere in loco." CIHM microfiche series; no. 34822. "Preface" 8 p. "Dedication to the Right Hon. Lord Russell" 5.5 p.

109. Haliburton, Thomas Chandler, 1796-1865. *The attaché, or, Sam Slick in England*. London: Richard Bentley, 1843. CIHM microfiche series; no. 45071. X 1 p.

110. Haliburton, Thomas Chandler, 1796-1865. *The attaché, or, Sam Slick in England*. Paris: A. and W. Galignani, 1843. NO: '"Tell you what, report my speeches ... "--Slickville translation.' CIHM microfiche series; no. 14034. "Valedictory Address" 2.5 p.

111. Haliburton, Thomas Chandler, 1796-1865. *Sam Slick's wise saws and modern instances, or, What he said, did, or invented* .. London: Hurst and Blackett, 1853. NO: "In two volumes. Vol. I." Part of a CIHM set. For individual microfiches in this set see CIHM microfiche nos. 67957-67959. Attributed to Thomas Chandler Haliburton--National Union Catalog, pre-1956 imprints. '"Quicquid agunt homines ..."--Juv.' '"The proper study of mankind is man"--Pope.' CIHM microfiche series; no. 67958. "Introductory Letter" 7 p.

112. Haliburton, Thomas Chandler, 1796-1865. *Sam Slick's wise saws and modern instances, or, What he said, did, or invented* ... London: Hurst and Blackett, 1854 (London: Schulze) NO: "In two volumes. Vol. I." Part of a CIHM set. For individual microfiches in this set see CIHM microfiche nos. 48968-48970. Attributed to Thomas Chandler Haliburton--National Union Catalog, pre-1956 imprints. '"Quicquid agunt homines ..."--Juv.' '"The proper study of mankind is man"--Pope.' CIHM microfiche series; no. 48969. "Preface to the New Edition" 2 p.

113. Haliburton, Thomas Chandler, 1796-1865. *Sam Slick's wise saws and modern instances, or, What he said, did, or invented*. London: Hurst and Blackett, 1859. NO: "'Quicquid agunt homines, votum, timor, ira, voluptas Gaudia'--Juv." "'The proper study of mankind is man'--Pope." CIHM microfiche series; no. 35973. "Preface to the New Edition" 2 p.

114. Haliburton, Thomas Chandler, 1796-1865. *The clockmaker: sayings and doings of Samuel Slick of Slickville*. New York: Hurd and Houghton; Cambridge: Riverside, 1872 (Cambridge: H.O. Houghton) NO: illustrated by F.O.C. Darley. Includes publisher's list. CIHM microfiche series; no. 34575. "Advertisement" X 4.5 p.

115. Haliburton, Thomas Chandler, 1796-1865. *Sam Slick, the clockmaker: his sayings and doings*. Toronto: Musson; London: G. Routledge, [19--?] NO: Author's name appears in introd. Includes publisher's list. CIHM microfiche series; no. 37475. X E.A. Baker 8 p.

116. Hickey, David. *William and Mary: a tale of the siege of Louisburg, 1745*. Toronto: W. Briggs, 1884. CIHM microfiche series; no. 05562. "Preface" 1.5 p.

117. Hanna, George W. (Spirito Gentil). *Earthborn!*. Montreal: J. Lovell, [1889?] NO: "A novel of the misty past - The story of a strange search - The tale of the beginning - A romance of the ending." Attributed to George W. Hanna--Canadiana 1867-1900. CIHM microfiche series; no. 29242. "Preface" Editor 2 p.

118. Harold, P. J. *Irene of Corinth: an historic romance of the first century*. Toronto: Hunter, Rose, 1884. CIHM microfiche series; no. 05365. "Preface" 1.5 p.

119. Hatton, Joseph, 1841-1907. *By order of the Czar: a novel*. New York: J.W. Lovell, c1890. CIHM microfiche series; no. 05208. "Introduction" 6 p.

120. Hawley, W. F. (William Fitz), 1804-1855. *The unknown, or, Lays of the forest*. Montreal: J.A. Hoisington, 1831. NO: "A tale of the times of old. Ossian." CIHM microfiche series; no. 35426. "Preface" 2.5 p.

121. Hilts, Joseph H. (Joseph Henry), 1819-1903. *Among the forest trees, or, How the bushman family got their homes: being a book of facts and incidents of pioneer life in Upper Canada, arranged in the form of a story*. Toronto: Printed for the author by W. Briggs, 1888. CIHM microfiche series; no. 05620. "Introduction" 4 p.

122. Holland, Fidele H. *"Waddie", A Christmas story*. Hamilton, [Ont.]: Times Print. Co., 1898. NO: "Sold for the benefit of the 'Duffield Flower Mission'." Includes: The dead baby's message, a Christmas etching. CIHM microfiche series; no. 07240. "Advertisement" 1 p.

123. Holmes, Abraham "A.S.H." *Belinda, or, the Rivals*. Toronto: Anansi, 1976. "Advertisement" 1 p.

124. Hooker, Le Roy, 1840-1906. *Baldoon*. Toronto: Poole Pub. Co., 1900. CIHM microfiche series; no. 08387. "Foreword" 4 p.

125. *The Hunted outlaw, or, Donald Morrison, the Canadian Rob Roy* ... Montreal: Montreal News, 1889. NO: "Truth is stranger than fiction." CIHM microfiche series; no. 08787. "Prologue" 1.5 p.

126. Hunter, Alfred Taylour, 1867-1957. *Stories told out of lodge*. Toronto: Carswell, 1898. NO: I. The counting out of Be-elzebub -- II. The lost organizer. CIHM microfiche series; no. 07054. "Preface" 2.5 p.

127. Huntington, L.S. (Lucius Seth), 1827-1886. *Professor Conant: a story of English and American social and political life*. Toronto: Rose Pub. Co., 1884. NO: "It is not that I adulate the people; Without me there are demagogues enough... -- Lord Byron." CIHM microfiche series; no. 07309. "Preface" 1.5 p.

128. J. E. *The old and the new home: a Canadian tale*. Toronto: J. Campbell, 1870. NO: '"But may dishonour blight our fame ..."' Original issued in series: Canadian prize Sunday-school books; v. 3. CIHM microfiche series; no. 35564. "Preface" 1 p.

129. Jenkins, Edward, 1838-1910. *Lord Bantam: a satire*. Montreal: Dawson, 1872. CIHM microfiche series; no. 13282. "Preface" 0.5 p.

130. Jenkins, Edward, 1838-1910. *The devil's chain*. Montreal: Dawson, 1876. CIHM microfiche series; no. 07431. "Dedication to Sir Wilfred Lawson, Bart., M.P." 2 p.

131. Jenkins, Edward, 1838-1910. *The captain's cabin: a Christmas yarn*. Montreal: Dawson, 1878. CIHM microfiche series; no. 07430. "Preface" 2 p.

132. Johnson, Frank. *The village of Merrow: its past and present*. Montreal: Lovell Print. and Pub. Co., 1876. NO: "The gods are just..." CIHM microfiche series; no. 07619. "Introduction to the American Edition" 8.5 p. "Dedication" 1.5 p.

133. Jones, James Thomas. *The Cromaboo mail carrier: a Canadian love story*. Guelph: Jos. H. Hacking, 1878. CIHM microfiche series; no. 25870. "Preface" 0.5 p.

134. Kennedy, Jas. B. (James B.). *Afloat for eternity, or, A pilgrim's progress for the times*. Toronto: W. Briggs; Montreal: C.W. Coates, 1893. CIHM microfiche series; no. 07840. "Preface" 1 p. "Introduction" Crossley & Hunter 1.5 p.

135. Kirby, William, 1817-1906. *Le Chien d'or: légende canadien*. tr. Pamphile LeMay. Montréal: L'Étendard, 1884. In Guildo Rousseau, *Préfaces des romans québécois du XIXe siècle* (Ottawa: Cosmos, 1970). "Pourquoi *Le Chien d'or* traduit en français" Les Éditeurs (Pamphile LeMay) 4 p.

136. Kirby, William, 1817-1906. *The golden dog (Le chien d'or): a romance of the days of Louis Quinze in Quebec*. [Montreal?]: Montreal News Co., [1897?] CIHM microfiche series; no. 29280. "Author's Prefatory Note" 1 p.

137. L. G. *Jessie Grey, or The discipline of life: a Canadian tale*. Toronto: J. Campbell, 1870. NO: "I've almost grown a portion of this place... -- Sangster" CIHM microfiche series; no. 01280. "Preface" 2.5 p.

138. L.S. *The Ladies' Benevolent and Industrial Sallymag Society: being a series of comic chapters, taken from an unpublished novel*. Charlottetown, P.E.I.: W.H. Bremner, 1868. NO: Includes bibliographical references. CIHM microfiche series; no. 13964. "Introduction" 0.5 p.

139. Lane, Edward. *The fugitives, or, A trip to Canada: an interesting tale, chiefly founded on facts, interspersed with observations on the manners, customs &c. of the*

colonists and Indians. London: E. Wilson, 1830. CIHM microfiche series; no. 59021. "Preface 2.5 p.

140. Lanigan, Richard. *They two, or, Phases of life in eastern Canada fifty years ago*. Montreal: J. Lovell, 1888. CIHM microfiche series; no. 28408. "Explanatory" Editor 1 p. "Canada" 4 ¶.

141. Lauder, Marie Elise T. T. (Marie Elise Turner T.). *At last*. Toronto: W. Briggs; Montreal: C.W. Coates, 1894. NO: "Teach me, my God and King..." CIHM microfiche series; no. 08892. "Preface" 1 p.

142. Laut, Agnes. *Lords of the North*. New York: P.F. Collier, 1900. "The Trapper's Defiance" 1 p. "Acknowledgement" 1 ¶. "Introduction" 2.5 p.

143. Lawson, J. Kerr (Jessie Kerr), 1838-1917. *Dr. Bruno's wife: a Toronto society story*. [London?]: Simpkin, Marshall, Hamilton, Kent, [1893?] NO: Copy autographed by the author. CIHM microfiche series; no. 01374. "Preface" 2 p.

144. Leisher, J.J. *The decline and fall of Samuel Sawbones, M.D., on the Klondike*. New York; London: Neely Co., c1900. CIHM microfiche series; no. 08647. "Preface" 1.5 p.

145. Leonard, May, b. 1862. *Zoe, or, Some day: a novel*. Saint John, N.B.: G.W. Day, 1888. CIHM microfiche series; no. 13064. "Preface" 1 p.

146. Leprohon, Mrs. (Rosanna Eleanor), 1829-1879. *Le Manoir de Villerai: roman historique canadien sous la domination française*. Montréal: Plinguet, 1861. NO: traduit de l'anglais avec la bienveillante permission de l'auteur par E.L. de Bellefeuille. -- Traduction de: The Manor House of Villerai. Errata--p. [407]. CIHM microfiche series; no 37236. "Note du Traducteur" E.L. de Bellefeuille 5.5 p.

147. Leprohon, Mrs. (Rosanna Eleanor), 1829-1879. *Antoinette de Mirecourt, or, Secret marrying and secret sorrowing: a Canadian tale*. Montreal: J. Lovell, 1864. NO: Also available in French. See CIHM microfiche nos. 52663 and 08562. CIHM microfiche series; no. 36349. "Preface" 1.5 p.

148. Leprohon, Mrs. (Rosanna Eleanor), 1829-1879. *Antoinette de Mirecourt ou Mariage secret et chagrins cachés: roman canadien*. Montreal: J.B. Rolland, 1881. NO: "(Traduit de l'anglais.)" Aussi disponible en anglais. Voir le numero de microfiche de l'I.C.M.H. 36349. CIHM microfiche series; no 08562. "Note des Editeurs" Editor 5.5 p.

149. Leprohon, Mrs. (Rosanna Eleanor), 1829-1879. *Armand Durand ou La promesse accomplie*. Montreal: C.O. Beauchemin, 1892. CIHM microfiche series; no 29523. X 2 p.

150. Leslie, Mary, 1842-1920. *The Cromaboo mail carrier: a Canadian love story.* Guelph [Ont.]: J.H. Hacking, 1878. NO: '"The theme is old, even as the flowers are old ..."' Followed by two reviews of the author's work. CIHM microfiche series; no. 25870. X 2 ¶.

151. Lighthall, W. D. (William Douw), 1857-1954. *The young seigneur, or, Nation-making.* Montreal: W. Drysdale, 1888. CIHM microfiche series; no. 24305. "Preface" 1.5 p.

152. Lighthall, W. D. (William Douw), 1857-1954. *The false chevalier, or, The lifeguard of Marie Antoinette.* Montreal: F.E. Grafton, 1898. CIHM microfiche series; no. 26273. "Prefatory Note" 0.5 p.

153. Lloyd, Wallace. *Houses of glass: a romance.* Toronto: W.J. Gage, 1899. NO: '"But the greatest of these is charity."' CIHM microfiche series; no. 26423. "Preface" 1.5 p.

154. Lowell, Robert, 1816-1891. *The new priest in Conception Bay.* Boston: Roberts, 1889. NO: "Woe! Woe! But right, at last, though slow." CIHM microfiche series; no. 28986. "Preface to the Revised Edition" 0.5 p. "Foreword to the First Edition" 0.5 p.

155. MacDonald, Flora. *Mary Melville, the psychic.* Toronto: The Austin Publishing Co., 1900. CIHM microfiche series; no. 09397. "Introduction" Wm. Newton Barnhardt 2.5 p. "A Foreword" B.F. Austin 3 p.

156. Macdonnell, Blanche Lucile, 1853-1924. *Diane of Ville Marie: a romance of French Canada.* Toronto: W. Briggs; Montreal: C.W. Coates, 1898. CIHM microfiche series; no. 09409. "Preface" 3.5 p.

157. Mackie, John, 1862-1939. *The heart of the prairie.* London: Nisbet, [1876?] CIHM microfiche series; no. 62078. "Preface" 1 p.

158. Malcolm. *The dear old farm: a Canadian story.* St. Thomas, Ont.: The Journal, 1897. CIHM microfiche series; no. 09517. "Preface" 1 p.

159. Mann, James (James William). *The victorious King: an allegory.* Richmond Hill, Ont.: J. Mann, 1878. CIHM microfiche series; no. 09524. "To the Reader" 1.5 p. "Introduction" John Potts 2 p.

160. Mayor, F. M. (Flora Macdonald), b. 1872. *Mary Melville.* Toronto: Austin, 1900. CIHM microfiche series; no. 09397. "A Foreword" 4 p. "Introduction" Wm. Newton Barnhardt 2 p.

161. McDonnell, William. *The heathens of the heath: a romance, instructive, absorbing, thrilling*. New York: D.M. Bennett, 1874. CIHM microfiche series; no. 12953. "Preface" 1 p.

162. McDougall, Margaret Dixon, 1826-1898. *The lady of the Beacon of Araheera: (a chronicle of Innishowen)*. Quebec: D. Carey, 1859. NO: In double columns. CIHM microfiche series; no. 39297. "Chapter I Introductory" 4 p.

163. McDougall, Margaret Dixon, 1826-1898. *The days of a life*. Almonte [Ont.]: W. Templeman, 1883. NO: "Erin, oh! Erin,..." CIHM microfiche series; no. 09466. "Preface" 1.5 p.

164. McKinnon, William Charles. *St. George: or, The Canadian League*. Halifax: Elbridge Gerry Fuller, 1852. "Introduction" 8 p.

165. McLennan, William, 1856-1904. *The span o'life: a tale of Louisbourg & Quebec*. New York; London: Harper & Bros.; Toronto: Copp, Clark, 1899. NO: illustrations by F. de Myrbach. "The span o'Life is nae lang eneugh...To part my Love frae me." CIHM microfiche series; no. 53209. "Preface" 1.5 p.

166. McSherry, James, 1819-1869. *Pere Jean, or, The Jesuit missionnary: a tale of the North American Indians*. Baltimore: J. Murphy; Dublin: R. Grace, 1847. NO: Original issued in series: Murphy's cabinet library; no. 9. CIHM microfiche series; no. 45906. "Preface" 1 p.

167. McSherry, James, 1819-1869. *Father Laval, or, The Jesuit missionary: a tale of North American Indians*. Baltimore: J. Murphy, [1860?]. CIHM microfiche series no. 18738. "Preface" Publisher 1.5 p.

168. Mercier, Jerome, Mrs. *The red house by the Rockies: a tale of Riel's rebellion*. Toronto: Musson, [1896?] NO: "'The very true beginning of wisdom is the desire of ...'" CIHM microfiche series; no. 32042. X 1.5 p.

169. Mercier, Jerome, Mrs. and Watt, Violet. *The red house by the Rockies: a tale of Riel's rebellion*. London: Society for Promoting Christian Knowledge, [1896?]. CIHM microfiche series no. 30614. "Preface" Anne Mercier 1.5 p.

170. Moodie, Susanna, 1803-1885. *Mark Hurdlestone, The Gold Worshipper*. London: Bentley, 1853. "Introduction" 2 p. In Douglas Daymond and Leslie Monkman, eds. *Canadian Novelists and the Novel* (Ottawa: Borealis, 1981). 50-52.

171. Moodie, Susanna, 1803-1885. *Roughing it in the bush, or, forest life in Canada*. (1852) Toronto/Montreal: McLelland and Stewart, 1962. "Introduction" 3.5 p.

172. Morel de la Durantaye, Mme. *A visit to the home of Evangeline: historical romance of the Acadians*. Detroit: [s.n.], 1898. CIHM microfiche series no. 04706. "Introductory" 3.5 p.

173. Morton, James. *Polson's probation: a story of Manitoba*. Toronto: William Briggs, 1897. CIHM microfiche series; no. 30393. "Prologue Chapter I".

174. Munro, Bruce W. (Bruce Weston), 1860-1900?. *A blundering boy: a humorous story*. Toronto: B.W. Munro, [1886?] CIHM microfiche series; no. 11310. "Note" 1 p. "Preface" 5.5 p.

175. Murray de Carteret Odevaine, James. *Papèta: a story: Abridged and arranged from the diary and private papers of Mr. Eugene Murat*. Saint John, N.B.: J. & A. McMillan, 1867. CIHM microfiche no. 34610. "To the Reader" 0.5 p.

176. Murray, Kate. *The guiding angel*. Toronto: Wesleyan Book Room, 1871. CIHM microfiche series; no. 11218. "Preface" 2 ¶.

177. *The Mysteries of Montreal: a novel founded on facts*. Montreal, C.E.: H.H. Cunningham, [1846?] NO: Text dated: Montreal, September, 1846. Intended to be published in 15 parts, CIHM no. 51448 contains part 1 only. CIHM microfiche series; no. 51448. "Preliminary Observations" 2 p.

178. Ogilvy, Maud. *Marie Gourdon: a romance of the Lower St. Lawrence*. Montreal: J. Lovell, 1890. CIHM microfiche series; no. 11502. "Introduction" 2 p.

179. Oxley, J. Macdonald (James Macdonald), 1855-1907. *Bert Lloyd's boyhood: a story from Nova Scotia*. London: Hodder and Stoughton, 1892. CIHM microfiche series; no. 29915. "Preface" 1.5 p.

180. Oxley, J. Macdonald (James Macdonald), 1855-1907. *The specimen hunters*. Toronto: Musson, [between 1894 and 1899?] CIHM microfiche series; no. 11678. "Note" 1 ¶.

181. Oxley, J. Macdonald (James Macdonald), 1855-1907. *On the world's roof*. London: J. Nisbet, [1896]. CIHM microfiche series; no. 11681. X 1 ¶.

182. Oxley, J. Macdonald (James Macdonald), 1855-1907. *The romance of commerce*. New York: T.Y. Crowell, c1896. CIHM microfiche series no. 29918. "Preface" 0.5 p.

183. Oxley, J. Macdonald (James Macdonald), 1855-1907. *The romance of commerce*. London; Edinburgh: W.R. Chambers, 1896. CIHM microfiche series no. 29917. "Preface" 0.5 p.

184. Page, Thomas Nelson. *Red Rock: a chronicle of reconstruction*. Toronto: The Publishers' Syndicate, 1899. CIHM microfiche series no. 11705. "Preface" 3.5 p.

185. Parker, Gilbert, 1862-1932. *The trail of the sword: wherein is set forth the history of Jessica Leveret, as also that of Pierre Le Moyne of Iberville, George Gering, and other bold spirits: together with certain matters of war, and the deeds of one Edward Bucklaw, mutineer and pirate*. London: Methuen, 1896. NO: Includes publisher's list. CIHM microfiche series; no. 51814. "Dedication" 2.5 p. "A Note" 1.5 p.

186. Petitt, Maud. *Beth Woodburn*. Toronto: William Briggs, 1897. X 1 ¶.

187. Phillips, J.A. *From bad to worse, hard to beat and a terrible Christmas*. Montreal: Lovell, 1877. CIHM microfiche series no. 12030. "Preface" 1 p.

188. Pickard, Hannah Maynard, 1812-1844. *The widow's jewels*. Boston: Waite, Peirce, 1844. CIHM microfiche series no. 45529. "Introductory" 1.5 p.

189. Potter, Austin, 1842-1913. *From wealth to poverty, or, The tricks of the traffic: a story of the drink curse*. Toronto: W. Briggs: Montreal: C.W. Coates, 1884. NO: "I will ask him for my place again...Othello, Act II." CIHM microfiche series; no. 12098. "Preface" 2.5 p.

190. Procter, J.J. *The philosopher in the clearing*. Quebec: Daily Telegraph, 1897. CIHM microfiche series no. 12276. "At the Gate of the Clearing" 3.5 p. "Pausing at the Gate. The Preface" 4.5 p.

191. Richardson, John, 1796-1852. *Wacousta, or, The prophecy: a tale of the Canadas*. London: T. Cadell; Edinburgh: W. Blackwood, 1832. NO: "In three volumes. Vol. I. CIHM microfiche series; no. 40221. "Chapter I Introductory" 24 p.

192. Richardson, John, 1796-1852. *Wacousta, or, The prophecy: a tale of the Canadas*. London: T. Cadell; Edinburgh: W. Blackwood, 1839. NO: Part of a CIHM set. For individual microfiches in this set, see CIHM microfiche nos. 50424-50427. "In three volumes, Vol. I." Attributed to John Richardson--National Union Catalog pre-1956 imprints. '"Vengeance is still alive ... and fires me with her charms." The Revenge.' CIHM microfiche series; no. 50425. "Chapter I Introductory" 25 p.

193. Richardson, John, 1796-1852. *The Canadian brothers, or, The Prophecy fulfilled: a tale of the late American war*. Montreal: A.H. Armour and H. Ramsay, 1840. CIHM microfiche series; no. 40103. "Preface" 4 p.

194. Richardson, John, 1796-1852. *The monk knight of St. John: a tale of the Crusades*. New York: Dewitt and Davenport, 1850. NO: Includes publisher's advertisements. CIHM microfiche series; no. 40454. "Chapter I Introductory" 6 p.

195. Richardson, John, 1796-1852. *Wacousta, or, The prophecy: an Indian tale.* New York: R.M. De Witt, [1851?] NO: '"Vengeance is still alive; from her dark covert, ..."--The Revenor.' CIHM microfiche series; no. 40644. "Introduction" 5.5 p.

196. Richardson, John, 1796-1852. *Wau-Nan-Gee; or, the massacre at Chicago: a romance of the American Revolution.* New York: H. Long, 1852. CIHM microfiche series; no. 64967. "Prefatory Inscription" 1.5 p.

197. Roberts, Charles G. D. (Charles George Douglas) Sir, 1860-1943. *The forge in the forest: being the narrative of the Acadian ranger, Jean de Mer, Seigneur de Briart: and how he crossed the Black Abbe: and of his adventures in a strange fellowship.* Toronto: W. Briggs; Montreal: C.W. Coates, [1897?] CIHM microfiche series; no. 32480. "A Foreword" 3 p.

198. Robertson, James. *Jickling's experiences: a reminiscence of Eton life.* Montreal: W. Drysdale, 1896. NO: Cover title. "A clever story; a mate for 'Tom Brown's Schooldays' -- F.W.M." -- cover. "The story...had its first appearance in "The Cornhill Magazine" a number of years ago...The present Editor has somwhat condensed the story...." -- Preface by the Editor. Attributed to James Robertson -- A checklist of Canadian literature, 1628-1960 / Reginald Eyre Watters. CIHM microfiche series; no. 12867. "Preface by the Editor" Editor 1 p.

199. Rogers, Frederick. *Le roman d'une pussie chat: a tale of ye olden times.* Detroit: American Pub. Co., 1900. NO: carefully, faithfully, and accurately translated from the original Sanscrit by Frederick Rogers. -- Original issued in series: Nonsense: being certain foolish tales told by a father to his children in 'The children's hour': v. 4. Duplicate of CIHM no. 09263. Includes bibliographical references. CIHM microfiche series; no. 25039. "Ye Poore Author's Apologia" 5.5 p.

200. Russell, James. *Matilda, or, The Indian's captive: a Canadian tale founded on fact.* Three-Rivers [Quebec]: Printed for the author by G. Stobbs, 1833. CIHM microfiche series; no. 52391. "Preface" 3.5 p.

201. Ryland, Richard. *The Coiners of Pompei: A Romance.* Toronto: H. and W. Rowsell, 1845. "To the Reader" 3 p.

202. Sanford, Mary Bourchier. *The romance of a Jesuit mission: a historical novel.* New York: Baker & Taylor, c1897. CIHM microfiche series; no. 12999. "Preface" 2 p.

203. Saunders, Marshall, 1861-1947. *Beautiful Joe: the autobiography of a dog.* London: Jarrold, 1895. NO: "Forty-second thousand." CIHM microfiche series; no. 64462. "Preface" 1 p. X Ishbel Aberdeen 1 p. "Introduction" Hezekiah Butterworth 2 p.

204. Saunders, Marshall, 1861-1947. *Der schöne Sepp: eine Selbstbiographie.* tr. A. Henrich. Philadelphia: Charles H. Banes, [c1896]. CIHM microfiche series; no. 13278. "Vorwort" 0.5 p. "Einleitung" Hezekiah Butterworth 3 p.

205. Saunders, Marshall, 1861-1947. *Her sailor: a love story.* Boston, 1900. CIHM microfiche series; no. 13010. "Publisher's Note" 0.5 p.

206. Savigny, Annie G. (Annie Gregg), d. 1901. *A romance of Toronto (founded on fact): a novel.* Toronto: W. Briggs, 1888. NO: "'I would like...not end well'--Darwin." "'What would the world do without story-books'--Dickens." CIHM microfiche series; no. 13188. "Note" 1 ¶.

207. Savigny, Annie G. (Annie Gregg), d. 1901. *Lion, the mastiff: from life.* Toronto: W. Briggs; Montreal: C.W. Coates, 1895. NO: '"If there are not reason ... they would say"--Beecher.' '"The power of control carries with it the obligation to protect"--H.H. Porter.' CIHM microfiche series; no. 13351. X 1 p. "Introductory" Wm. Caven 2 p.

208. Savigny, Annie G. (Annie Gregg), d. 1901. *Lion, the mastiff: from life.* Toronto: W. Briggs, 1900. NO: with introduction by Rev. Principal Caven. -- '"If there are not reason ..."' '"The power of control carries with it the power to protect"--H.H. Porter.' CIHM microfiche series; no. 32903. "Prefatory Note" 1 p.

209. Sellar, Robert, 1841-1919. *Gleaner tales.* Huntingdon, Quebec: 1895. CIHM microfiche series; no. 33029. X 0.5 p.

210. Sheppard, Edmund E. (Edmund Ernest), 1855-1924. *Dolly, the young widder up to Felder's.* Toronto: Rose, 1886. CIHM microfiche series; no. 09271. "Preface" 2 p.

211. Sheppard, Edmund E. (Edmund Ernest), 1855-1924. *Widower Jones:a faithful history of his "loss" and adventures in search of a "companion": a realistic story of rural life.* Toronto: Sheppard Pub. Co., 1888. CIHM microfiche series; no. 13563. "Note" 1 ¶.

212. Shinnick, J. *The banker's daughter, or, Her first and last ball: a novel.* Montreal: Gazette Print. Co., 1891. CIHM microfiche series; no. 13611. "Introduction" 1 p.

213. Shrimpton, Charles. *The black phantom, or, Woman's endurance: a narrative connected with the early history of Canada and the American revolution.* New York: J. Miller, 1867. CIHM microfiche series; no. 13614. X 1 p.

214. Skelton, Henrietta. *Grace Morton.* Toronto: A.S. Irving, 1873. CIHM microfiche series; no. 13633. "Preface" 0.5 p.

215. Skelton, Henrietta. *A man trap; and, The fatal inheritance: two temperance tales.* Toronto: J.B. Magurn, [1876?] CIHM microfiche series; no. 13634. "Preface" 0.5 p.

216. Slivers. *Fables of the Nechaco: a complete novel of one of the most remarkable and romantic districts on the American continent.* Vancouver: Produced by the Dominion Stock and Bond Corp., [18--?] CIHM microfiche series; no. 14205. "Dedication" 1 ¶.

217. Smith, Thomas B. (Thomas Barlow), 1839-1933. *Young lion of the woods, or, A story of early colonial days.* Halifax, N.S.: Nova Scotia Print. Co., 1889. NO: "Here in Canadian hearth, and home, and name ..." CIHM microfiche series; no. 15222. X 1 p.

218. Smith, Thomas B. (Thomas Barlow), 1839-1933. *Rose Carney: a story of ever shifting scene on land and sea.* Windsor, N.S.: J.J. Anslow, 1890. CIHM microfiche series; no. 13750. X 6 p.

219. Smith, Thomas B. (Thomas Barlow), 1839-1933. *A seraph on the sea, or, The career of a Highland drummer boy.* Windsor, N.S.: J.J. Anslow, 1891. NO: Cover title: A seraph on the sea, or, The fall and rescue of a Highland drummer boy. CIHM microfiche series; no. 25399. "Dedication" 0.5 p.

220. Sparrow, Malcolm W. (Malcolm Weethie), 1862-1936. *The lady of Chateau Blanc: an historical romance.* Toronto: Brough, 1896. CIHM microfiche series; no. 13882. "Acknowledgements" 1 ¶.

221. Stevenson, Wentworth S. Mrs. *The ladies' benevolent and industrial Sallymag society, being a series of comic chapters, taken from an unpublished novel.* Charlottetown, PEI: W.H. Bremner, 1868. CIHM microfiche series; no. 13964. "Introduction" 0.5 p.

222. Stroud, Amelia Panton. *Daisy Dalton's decision.* Toronto: J. Bain, 1894. CIHM microfiche series; no. 24403. "Preface" 1.5 p.

223. Tennant, Margaret E. *The golden chord: a story of trial and conquest.* Almonte [Ont.]: McLeod & McEwen, 1899. CIHM microfiche series; no. 15813. X 1 p.

224. Thompson, Phillips. *The Political experiences of Jimuel Briggs.* Toronto: Flint, Morton, 1873. Attributed to Phillips Thompson. CIHM microfiche series no. 25169. "Dedication" 0.5 p. "Preface" 1.5 p.

225. Traill, Catherine Parr, 1802-1899. *Canadian Crusoes: a tale of the Rice Lake plains.* London: A. Hall, Virtue, 1852. NO: edited by Agnes Strickland; illustrated by Harvey. -- Later published under title: Lost in the backwoods. Includes publisher's list. CIHM microfiche series; no. 26500. "Preface" Agnes Strickland 6 p.

226. Traill, Catherine Parr, 1802-1899. *Lost in the backwoods: a tale of the Canadian forest*. London: New York: T. Nelson, 1882. CIHM microfiche series; no. 34025. "Preface" 0.5 p.

227. Waitt, Georgina Seymour, 1866-1933. *Three girls under canvas*. Victoria, B.C.: "In black and white", publishers, [c1900]. CIHM microfiche series; no. 09282. "Preface" 2 p.

228. Warman, Cy, 1855-1914. *Snow on the headlight: a story of the great Burlington strike*. Toronto: W. Briggs, 1899. CIHM microfiche series; no. 50394. "Preface" 0.5 p.

229. Warman, Cy, 1855-1914. *The white mail*. New York: C. Scribner's Sons, 1899. CIHM microfiche series; no. 25512. "Preface" 0.5 p.

230. Weaver, Emily P. (Emily Poynton), 1865-1943. *Soldiers of liberty, or, "From the great deep"*. London: C.H. Kelly, 1893. CIHM microfiche series; no. 17033. "Introduction" 0.5 p.

231. Wilson, Anna May. *The days of Mohammed*. Elgin, Ill.; Chicago: D.C. Cook, 1897. NO: Cover title. At head of title: Christmas souvenir. Original issued in series: Sabbath library; v. 10, no. 295. " 1,000 prize story." In double columns. CIHM microfiche series; no. 25972. X 1 p.

232. Wilson, Cornelius, d. 1909. *Rescued in time: a tale*. Toronto: W. Briggs; Montreal: C.W. Coates, 1894. CIHM microfiche series; no. 25976. "Preface" 1 p.

233. Wilson, Robert. *Never give up, or, Life in the lower provinces*. [Saint John, N.B.?: s.n.], 1878 (Saint John, N.B.: Daily News). CIHM microfiche series no. 32337. "To the Reader" 1.5 p.

234. Withrow, W. H. (William Henry), 1839-1908. *The king's messenger, or, Lawrence Temple's probation: a story of Canadian life*. Toronto: S. Rose, 1879. CIHM microfiche series; no. 34392. "Preface" 0.5 p.

235. Withrow, W. H. (William Henry), 1839-1908. *Neville Trueman, the pioneer preacher: a tale of the war of 1812*. Toronto: W. Briggs, 1880. NO: Includes bibliographical references. CIHM microfiche series; no. 34398. "Preface" 1.5 p.

236. Withrow, W. H. (William Henry), 1839-1908. *Valeria, the martyr of the catacombs: a tale of early Christian life in Rome*. Toronto: W. Briggs; Montreal: C.W. Coates, [1882?] CIHM microfiche series; no. 34407. "Preface" 1 p.

237. Withrow, W. H. (William Henry), 1839-1908. *Life in a parsonage, or, Lights and shadows of the itinerancy*. Toronto: W. Briggs; Montreal: C.W. Coates, 1886. NO:

'"Play thy part and play it well ..."' CIHM microfiche series; no. 34395. "Preface" 1 p.

238. Withrow, W. H. (William Henry), 1839-1908. *The king's messenger, or, Lawrence Temple's probation: a story of Canadian life.* Toronto: W. Briggs; Montreal: C.W. Coates, 1897. NO: Includes advertising matter. CIHM microfiche series; no. 34393. "Preface" 0.5 p.

239. Young, Egerton R. (Egerton Ryerson), 1840-1909. *Winter adventures of three boys in the great lone land.* New York: Eaton & Mains; Cincinnati: Jennings & Pye, c1899. NO: with illustrations from drawings by J.E. Laughlin and from photographs. -- A sequel to the author's "Three boys in the wild north land." '"The visions of memory are the dreams of youth ..."' CIHM microfiche series; no. 34527. "Explanatory" 1.5 p.

FRENCH-CANADIAN NOVELS WITH PREFACES

1. Aubert de Gaspé, Philippe, 1786-1871. *Les anciens canadiens.* Québec: Desbarats et Derbishire, 1863. NO: "Publié par la direction du "Foyer Canadien". "Les hommes se réjouissent lorsque le soleil se lève ... Ramayana." CIHM microfiche series; no 28743. "Chapitre Premier" 10 p.

2. Aubert de Gaspé, Philippe, 1786-1871. *The Canadians of Old: an historical romance.* tr. Charles G.D. Roberts. Toronto: Hart, 1891. CIHM microfiche series; no. 26284. "Introduction" 4 p.

3. Aubert de Gaspé, Philippe, 1814-1841. *L'influence d'un livre: roman historique.* 1837 (Québec: W. Cowan) NO: "'Ah! quand le songe de la vie sera terminé, à quoi ...'"--Volney.'" CIHM microfiche series; no 33273. "Préface" 3 p.

4. Barthe, Georges Isidore. *Drames de la vie réelle: roman canadien.* Sorel, P.Q.: J.A. Chenevert, 1896. CIHM microfiche series; no 03023. "Notes de l'auteur" 1 p.

5. Beaugrand, Honoré 1849-1906. *Jeanne la fileuse: épisode de l'émigration franco-canadienne aux États-Unis.* 1878. CIHM microfiche series; no 03033. "Introduction" 3.5 p.

6. Beaugrand, Honoré, 1849-1906. *Jeanne la fileuse: épisode de l'émigration franco-canadienne aux États-Unis.* Montréal: La Patrie, 1888. CIHM microfiche series; no 26490. "Préface" 2 p.

7. Berthelot, Hector, 1842-1895. *Les mystères de Montréal: roman de moeurs.* [Montréal?: A.P. Pigeon?, 189-?] NO: Titre de départ. CIHM microfiche series; no 29429. "Prologue" 1.5 p.

8. Boucherville, Georges Boucher de, 1814-1894. *Une de perdue, deux de trouvées*. Montréal: E. Senécal, 1874. NO: "Tome premier." La microfiche fait partie d'une collection de l'I.C.M.H. Pour obtenir les microfiches particulières de cette collection, voir les numéros de microfiches de l'I.C.M.H. 06599-06601. CIHM microfiche series; no 06600. "Avertissement de l'Éditeur" Eusèbe Senécal 2 p.

9. Bourassa, Napoléon, 1827-1916. *Jacques et Marie: souvenir d'un peuple dispersé*. Montréal: E. Senécal, 1866. CIHM microfiche series; no 03809. "Prologue" 4 p.

10. Brémond, Georges. *Les jumeaux de Montréal: épisode de la guerre du Canada*. Tours (France): A. Mame, 1887. CIHM microfiche series; no 04178. "Préface" 2 p.

11. Brémond, Georges. *Les jumeaux de Montréal: épisode de la guerre du Canada*. Tours [France]: A. Mame, 1889. CIHM microfiche series no. 27817. "Préface" 1.5 p.

12. Chauveau, Pierre-J.-Olivier (Pierre-Joseph-Olivier), 1820-1890. *Charles Guérin: roman de moeurs canadiennes*. Montréal: G.H. Cherrier, 1853. NO: Table. Comprend: Notes de l'auteur. CIHM microfiche series; no 48457. "Avis de l'éditeur" G.H. Chevrier 5 p.

13. Chauveau, Pierre J.O., 1820-1890. *Charles Guérin: roman de moeurs canadiennes*. Montréal: Revue Canadienne, 1900. NO: introduction de Ernest Gagnon; illustrations de J.-B. Lagacé. -- "L'auteur en fit paraître la première partie en 1846-47, dans l'Album de la Revue Canadienne ... En 1852, M. Cherrier en donna une édition régulière et complète, par livraisons mensuelles"--Introd. CIHM microfiche series; no 11864. "Introduction" Ernest Gagnon 2 p.

14. Chevalier, H. Émile (Henri Émile), 1828-1879. *L'enfer et le paradis de l'autre monde*. Paris: Librairie centrale, 1866. CIHM microfiche series; no 04420. "Préface" 2.5 p.

15. Chevalier, H. Émile (Henri Émile), 1828-1879. *L'Ile de Sable*. Paris: Lévy, 1878. CIHM microfiche series no. 00603. "A.M. Adolphe Guéroult" 0.5 p. "Envoi" 0.5 p.

16. Chevalier, H. Émile (Henri Émile), 1828-1879. *La fille des Indiens rouges*. Paris: C. Levy, 1888. NO: L'original publié dans la collection: Drames de l'Amérique du Nord. CIHM microfiche series; no 04746. X 1.5 p.

17. Choquette, Ernest, 1862-1941. *Les Ribaud: une idylle de 37*. Montréal: E. Senécal, 1898. CIHM microfiche series; no 02270. "Dedication" 2 p.

18. Conan, Laure. *Angéline de Montbrun*. [Québec?: s.n.], 1884 (Québec: L. Brousseau). CIHM microfiche series no. 00738. "Étude" l'Abbé Casgrain 20 p.

19. Cynosuridis, Alph. (Alphonse). *Memoires d'un vieux garcon*. 1865. NO: En tête du titre: Foule et solitude. CIHM microfiche series; no 26079. "Un Mot de Préface" 1 p.

20. D'Ennery, Adolphe. *A martyr; or, a victim of the divorce law: a novel*. tr. Aristide Filiatreault. Toronto: Rose, 1886. CIHM microfiche series; no. 04501. "To the Reader" Aristide Filiatreault 2.5 p.

21. Dick, V.-Eugène (Vinceslas-Eugène), 1848-1919. *L'enfant mystérieux*. Québec: J.A. Langlais, [1890?] NO: En tête du titre: Littérature canadienne. La microfiche fait partie d'une collection de l'I.C.M.H. Pour obtenir les microfiches particulieres de cette collection, voir les numéros de microfiche de l'I.C.M.H. 05666-05668. CIHM microfiche series; no 05668. "Prologue" 10 p.

22. Doutre, Joseph, 1825-1886. *Les fiancés de 1812: essai de littérature canadienne*. [Montréal?: s.n.], 1844 (Montréal: L. Perrault). CIHM microfiche series no. 34770. X 16 p.

23. Duquet, Edouard. *Pierre et Amélie*. Québec: J.N. Duquet, 1866. CIHM microfiche series; no 23342. "Préface" 2 p.

24. Durandal, Pierre. *Le vengeur de Montcalm*. Paris: H. Lecène et H. Oudin, 1887. NO: Faux-titre. Comprend un index. CIHM microfiche series; no 02272. "Prologue" 17 p.

25. Fortier, Auguste, 1870-1932. *Les mystères de Montréal: roman canaden. [sic]*. Montréal: Leprohon & Guilbault, [1894?] NO: Titre de la couverture. L'original publié dans la collection: La bonne littérature française: publication mensuelle; no 2. CIHM microfiche series; no 12609. "Prologue" 3.5 p.

26. Gauvreau, Charles-Arthur. *Captive et bourreau*. Québec? [189-?]. CIHM microfiche series; no 03297. "Prologue" 2 p.

27. Gérin-Lajoie, Antoine, 1824-1882. *Jean Rivard, le défricheur: récit de la vie réelle*. Montréal: J.B. Rolland, 1874. CIHM microfiche series; no 33005. "Préface" Editor 1.5 p. "Avant-Propos" 2 p.

28. Girard, Rodolphe, 1879-1956. *Florence: légende historique, patriotique et nationale*. Montréal: 1900. CIHM microfiche series; no 12583. "Préface" Firmin Picard 4.5 p.

29. Lacombe, Patrice Trullier, 1807-1863. *La terre paternelle*. Québec: A. Côté, 1877. CIHM microfiche series; no. 08376. "Conclusion" 5 p.

30. *Le chasseur canadien* . --. Montréal: "L'Etendard", 1885. NO: En tête du titre: Feuilleton de l'Etendard. CIHM microfiche series; no 03018. "Prologue" 18 p.

31. Lemay, Pamphile, 1837-1918. *Picounoc le maudit*. Québec: C. Darveau, 1878. NO: "Tome I." La microfiche fait partie d'une collection de l'I.C.M.H. Pour obtenir les microfiches particulières de cette collection, voir les numéros de microfiches de l'I.C.M.H. 08625-08627. Suite du "Pèlerin de Sainte-Anne." CIHM microfiche series; no 08626. "Prologue" 14 p.

32. L'Epine, Charles. *Le secrétaire d'ambassade*. Montréal: E. Senécal, 1878. NO: "Laisse-moi soupirer en même temps mes peines et mes plaisirs--Montesquieu, Temple de Gnide." CIHM microfiche series; no 08563. "Avant-Propos" 4 p.

33. Marcil, Charles. *L'héritière d'un millionaire: roman historique*. Montréal: J.A. David, 1867. NO: 1ère et 2ème livraisons du roman. L'action se passe à Montréal vers 1837. CIHM microfiche series; no 09770. "Préface" 0.5 p. "Avis au Lecteur" J.A. David 2 p.

34. Marmette, Joseph, 1844-1895. *François de Bienville: scènes de la vie canadienne au XVIIᵉ siècle*. Québec: L. Brousseau, 1870. CIHM microfiche series; no 09904. "Introduction" 7 p.

35. Marmette, Joseph, 1844-1895. *L'intendant Bigot*. Montréal: G.E. Desbarats, 1872. NO: En tête du titre: Roman canadien, reproduit de "l'Opinion publique". Texte sur deux colonnes. CIHM microfiche series; no 09780. "Prologue" 14 p.

36. Marmette, Joseph, 1844-1895. *Le chevalier de Mornac: chronique de la Nouvelle-France, 1664*. [Montréal?: s.n.], 1873 (Montréal: "L'Opinion publique"). CIHM microfiche series no. 09903. "Introduction" 2.5 p.

37. Marmette, Joseph, 1844-1895. *Les Machabées de la Nouvelle-France: histoire d'une famille canadienne, 1641-1768*. Québec: Léger Brousseau, 1882. CIHM microfiche series no. 09781. "Introduction" 3.5 p. "Sources" 1.5 p.

38. Marmette, Joseph, 1844-1895. *François de Bienville: scènes de la vie canadienne au XVIIe siécle*. Montréal: Beauchemin & Valois, 1883. CIHM microfiche series; no 09779. "Introduction" 7.5 p. "Préface" 7 p.

39. Morissette, J.F. (Joseph-Ferdinand), ca. 1858-1901. *Au coin du feu: nouvelles, recits, et légendes*. Montréal: Piché, 1883. CIHM microfiche series; no 04710. "Préface" 1 p.

40. Myrand, Ernest. *Une fête de Noël sous Jacques Cartier*. Québec: L.-J. Demers, 1890. CIHM microfiche series no. 52527. "Préface" 13.5 p. "Prologue" 37 p.

41. Orsonnens, Eraste d', né 1836. *Une apparition: épisode de l'émigration irlandaise au Canada*. Montréal: Cérat et Bourguignon, 1860. NO: En tête du titre: Littérature

canadienne. CIHM microfiche series; no 22831. "A Mm. les propriétaires de la Guêpe (Servant de Préface)" 1.5 p.

42. Prévost, Paul-Emile, 1864-1908. *L'épreuve.* Montréal: A. Pelletier, 1900. CIHM microfiche series; no 12166. "Préface" 9 p.

43. Proulx, J.-B. (Jean-Baptiste), 1846-1904. *L'enfant perdu et retrouvé ou Pierre Cholet.* Mile-End, [Québec]: Institution des Sourds-Muets, 1887. CIHM microfiche series; no 11905. "Préface" 10 p.

44. Proulx, J.-B. (Jean-Baptiste), 1846-1904. *Pierre Cholet, or, The recovered kidnapped child.* Mile End, P.Q.: Institution for Deaf Mutes, 1888. NO: Cover title. Preface signed: J.B. Proulx. CIHM microfiche series; no. 04848. "Preface" 12 p.

45. Rousseau, Edmond, 1850?-1909?. *Le château de Beaumanoir: roman canadien.* Levis, [Québec]: Mercier, 1886. CIHM microfiche series; no 12940. "Préface" 2 p.

46. Rousseau, Edmond, 1850?-1909?. *Les exploits d'Iberville.* [Québec: s.n.], 1888 (Québec: C. Darveau). CIHM microfiche series no. 12677. "Préface" 6.5 p.

47. Rousseau, Edmond, 1850?-1909? *La monongahéla.* Québec: C. Darveau, 1890. NO: L'original publié dans la collection: Histoire du Canada popularisée. Comprend des références bibliographiques. CIHM microfiche series; no 57100. "Dédication" 1 p.

48. Singer, F.B. (François-Benjamin), 1830-1876. *Souvenirs d'un exilé canadien.* Montréal: J. Lovell, 1871. CIHM microfiche series; no 13628. "Préface" 3 p.

49. Sulte, Benjamin. *Au coin du feu: histoire et fantasie.* Québec: Blumhart, 1877. CIHM microfiche series no. 24412. "Au Lecteur" 3 ¶.

50. Tardivel, Jules Paul, 1851-1905. *Pour la patrie: roman du XXe siècle.* Montréal: Cadieux & Derome, 1895. NO: "Ne laeteris inimica mea super me, quia cecidi ..." CIHM microfiche series; no 24462. "Pour la patrie: Avant-Propos" 9 p.

51. Thomas, A. (Alphonse), 1841-1905. *Gustave ou Un héros canadien: roman historique et polémique.* Montréal: Gernaey & Hamelin, 1882. CIHM microfiche series; no 25106. "Avis des éditeurs" Editor 1.5 p.

52. Thomas, A. (Alphonse), 1841-1905. *Albert ou L'orphelin catholique.* Montréal: Beauchemin & Valois, 1885. NO: "Publié avec l'approbation de Sa Grandeur Monseigneur de Montréal." CIHM microfiche series; no 25105. "Préface" 3 p.

INDEX

Biographical Detail about the Author

Steven TÖTÖSY de ZEPETNEK

1950	Born in Budapest, Hungary
1964—1976	Secondary schools in West Germany, Austria, and Switzerland; Language Training at Oxford and Genève; Bank Employee in Bern and Basel, Switzerland
1976—1980	B.A. in History and German, The University of Western Ontario (London, Ontario)
1980—1982	M.A. in Comparative Literature, Carleton University (Ottawa, Ontario)
1982—1983	Stay-home Parent
1983—1984	B.Ed. in English as a Second Language and History, Université d'Ottawa (Ottawa, Ontario)
1984—1989	Ph.D. in Comparative Literature, University of Alberta (Edmonton, Alberta); Sessional Lecturer in the Departments of Comparative Literature and Germanic Languages; Secondary School Teacher with the Edmonton Public School Board
1989—1992	Research Associate, Research Institute for Comparative Literature, University of Alberta and Sessional Lecturer with the Departments of Comparative Literature and Film Studies, English, and Germanic Languages, University of Alberta
1992—	Visiting Assistant Professor, Research Institute for Comparative Literature, University of Alberta

Works in the areas of Literary Theory, Feminist Criticism, the Modern novel, Mainstream Canadian and Canadian Ethnic Minority Literatures, Intra- and Interdisciplinary Studies, and Readership research. Publications in *TTR — Traduction, Terminologie, Rédaction* (1988), the *Canadian Review of Comparative Literature / Revue Canadienne de Littérature Comparée* (1989, 1990, 1992), *SPIEL — Siegener Periodicum zur Internationalen Empirischen Literaturwissenschaft* (1990), *Men's Studies Review* (1991), *Poetics* (1992), *TSC/ETC — Textual Studies in Canada / Études Textuelles au Canada* (1993), *Neohelicon* (1993), *Seminar* (1993), *Hungarian Studies* (1993), *Dictionary of Canadian Biography / Dictionnaire biographique du Canada* (1993), etc. Research and several articles also in Canadian Ethnic History and a compilation of Latin, Hungarian, and German archival documents 1587 to present, *A Zepetneki Tötösy család adattára / Records of the Tötösy de Zepetnek Family* (Szeged: József Attila University, 1993). Assistant Editor and desk-top publisher of the *Canadian Review of Comparative Literature / Revue Canadienne de Littérature Comparée*. Recent projects include readership research, contemporary Canadian literature, the narrative in film and literature, and Neurophenomenology and literature.

Vieweg – Scientific Publishing since 1786

In 1786, *Friedrich Vieweg* founded his publishing house in Berlin.

For more than 200 years, many authors and many more readers have dealt with Vieweg. The domicile of the publishing company has remained in Germany: Berlin, Braunschweig, Wiesbaden. Very soon, however, its sphere of activity extended into Europe and nowadays spreads throughout the world. The raison d'être for this successful undertaking may be found in the scientific fields chosen by Vieweg for coverage in its program: mathematics, sciences and engineering do not recognize national borders. A few names taken from the long list of authors will be able to demonstrate Vieweg's important contribution to the scientific community, better than any extended review: *Liebig, Lavoisier, Berzelius, Wöhler, Dedekind, Riemann, Helmholtz, Clausius, Rutherford, Einstein, Laue, Bohr, Heisenberg, Staudinger, Faltings.*

Verlag Vieweg · Postfach 58 29 · 65048 Wiesbaden